THE BEST IN RETAIL ADS

Vol. 1

401 Newspaper Ads and Why They Work

J. Paganetti
M. Seklemian

Retail Reporting Corporation • New York

CONTENTS

FOREWORD

How would you go about selecting the best advertisements of the past two decades? Who is to judge? Advertising as a science, a craft, or a business is a highly personal matter. What will be caviar to one will be salami to another. Moreover, the final and only judge is the ultimate customer and that person is rarely consulted in our mad whirl of making ads and meeting deadlines. The miracle is that we do as well as we do and sometimes something truly great happens.

This book is a selection from those truly great, reproduced here as a permanent record. I have to congratulate Jo Ann Paganetti for her thoughtfulness and keen judgement in the choices she has made. Her's was not an easy task. She will be the first to say that many superb examples had to "hit the cutting room floor" for one reason or another. Often it was because the material was not available in a form that would reprint clearly. And she will also tell you that there is no such thing as the perfect advertisement. But each selection shown exhibits some qualities, some features that make it worthy of this permanent record.

This book is more than simply a record. It is more than useful reference material. Above all it is studying-learning material. Here you are exposed to the practical published work by some of the best advertising minds of our generation. A monument to those individuals, many unknown and unsung, who have done so much for the advancement of retail advertising.

Please note that this collection incorporates mainly what I call Class B and C advertisements. To clarify, Class B is "advertising to build"--to build a classification of merchandise, to build a department, to identify a fashion trend, to build a growing business. Class C is "advertising for character"--the character of the store, the store's policies, the store's relationship to its customers, its marketplace, its community. (Class A, "advertising for action"--sales, price appeal, and immediate action advertising--appears to a minor extent.)

There is reason for making this distinction and bringing you this Class B-C collection first. We've just come through a decade of sales, off-price, volume-producing efforts. Please understand that there is vital need for Class A advertising. A store--any store--must find ways to stimulate sales and develop advertising for immediate action. But we've come through a decade of that. We have people in our stores who hardly know that advertising, in the long run, must serve purposes that reach beyond tomorrow's sales. A balance of Class A, B and C advertising is essential if a store is to survive and make a profit. "Selling the store" is advertising's Number One assignment. It always was, it always will be. This collection points the way.

The comments on each advertisement shown in this book have been written in part by Jo Ann Paganetti and in part by me. We hope these editorial notes will contribute a modicum of interest and explain why that particular selection was made.

And we aren't through selecting! There's another compilation of "Best Ads" in the works. This time it will be "The Best in Sale Ads, Volume I". We are proud of the "Best Ads" concept and confident that we are providing information that has been needed for the complete retail advertising library.

M. Seklemian

INTRODUCTION

The thousands of ads I have poured through to select ''The Best in Retail Ads, Volume I'' have set forth visions of the many men and women who made those ads. Talented people who, faster than the speed of an approaching deadline, are able to pull together powerful messages for their stores—ads that get read, remember-ed—ads that sell merchandise, store services and most important of all, the store itself. It is to these people that this book is dedicated.

Just as nature makes no two snowflakes alike, believe it or not, it also makes no two creatives alike. And it is this precious individualism that made the ads you see here work for their stores. Through this intensively attractive individuality, (no, we don't mean perverse or unnecessary eccentricity), a chord of the universal is struck, because the advertising message that is presented is the truth! And the reader stops, reads, remembers and reacts.

As always, the French have just the right phrase for it: ''Le style est l'homme même''—''The style is the man''. And this style is not only that of the individual creative but obviously, first and foremost the style—the true image—of the retail establishment that signed the ad with its logo.

Mr. Seklemian advises, and I reemphasize that this volume is more than just a record of retail advertising creativity over the past 20 years. It is a practical reference manual—meant to be used over and over again. When faced with an immediate advertising problem—or when just speculating about what you would like to do for a client—it is useful to study the successful work of others. Look for the clarity and the simplicity of the message, the human appeal, the unified whole created by the visual and the copy to inspire you to do your own ''Best''.

Jo Ann Paganetti

CHAPTER I

WOMEN'S FASHION

What a confusing time the past two decades have been for the American fashion customer! Fashion dictatorship died hard! But when it died, women were set free—free to look fabulous—or free to look like total disasters. And ironically after all the bras had been burned and all the jeans had been patched, women again turned to their favorite store for direction. But this time, they weren't interested in heavy-handed dictatorship. They wanted the advice of an intelligent, trusted friend.

More changes came. The number of women in the work force of the United States grew until in 1981, 50.4 percent of all women were employed. And the emphasis of advertised merchandise changed with the statistics. Separates, suits and dresses that could be worn to work took precedence. The tone of the ads changed also. Poses and words were carefully chosen to appeal to the women who now had their own discretionary income.

And another change. According to the most recent study by Celanese, in 1981 the largest group of female customers fell into the 25-to-34-year age range (23 percent of the total), evidencing the growing up of the Post World War II Baby Boomers. And another important statistic from the Celanese study: 56 percent of the total market is now over the age of 35. Customers have become more sophisticated, more affluent and retail advertising has reflected these changes.

Readers of this ''Best Ads'' volume will see how the astute retailer has coped with all of these changes: how he has replaced fashion dictatorship with advertising messages from a trusted friend; how he speaks to the working woman with a new respect and how he has approached a more sophisticated, affluent audience.

Getting talked about is half the battle—even if you're Bloomingdale's. And what was talked about in the summer of '82 was a sensational series of fall fashion introduction ads modeled by Raquel Welch and photographed by Francesco Scavullo. What made the concept so perfect was its timeliness. Welch had just taken over the Broadway lead of "Woman of the Year". Her spectacular on-stage wardrobe is designed by Norma Kamali—and here she is modeling for Bloomingdale's in cape and dress by the same designer. This ad is just one from a memorable series.

Adolfo Now

Adolfo for her: all dazzle, all glamour at night. It begins with the cardigan, hand-crocheted of the finest wool, trimmed with silk ribbon. It continues with the stock-tie blouse...a wash of cream silk charmeuse against the skin. And it finishes—beautifully!—with the long skirt of pure silk charmeuse. Ours alone, in champagne, for sizes 4 to 14, $1300. In Designer Collections, Third Floor—where we are all the things you are! *Adolfo on Three: meet him on September 21st, 22nd and 23rd at 11 to 4, informal modeling of the collection from 12 to 4*

Saks Fifth Avenue

Adolfo Here

Adolfo for him: a sense of quiet elegance...for day, for night. The single-breasted suit, deeply back-vented, impeccably tailored in the finest worsted wool. In a subtle charcoal grey pinstripe, $555. And it's just one from a superb collection of suits in exclusive fabrics—worsteds, cashmere, silk, alpaca, camel hair and worsted wool—imported from Europe expressly for SFA. Find them in Designer Suit Collections, The Men's Store, Sixth Floor—where we are all the things you are!

Saks Fifth Avenue

Adolfo Tomorrow

Adolfo. Sorcerer of fashion that dazzles the senses of sight and touch...creator of fashion that's elegant, timeless, always classic. Now, Adolfo goes one step further...explores still more realms...and his new vision is realized tomorrow at Saks Fifth Avenue—where we are all the things you are.

Saks Fifth Avenue

Adolfo Today

Adolfo. Master creator of elegant design for men, beautiful clothes for women...and now, fragrance for both. Introducing Adolfo for Men: a handsome new fragrance created expressly for the man who is quite simply, quite discerning in his habits and his tastes. A fragrance that is discreet, that has...manners. Rich and warm, lasting long, Adolfo for Men begins with a fresh green topnote, continues with smoky tabac, bergamot and leather, and finishes with warm woody tones. The result is a man's fragrance unlike any other...singular in style! Adolfo for Men, first at SFA. Long Wear Cologne, 2 oz., 18.50. Long Wear After Shave, 2 oz., $12. Hair Cleanser, Normal to Dry or Normal to Oily, 6 oz., $8 each. And this week, today through the 26th, you'll receive an elegant black leather card case with any purchase from the collection...in the Gentleman's Quarter, Street Floor—where we are all the things you are! *Adolfo, here in person in New York. Meet him when he presents his new fragrance collection for gentlemen tomorrow from 12 to 1.*

Saks Fifth Avenue

Three of these full-page ads appeared in a September 1981 Sunday edition of the New York Times. The fourth appeared the following day to introduce the new Adolfo fragrance for men. The powerful campaign demonstrates the commitment Saks has made to one of the most popular designers of the early '80s. The ads also served to invite customers to a mini fashion show and to a meeting with the designer at the Rockefeller Center store.

SCOTT BARRIE FOR SBF

It's a long way from Philadelphia to New York's Seventh Avenue. Scott Barrie can tell you that. He's a talented black designer who made the trip and has definitely "arrived." Six years ago he was designing for his own small dress firm. Today, at 530 Seventh Avenue, he's still at dresses, and his collections are watched everywhere.

Because what Barrie does well—soft, sensuous dresses—he does better than almost anyone. And how does he do it, create a dress that moves, flows, and feels like a waterfall on? Call it what you will, it's the Scott Barrie genius, seen here in a ripple of matte rayon jersey, liquid and lean. In navy or mauve, 6-14, $178. Miss SBF, Westroads only.

Stix, Baer & Fuller

A tribute to Scott Barrie, one of the truly great talents of our day. A beautiful layout, a thoughtful and sincere copy job and a distinguished photograph. The printing job by the St. Louis Globe-Democrat is fantastic.

Five innovative designers, "five bundles of talent," each fondly embracing a favorite object. What a wacky, wonderful way of projecting an idea and announcing a fashion show. Saks Fifth Avenue saluted its Fifty Years of Fashion in 1974.

Horne's fashion director is holding a series of conversations
with the leading fashion designers of the day. This
tete-a-tete with Chester Weinberg is exciting, fascinating
and revealing. The copy is beautiful. Thank you,
Jane Vandermade, we love it all.

Bullock's invites you to a morning of person-to-person fashion with California designer

HARRIET SELWYN

Bullock's

WHAT: Bring your favorite piece of clothing—a blazer, blouse, skirt—then watch Harriet work! She'll show you how to stretch your wardrobe, make endless new looks, and how her designs, Fragments, mix with what you've brought. There'll be a fashion show and clinic. You may be picked to work with Harriet right then and there! $5 Benefiting the Preservation of the Variety Arts.

WHEN: Wednesday, November 29. The day begins at 9 with breakfast snacks. What a nice way to start the day!

WHERE: The Encino Dining Room at Bullock's Sherman Oaks.

RSVP: Benefiting the Preservation of the Variety Arts. Call them at 623-9100. Or call us, 788-8350 ext. 372 for reservations and information. Tickets are $5 each.

SHOP MON-FRI TILL 9:30 PASADENA LA HABRA LAKEWOOD SANTA ANA TILL 9 DOWNTOWN TILL 6 EXCEPT FRI TILL 7:30 SUN 12 TILL 5. EXCEPT DOWNTOWN
DOWNTOWN PASADENA WESTWOOD SANTA ANA SHERMAN OAKS LAKEWOOD DEL AMO LA HABRA NORTHRIDGE SOUTH COAST PLAZA SAN DIEGO WEST COVINA CENTURY CITY

It was 1977 and Harriet Selwyn was one of the first designers to be concerned about investment dressing for the working woman. Bullock's does a smart promotion in four parts. First, the reader is asked to bring her favorite piece of clothing (blazer, blouse or skirt) and watch Harriet work with it, stretching that customer's wardrobe with all her Fragment looks. Second, breakfast snacks were served with the event. Third, Bullock's sold tickets and turned the seminar into a benefit. Fourth, the ad had maximum visibility on the back page of the Los Angeles Times Friday fashion section.

15

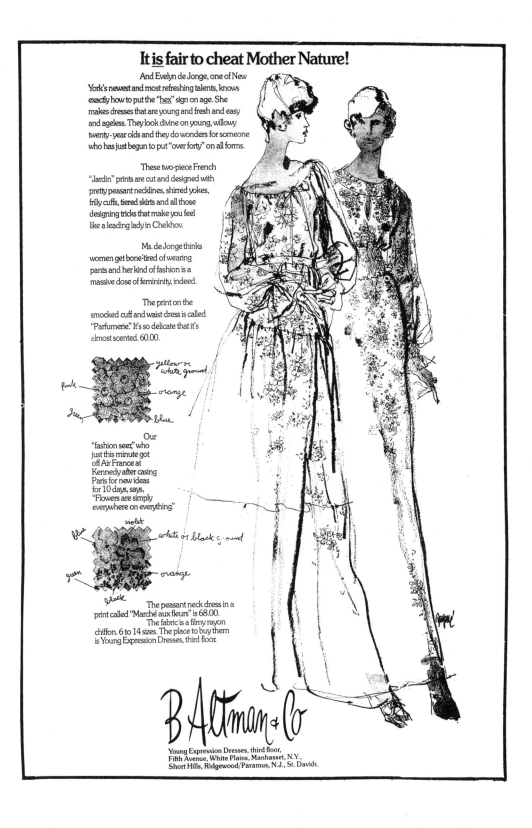

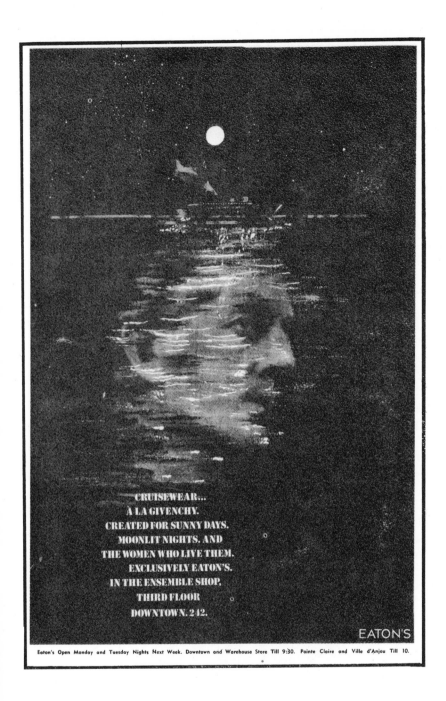

CRUISEWEAR...
A LA GIVENCHY.
CREATED FOR SUNNY DAYS.
MOONLIT NIGHTS. AND
THE WOMEN WHO LIVE THEM.
EXCLUSIVELY EATON'S.
IN THE ENSEMBLE SHOP,
THIRD FLOOR
DOWNTOWN. 242.

EATON'S

Eaton's Open Monday and Tuesday Nights Next Week. Downtown and Warehouse Store Till 9:30. Pointe Claire and Ville d'Anjou Till 10.

Those imaginative people in Eaton's, Montreal, have come up with a dream of an ad on Givenchy and cruisewear. A great idea carefully carried out. Read the copy. It says so much in a few words.

Left:
Please read this copy from first word to last. This is how a fashion expert explains fashion. Does fashion need explaining? You'd better believe it and Altman's does it with authority and verve plus a fantastic realism. How can you resist?

17

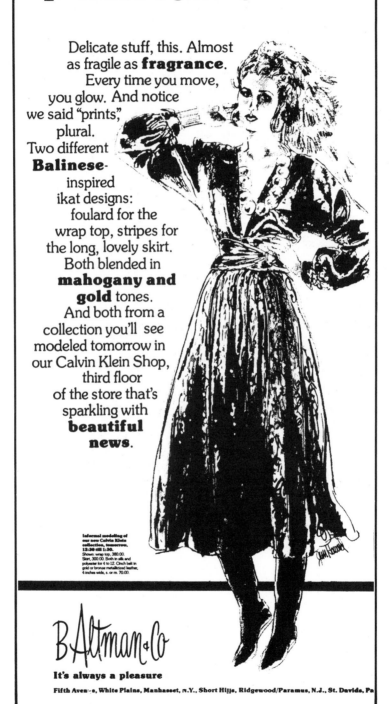

Left:

The traditionalist among us may cringe at what Altman's is doing with type. But Altman's isn't concerned with tradition. Their only concern is customer message, customer impact. The stepped-up type has a new sense of news, a new urge to read. Unity is maintained by arranging the words around the art, making a graphic total. Without doubt the best seen advertisement in the paper that Sunday.

Below:

As a department store, Dayton's firmly believes it should offer fashion to all price categories and to all levels of fashion acceptance. In fulfilling the wants of the woman who appreciates and can afford the haute couture creations of Yves St. Laurent, Dayton's offers, along with the fashions themselves, an elegant and exclusive shopping environment. Rive Gauche with its striking red and black decor and contemporary-style chromed fixtures also provides Dayton's with the opportunity to check the pulse of trends that will some day be translated into mass market ready-to-wear. This full-page ad dramatically announced to customers the date and place of the informal modeling of Rive Gauche fashions.

Nordstrom Best

NOT EVERYONE IS LONG AND LEAN YOU DON'T HAVE TO BE

the new fashions are longer than you're used to, but how long depends on you. Nordstrom Best can not dictate a length. we can make the longer looks right for you . . . adapt them to you alone. find the length, fabrics, silhouettes, accessories keyed to your size, attitude, lifestyle. that is what fashion is all about at Nordstrom Best . . . dedicated to the fashion individualist.

A sensible approach to the mini-midi hassle of 1970. Nordstrom Best
makes a lot of sense in a few words and wraps it up in a layout
nobody can miss.

You'd better believe it because Neiman-Marcus makes it official with this delightful ad. The scene-stealer for spring 1970 was mid-way length.

"I think it's perfectly shocking!"

Nevertheless the scene-stealer for Spring is the mid-way length. *Neiman-Marcus*

A woman of 40 will never look 30 dressing like 20.

The outfit you see above would look terrific on a different woman. And the woman you see above would look terrific in a different outfit. But when you put them together, they both end up looking a little foolish.

That's why Ohrbach's doesn't try to sell everybody the same style. We know that a mother can't always wear the same clothes her daughter wears. And vice versa. So we make sure we have the right look for each of them, no matter what their age. By filling our stores with thousands and thousands of great fashions. And pricing them at Ohrbach's famous low prices.

So if you want something that will make you look a little younger, you'll probably find it at Ohrbach's. But please don't try to push it. We want you to look like an ad for our store, but this isn't the ad we have in mind.

OHRBACH'S Where you always find the fashion and the price that's right for you.

New York: 34th St., Newark, N.J.: Market & Halsey. Westbury, L.I.: at the Raceway. Paramus, N.J.: Bergen Mall. Wayne, N.J.: Willowbrook. Woodbridge, N.J.: Woodbridge Center.

Ohrbach's message is as important today as it was back in 1971. It reads in part: "The outfit you see above would look terrific on a different woman. And the woman you see above would look terrific in a different outfit. But when you put them together, they both end up looking a little foolish. That's why Ohrbach's doesn't try to sell everybody the same style...." The institutional goes on to sell the selection and low prices, two qualities for which the store is famous. This is true fashion direction.

22

Ohrbach's works on the premise that fashion is a competitive sport for women, that all women vie for the male eye! And that's honesty in advertising, isn't it?

In the most recent page from this competitive campaign, Ohrbach's talks to the woman whose husband just can't wait for the next chance to visit the children's school. The reason? A fantastic-looking teacher who gets her clothes at Ohrbach's.

Maybe Johnny's teacher can teach you a thing or two.

Knowing how to keep the kids' minds on new math is easy. Getting their fathers to come to PTA meetings takes something else.

And she's got what it takes.

Ohrbach's. That's where she gets the clothes that make her look so fantastic day after day. Even on a teacher's salary.

If your husband has been counting the days to Open

School Week, don't be jealous. It's never too late to learn. Just come to Ohrbach's too.

A few wild things from us and your husband will get to be crazy about homework.

What a little money can do at Ohrbach's.

23

When this doubletruck ran the fall of '77, phone lines were buzzing with women calling each other to say: "Did you see Barney's ad?" The opening of the store's new Woman's Place floors became an historic event, bringing equality to another men's-only territory. We love the references to the first woman to ride at Aqueduct, the first unescorted woman at P.J. Clarke's, the first woman West Pointer. In each recreated scene, the model wears Barney's fashions.

My Garfinckel is showing?

It turns me on.

Garfinckel's

Garfinckel's was turning everyone on in 1969.
Big beautiful things were happening and the scenery
in Washington was improved considerably.

MEN

are you distraught about the disappearance of the Beautiful American Knee?

MACY'S HAS GOOD NEWS FOR YOU

Just relax. Close your eyes. Breathe deeply and think positively. Think of words like Slinky...and Slender... and Smooth. Think of Clingy...and Close-fit. Think of the flash of Dark-Stockinged legs...and Higher Heels. *Think of Shape. Think of Soft. Think of Feminine.* That's really the fashion news, more than length. Remember, "It's not how long you make it, it's how you make it long."*

*Feel a little better? Here's even more cheer from Macy*s.*

We believe in *fashion freedom* for your lady. We believe she should be able to choose whatever length is right for her, whichever of the many new looks the moment calls for. That's why we're offering her more *freedom of choice* than she's ever had before. She loves the long and luscious looks? She'll find shop after shop of them. She wants a skirt that's "Not that long"? We have the new silhouettes in dozens of different proportions. She still wants to show off those nifty knees? She'll find head-turning collections of short skirts here. Because we're the World's Largest Store. And you can be sure *she'll get good value for her—or your—money.* You know our motto: "It's smart to be thrifty."

To quote one of your favorite t-v commercials.

In fashion too...more freedom of choice at Macy's, the store with more of just about everything.

Yes, along with all Americans, Canadians, and the world at large we, too, were distraught about the disappearance of the Beautiful Knee in 1970. "Macy's has good news for you," it says here. For this we are glad. It's a great editorial.

Ladies, be seated.
The tug of yore is over!

All over, the surreptitious tug of skirt when you sit down. All over the secret nag that possibly the back (and maybe even the front) of your knees are not entirely aesthetic!

Once again, you can sit, rise, walk . . . even get in and out of a car . . . gracefully. Even the skirt that halts only an inch or two below the knee permits it.

Longer length is one of the nicest things that could have happened to fashion . . . and you. And, still the nicest place to discover it is Neiman-Marcus.

Speaking of discoveries, our Jeremy wool knit is one. Beige, asymmetric buttons and belt of fake snake . . . soft, just below knee day dressing 75.00 in Galleria, Downtown and NorthPark

Neiman-Marcus

Leave it to Neiman-Marcus to approach fashion honestly, simply, and with consummate skill. "Longer length is one of the nicest things that could have happened to fashion . . . and you." A practical thought, well told.

COHNS PRESENTS SPRING'S MOST PROPHETIC TRENDS*

the oversize blouse
Free-flowing simplicity. Blousons, bubbles, tunics, big shirts. Voiles, gauzes, string knits

the unconstructed jacket
Unlined, uncluttered, unstudied. Small, slim, lean, soft natural fabrics

soft suits
Unconstructed jackets with easy, elasticized dirndl skirts. Silks, linens. Natural hues

sundresses
Layered tunic looks, side slits, contrast prints, smocks, bare shoulders

peg-leg pants
Fullness that funnels down to hug the ankles. Best with huge oversized tops

gauze dressing
Cool, textured, natural. A look, a feel finding its way into so much that's new

the petticoat look
Hemlines flounced, tiered, tucked. Tenderly romantic. Lavish lace, ribbon, eyelet

Victoriana
Innocent, nostalgic. Sweet chemises, bellowy dresses. Lace and eyelet

soft blousing
Unfussy, free-spirited, often floaty. Plunge, petrol, peasant necklines. Airy fabrics.

m.m. Cohn

*See these trends at Memphis' first major Spring Luncheon-Fashion Extravaganza benefitting St. Jude's Hospital
Join the festive excitement Wed., Feb. 1st, 11:30 a.m. in the Holiday Inn Ballroom-Rivermont

The Ladies of St. Jude will be at M.M. Cohn Laurelwood and Germantown stores 11 to 3, Mon.-Wed., Jan. 23-25 to accept reservations.
You may also call M.M. Cohn daily to make reservations by phone. Tickets will be mailed upon receipt of check.
Luncheon-Fashion Show tickets (donation): Each $10. Table of ten $100.

Long dresses: the elegant long evening dress is still in.

FASHION PROPHECY '69 FROM ESTHER WOLF

Post Oak at San Felipe

Lengths: remain short—status quo!

Silhouette: more figure flattering, closer to the body, not necessarily belted.

Pants: greater than ever—city pants for day, glamorous pants for night.

"Do your own thing": still big for swingers.

Colors: pastels, white, and perennial navy.

Fabric: big news—from the sculptured to the extravagant.

Accessories: lots of them—bags are shiny and sleek.

Total picture: I like the fashions for '69—they are elegant, feminine, and exciting.

How does a store emphasize fashion authority? By letting a fashion authority talk about fashion. Fabulous photography and fashion prophecy from Esther Wolf.

Left:
"Spring's most prophetic trends" is M.M. Cohn's way of showing the customers what's new, what's right and what they should look for. Nine trends are sketched and described. The descriptions are brief but amazingly complete, all a person needs to know at the start of a season. This is a practical, simple approach to an opportunity many stores miss doing entirely. Tied-in is a fashion show and a charity benefit which wraps up a good performance.

There is a new look on the streets of Winnipeg these days. It's Eaton's packaging for the new Number 1 shop, the shop for "Young woman on the go. Pace Setter. Action person. Walking to the beat of your own drum." A fantastic box design in tan and orange-red. A fantastic ad to show it off.

Good news. The indomitable two-piece dress. Liquid. Soft. Torso-skimming. Because that's the way fabrics are this season (to wit: January Vogue's fashion dictates, page 53). Carol Horn does it first for the John Wanamaker Contemporary Shop, Philadelphia and all JW stores, in banner-bright art-deco-printed green rayon georgette. Shirt with delicately gathered shoulders. 38.00. Matching front-pleated skirt. 40.00
JOHN WANAMAKER HAS GOOD NEWS: TWO-PIECE DRESSES.

The ultimate in fashion layouts! John Wanamaker sets larger close-up figure against a page of white. Smaller full figure is set close to copy, giving the reader a second view of the outfit. Also note the intelligent headings: "John Wanamaker has good news: Two-piece dresses." This ad is just one from a campaign.

Henri Bendel 10 West 57th Street

ON THE CHANCE THAT THIS MAY BE OVER-AND-OUT FOR A WHILE...A PAGE
FOR YOU TO CLIP, REFER TO. A SORT OF WHAT'S HAPPENING AT BENDEL'S.

APRIL 13
Glorious costume of striped silk chiffon...gathery skirt, skivvy, whisper of a jacket. White with tobacco or smoke. $285. on the 2nd Fl.

APRIL 1
Mini-kaftan for the sand pile set...striped seersucker in navy, yellow or orange with white, fringe at the neck and cuffs. 3-6X, $12.00; 8-14, $14.00. Seventh Floor.

VERNISSAGE WILL HAVE AN EXHIBITION OF SMALL, DECORATIVE PAINTINGS BY SCOTT ELLIOT. ALL FRAMED— (SOME ARE HANDMADE) THE GROUP STARTS AT $25.

APRIL 1
Pleated Arnel to wear at home...violet, cherry or deep brown, all white dotted. To the floor, P,S,M, $35.00. The Fifth Floor.

APRIL 24
So what about that curly, tossy little haircut you were going to get. Have it. And don't forget your skin. Or your nails. Or your muscles. Mustn't let things go to rack and ruin, you know.

a new white paper with shiny, slick borders of green, blue or coral. With envelopes. $18.00

On the Fourth Floor— John Kloss's new thinner... In Linen. Dresses with shape, with small high bosoms. With narrow ribcages. In white. In lilac. In orange. In green. In turquoise. In navy. In short from $75.00. Long ones $115.00

APRIL 25

Gleamy patents, brown, navy, and black arrive from Italy... Spectator pumps with squarish, low heels and white inlays on the wing-tippy toes. $42.00

APRIL 10
IN THE STOCKING SHOP...MARVY NEW STOCKINGS THAT STAY UP BY THEMSELVES, REALLY. AGILON IN CREME PUFF. SIZES 8-10 SHORT; 8½-11 MED.; 9½-11 LONG. THIGH-HI, $2.00 THE PAIR.

AND THE BAG SHOP HAS THE SUPER-EST SUMMER BAG AROUND, WE THINK. A SATCHEL-SHAPED BAG JUST FOR CARRY-DONE JUST LIKE THE BAG DOCTORS US OF CANVAS WITH MOCK LIZARD STRAPS AND HANDLES. HAVE IT IN NATURAL WITH BROWN OR BLACK, OR HAVE IT IN BLACK WITH BLACK. OR HAVE THEM ALL. $8.00.

Cotton duck cut like a super little French shirt, tiny at the top, sprouty skirt. White, red, yellow, brown or turquoise. Sizes 3 to 13, $35. Fourth Floor.

APRIL 19
Linen, wrapped like a kimono, tied high under a small bosom. In white, navy, brown or poppy, $45.00, 3 to 13. To the floor at $55.00. On the Fourth Floor.

APRIL 28
THE JEWELER GETS THE ST. LAURENT WATCH FROM PARIS. WAFER-THIN 18K GOLD, THE STEM STUDDED WITH A CABOCHON SAPPHIRE. ON BLACK OR WHITE LEATHER BANDS. 1" SQUARE, $160. A MITE SMALLER, $150.

APRIL 1
Perfectly cut little pants of oatmeal linen, jacketing of deep chocolate linen... Cachet's suit. Sizes 6-12. $65. Third Fl.

Can clothes revive society?

My fabulous outfits outwit the snootiest social climbers. Shahs and states-men throng to my salon. Rave over my latest creation from Sealfon's. My clothes have the snobs agog. I'll tell the Count not to count on me; then I'll stroll back to Sealfon's. Buy a cigarette holder to wave at an old gossip, some stunning jewelry I'll say is real. I'll find clothes and accessories sure to assure a hostess the most fashion finesse.

certainly its **Sealfon's** *established way back in 1952*
ridgewood

Page left:
Henri Bendel is noted for its beautiful "shops". Here are items from several of these boutiques, each handled with individual conversational copy and distinctive typography.

There's talk of a possible newspaper strike and Bendel makes this the theme. An imaginative idea.

This page:
While every other store is smashing away with Summer sales Sealfon's is reviving society with clothes and giving customers something to talk about. This approach to advertising is helping to keep this store exciting, original, and out in front. We love the last line, "established way back in 1952". A store that thinks this way is going places.

IT'S IN THE AIR...

HIGBEE'S SAYS : THERE'S A WHOLE NEW ERA OF FEMININITY IN FASHION.

NOT IN YEARS HAS THERE BEEN SUCH A REVOLUTION IN SILHOUETTE.

EVERYTHING'S GOING CURVIER. MORE BODY CONSCIOUS...THE SHAPE IS BACK.

DRESSES ARE SOFTER AND BELTED, IN SILKY CREPES AND FLUTTERY RUFFLED CHIFFONS

FOR EVENING. COATS CURVE CLOSE TO THE BODY AND ARE OFTEN BELTED...SUITS ARE CUT

WITH SMALL, NARROW LITTLE JACKETS, DIRNDL AND FLARING SKIRTS WITH

MOTION AND AGAIN, THE ALL-IMPORTANT BELT! AND EVERYWHERE THERE'S THE IRRESISTIBLE

FLATTERY OF THE SHIRT LOOK. . . IN THE NEW PARIS-INSPIRED BODY SHIRTS,

IN MARVELOUS SHIRTDRESSES. . . AND SPEAKING OF BODIES . . .

THERE'S THE WHOLE NEW BONNIE AND CLYDE LOOK, REMINISCENT

OF THE 30'S BUT VERY MUCH 1968. THE HEMLINE? THE SHORT

SKIRT...YES, BUT WATCH THE ULTRA-FEMININE NEW

MIDI-LENGTH SKIRT. HAIR, SHORT OR LONG,

IS TOUSLED WITH CURLS. AND ACCESSORIES

ARE ON A NEW WAVE LENGTH...THE

HEAD-HUGGING CLOCHE, THE SHOE

WITH CURVED TOE. EVERYWHERE

SOFTNESS, CURVES, FEMININITY.

WATCH FOR IT ALL

AS SPRING UNFOLDS

AT HIGBEE'S. AND

IF THE MAN

IN YOUR LIFE SEEMS

SUDDENLY MORE ATTENTIVE...

THAT'S ALL PART OF THE

PLAN, ENJOY IT.

HIGBEE'S

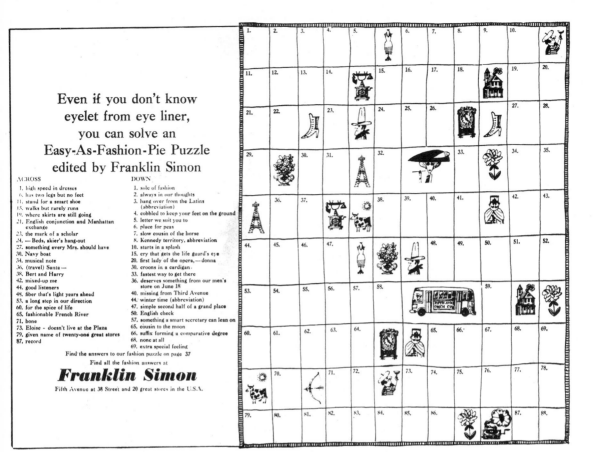

Even if you don't know eyelet from eye liner, you can solve an Easy-As-Fashion-Pie Puzzle edited by Franklin Simon

ACROSS

1. high speed in dresses
6. has two legs but no feet
11. stand for a smart shoe
15. walks but rarely runs
19. where skirts are still going
21. English conjunction and Manhattan exchange
23. the mark of a scholar
24. — Beds, skier's hang-out
27. something every Mrs. should have
30. Navy boat
34. musical note
36. (travel) Santa —
38. Bert and Harry
42. mixed-up me
44. good listeners
48. fiber that's light years ahead
53. a long step in our direction
60. for the spice of life
65. fashionable French River
71. bone
73. Eloise - doesn't live at the Plaza
79. given name of twenty-one great stores
87. record

DOWN

1. sole of fashion
2. always in our thoughts
3. hang over from the Latins (abbreviation)
4. cobbled to keep your feet on the ground
5. letter we suit you to
6. place for peas
7. slow cousin of the horse
8. Kennedy territory, abbreviation
10. starts in a splash
15. cry that gets the life guard's eye
20. first lady of the opera, — donna
30. croons in a cardigan
33. fastest way to get there
36. deserves something from our men's store on June 18
40. missing from Third Avenue
44. winter time (abbreviation)
47. simple second half of a grand place
50. English check
57. something a smart secretary can lean on
65. cousin to the moon
66. suffix forming a comparative degree
68. none at all
69. extra special feeling

Find the answers to our fashion puzzle on page 37

Find all the fashion answers at

Franklin Simon

Fifth Avenue at 38 Street and 20 great stores in the U.S.A.

There are times when advertising can be pure entertainment. This is particularly appropriate when it's Sunday morning, it's pelting rain outside, and the reader sits back in leisure to scan the newspaper. Franklin Simon believed a store must penetrate into the consciousness of every such reader, must make itself felt, must make that reader turn to her spouse and say, "That Franklin Simon! What will they do next!" (Yes, it rained.)

Left:
Higbee's takes a strong stand on what's new in fashion. It's an exciting statement, informative, practical, and positive. A great piece of copy.

Once again, Ohrbach's demonstrates fashion leadership by presenting plain talk about the high fashion ideas of 1967. As usual, Ohrbach's uses strong graphics to make the store's message come alive.

But where did all the "grandmothers" go? Fashion in America today has created two groups of women. The ageless. And the young. It is a clean-cut distinction and out of it, there has evolved what amounts to a two party system. Look about you at the next social gathering. Quite possibly, in fact, quite probably, you will see a woman beautifully in her forties, and a girl beautifully in her late teens, each wearing a dress of the same simple body shaping. While color and fabric may differ, shaping can be identical to the last seam. Today, designers stand accused of designing just for the young. This is madness, for the truth is that almost all that goes on between neck and hem is for anyone and everyone. This is truly the day of no-age clothes. What separates the women from the girls is the way they put fashion together. For example, let's take our simple, well-cut dress. Nobody says it must be worn four inches above the knee with the gloveless glove, a plastic cube watch, giant patterned panty hose and an almost no-heel, squared-toe kid shoe. Sweet sixteen can wear it and bring it off in great swinging style. Now, bring to this same shaping, a hem discreetly above knee, a mini-glove, a handsome bracelet watch, rib-mesh hose and superb turtle shoes . . . and sweet forty-nine will bring this off too in every bit as great style. Swinging? No, not swinging . . . chic and ageless. This is indeed the two party system. We believe in it. We believe in it so hard we have a store filled with two party fashion. Total looks for the modern ageless woman . . . total looks for the young, and these looks are, as they should be, totally different yet each is new, in fashion and most important of all, right! For if you can't count on Neiman-Marcus to bring you what is fashionable and right, who can you count on?

Neiman-Marcus makes a significant observation on fashion in America in 1967. Read this editorial. Neiman-Marcus has what it takes to be a world fashion leader.

Right at this moment Alexander's is doing a fur coat campaign the like of which has never been seen. There is always some mystery, some emotional tension, for wanting to buy a fur. Alexander's advertising is starting from that point and getting directly into the common sense practicality of it all. In each ad Fred the Furrier does the conversation and it's great.

Any fashion-appeal store worthy of the designation knows it can never cease to make strong fashion registration. This calls for many things including outstanding advertising, one fashion idea at a time. Dayton's does a super job and this page on The Big Coat is tops. Informative reason-why conversational copy supported by sensational graphics.

The Big Coat

It takes something pretty spectacular to convince any diet conscious woman (and aren't we all) just how much better bigger can sometimes be. But our new shapely trench coats should do the trick. They're big, all right. Even bigger than your biggest bigtop. And they're loose. At least as loose as the dresses you'll be wearing under them. But most of all they're proportioned. So that the looseness flows, instead of, hangs. So that big or small you can wear this kind of coat. Rather than have the coat wear you. We think it's definitely the shape of things to come. And once you try it on, we think you'll think that way too! Examples from our whole big selection: By Luba, in honey, 6-14, $80; Contemporary Coats, all stores. By Margit Brandt for Drizzle, hooded trench in navy/walnut, 8-14, $120; Misses' Casual Coats, all stores except Rochester and Fargo.

DAYTON'S

CATCH · SPRING · FEVER · AT · DAYTON'S

Bergdorf Goodman looks back fifty years and finds smart opera wraps are still smart opera wraps. The 1912 vintage advertisement is revelation. It shows that styles may have changed a bit but women's passion for "fashions of inimitable beauty, charm and originality" has not changed at all. Bergdorf Goodman, of course, goes on forever.

glamour *today*

American. Vital.
Original. Recognizable
anywhere in the world.

The theatre suit.
Beaded. Belted.
Peplumed. High drama.

Moonbeam beading traces the shoulder of a fitted jacket
over slim, back slit skirt. By Evelyn de Jonge in
dark navy tissue faille of acetate-nylon, 4 to 12, 196.00
Contempora, Third Floor, Lord & Taylor, Fifth Avenue
at 39th Street—call (212) 391-3300. Open daily 10 to 6,
Thursday 10 to 8. And at Manhasset, Westchester,
Garden City, Millburn, Ridgewood-Paramus and Stamford
Shop Sundays 12 to 5 at our Manhasset, Westchester,
Garden City and Stamford stores.

"Glamour today" has been the highlight of the fashion scene this fall. Lord & Taylor's campaign has been distinguished three ways: beautiful, consistent, and fashion-authoritative. Each presentation in the newspaper has made one fashion statement, one at a time. This is how a great fashion store maintains customer acceptance. Note the layout simplicity, the sparse and telling copy, the visible typography and the dynamic art. Authority all the way.

W2

Our exciting new shop for one special person: the Woman who Works.

It's here now. A marvelous new shop that's geared to your tight schedule, your tight budget, and your very particular sense of style. You're a super special person with special needs, and we're here to devote ourselves just to you.

We've stocked our new W2 (that stands for the Woman who Works) with fashions that are fresh and immediate for active women. Not just cute little juniors or matronly mothers, but clothes for the wide spectrum of women who work. And look good at it. We've geared our staff to take care of you the

way you want and need: quickly and knowledgeably. W2: the kind of shop you've always hoped would happen. (Shown here: our double-breasted suit with a

side-pleated skirt, in bisque or snow linenweave at $96. And our blazer suit with a side-slit skirt, in navy or fudge linenweave at $90. Both in sizes 6 to 16.)

HUGHES & HATCHER
Available in our stores at the end of March

Hughes & Hatcher, Detroit, opens it's W2 shop for "the Woman Who Works." The emphasis is on moderately priced fashion, on meeting the needs of all women who work... "not just the cute little juniors or matronly mothers". And the shop promises to have a staff geared to the special needs of the career woman. This black-and-white page appeared in the Detroit News Sunday roto for spring fashion.

The Paris Couture suit... in all its quiet glory

Fashion Council
...a group of stores and people who think fashion

Q-How can a smaller store look big in the newspaper?

A-Join up with other smaller stores and run full pages.

Watch Fashion Council. This group of smart fashion shops in Ontario is doing a notable advertising campaign featuring outstanding photography and copy. One store at a time, one over-all look.

Of course, everyone uses election themes to dramatize fall fashion promotions during a presidential election year. But Carsons does the extraordinary. The store goes to great lengths to find Nixon and McGovern look-alikes and poses them with four fashion models in front of the store. "Carsons Blazer Campaign" was sure to have been the most talked about ad in the Tuesday, August 15, 1972 Chicago Tribune!

COUNTRY GENTRY. The tailored hacking jacket and trousers in cotton corduroy, dashed with a soft, plaid shirt. All from TWCC. Most properly pulled together with kiltie moccasins and a lean loop of a muffler. Jacket, $76; pants, $36; shirt, $25. All in sizes 6 to 14 in Indeed † at Dayton's.
†Registered, State of Minnesota

DAYTON'S

The all-together look of country gentry focused attention on the classy separates to be found in Dayton's medium-priced Indeed Shop. It ran in a fall 1977 issue of Mademoiselle.

Hudson's recreates the pin-up attitude of the W.W. II years and everyone in Detroit sits up and takes notice. There's Greta with her back to us, Lauren ready for Bogie's whistle, Betty sans legs, Rita looking lovely, Marilyn ready to trade in her diamonds for parrots. A warm peach spot color background gives the page even more importance. The ad is part of Hudson's "Lights…Camera…Action" California promotion.

46

Girls in the Locker Room? "You bet your socks," says Miller & Rhoads and does an ad to be seen and remembered. The Locker Room, a shop within a shop, is "where you'll find all the raciest looks" and to do it justice the ad department has come up with the raciest concept for an ad we've seen in a long time. Down below it says "to be continued". We can hardly wait.

There is something special and delightful about this one from Joseph Horne. Judy Bond turns out to be "your favorite poet" and the copy is poetic about bigger bows, fuller sleeves, and all the details of smart merchandise. All this for $15? This kind of gentle elegance, subtly romantic (the big hat!) and utterly nostalgic relates totally to today's customer. Horne's never misses.

Page right:
Lord & Taylor is famous for making fashion statements and utilizing the power of double-trucks for supreme emphasis. This one, on Romantic Pants, is the most exciting of them all. Not only the incredible layout and the beautiful artwork but the essential copy — crisp, logical and inform-ative, talking to You, the One Customer. In a New York Sunday Times, filled with fine advertising and competing doubletrucks, this spread stood out far in front. A masterpiece.

Joseph Horne Co.

$15 Your favorite poet Judy Bond fluffs the bow bigger, billows the sleeve fuller, cuffs a dainty wrist three buttons deep for a blouse idyllic with spring suits and bigskirting. Romantic lines worth repeating in white, ivory, blue, mint, pink. Another touch of the poet: silky-feeling Ultressa® Dacron® polyester, spinning-wash, spinning-dry. Sizes 10 to 18. Street Floor Sportswear, Downtown, and all stores.

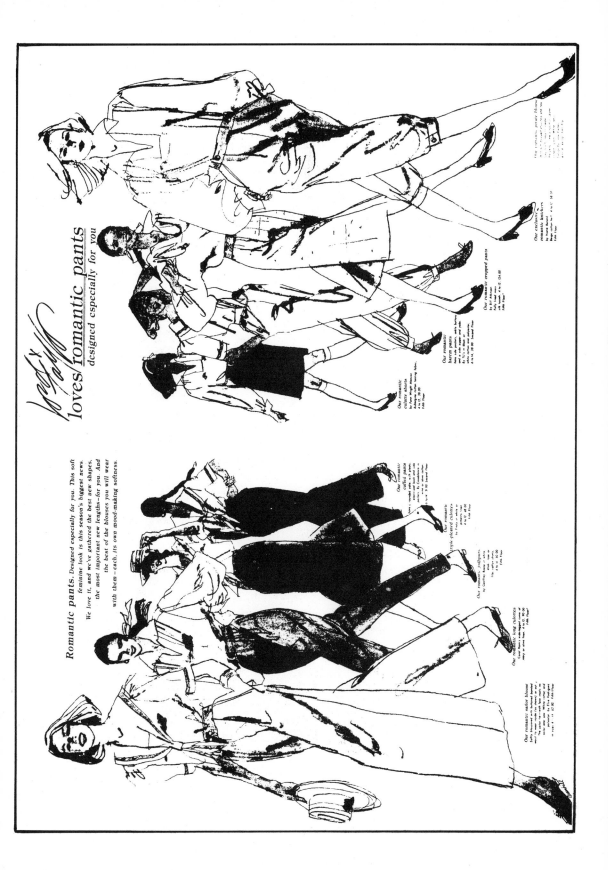

loves/romantic pants
designed especially for you

Romantic pants. Designed especially for you. This soft feminine look is this season's biggest news. We love it, and we've gathered the best new shapes, the most important new lengths—for you. And the best of the blouses you will wear with them—each, its own mood-making softness.

Our romantic culotte shorts
by Pam Wright Maison

Our romantic harem pants

Our romantic cropped pants
by Bill Atkinson

Our exclusive romantic knickers
by Pierre Berard

Our romantic sailor blouse
by Geoffrey Beene

Our romantic long culottes

Our romantic jodhpurs
by Geoffrey Beene

Our romantic triple-pleated culottes

Our romantic cuffed pants

49

It was sure to happen. One of the New York stores was bound to tie in with the Chorus Line. But we were not prepared for such a super job. Abraham & Straus does it fabulously. The models, the poses, the masks, the background—to say nothing of the merchandise which is shown to great advantage. This was without doubt the best seen and most talked-about ad of the week.

50

Joseph Magnin sells optimism as well as merchandise in this "Sunny Side of the Street" page. We love the way the figure stretches to the top of the page, the sun symbol in her hand directing us right to the headline and copy. JM sells an $18 striped t-shirt—and so much more in this page. It sells itself as the lively, exciting place to shop in San Francisco.

52

In San Francisco summer comes earlier and the good citizens there have a right to know what the beaches and favorite spas will look like. Macy's, ever ready to oblige, gave with a handsome revelation. From here on in when anybody thinks swimwear this scene featuring the maillot will not be forgotten.

Page left:
Our reproduction of this ad hardly does justice. You don't see the perfect shade of blue perfectly printed by the Los Angeles Times. The May Company's art is good as we've ever seen and the type overlay has been expertly handled, a beautiful blending of all elements. Surely the best seen and best remembered ad of the week.

53

This has to be one of the most
powerful eye-compelling
photographs of the year. The
perspective and converging
lines are irresistible. Lately
most major New York stores
are depending on full page or
near-full page photography
with the inevitable result that
ads begin to look alike. Saks
Fifth Avenue, by virtue of extraordinary lifestyle settings,
is gaining distinction.

The maillot. One shimmering piece that's twice as sexy as two. Monika Tilley for Elon
cuts it high on the legs. Bare on the shoulders. Straight across the back.
Black nylon and spandex, lashed with brights, sizes 6 to 14, $36.
Sand and Sea Shop, Third Floor.

Saks Fifth Avenue

Monika Tilley. Here today, March 28. Informal modeling of the collection, today and Tuesday, from 12 to 4.
New York (212) PL3-4000 open Thursday until 8.30 p.m. • White Plains, Springfield and Garden City open Monday and Thursday until 9 p.m. • Bergen open Monday, Thursday and Friday until 9.30

JM SWIMSUITS ARE FOR SUN WORSHIP-PERS WHO THINK A LITTLE LEFT TO THE IMAGINATION (AND WE DO MEAN JUST A LITTLE) IS BETTER THAN THE NAKED TRUTH!

Not just two or three wicked numbers, but a sexy selection (in depth) of swimsuits sure to snare every eye. Here, our cut-out maillot in slate or paprika for 6 to 14 sizes 33.00. JM Swim Shop.

JM deliberately sells sex appeal as the motivating factor in swimsuit promotion. There is no question about this advertisement. It gives the reader an eye-full but much more than that. The headline tells it like it is and it's a smash hit. This advertisement should be pinned up in the ad office as the first and most far-out swimsuit advertisement for the season just ahead. Great layout art. A winner in every way.

ALL
THE THINGS
YOU
LOVE ABOUT
SUMMER
ARE FOCUS
RIGHT IN
YOUR OWN
BACKYARD
AT
JOSEPH
MAGNIN

look the world over and you won't find a happier summer landscape than the one airbrushed on our long cotton t-shirt for s-m-l sizes, 24.00, in jm & sun.

Some stores have a talent for making readers happy. Joseph Magnin, for example. Here's a four-color presentation that sells summer fashion generically and a $24 t-dress in particular. The brightest of butterflies, beach umbrellas, double-dip ice creams, sunglasses, beach chairs, picnic baskets, sunfaces, shells dot the background grid. The fashion art is page-high and dramatic. What an invitation to summer fashion shopping!

Making the whole page a mail-order coupon is not a new idea but Nordstrom has done it better than ever. For once the customer can read the "small type". Most coupons appearing in retail store ads are poorly done, hard to read, and rarely provide enough space for a name and an address. Nordstrom's ad, of course, is more than a coupon. It is a strong selling ad with a good headline and appealing artwork. Surely the best seen ad of the week.

This captivating approach to Juniors is one of the best. A smashing headline and everything from Weather ("Halters continue very cool with occasional jackets. Sun today, moonlight tonight") to Hot Line!!! ("Any item on this page will get immediate action if you call 372-6800"). The telephone orders were heavy. Love the "Thought for Today: Never turn your back on the opportunity to turn your back." Great copy. Great layout.

The hat is off to Bloomingdale's as well as to the New York Times this week. For sheer excitement this photograph plus Bloomingdale's distinguished copy is absolute tops. Add to this a perfect reproduction job in the newspaper. Breathtaking.

... this is the way to look. Modern. Attractive. Totally at ease. In sweaterskirts and sweatertops that are knitted in soft, thin wool in fragile sea-island colours. Here, sweaterdressing from Ciao: houndstooth skirts with, at the left, a short-sleeved polo, or, at the right, a turtleneck. Both in coral gables, bermuda pink or caribbean green, for sizes 6 to 16, $70.00 each in Town and Country Dresses, 3rd Floor, New York and all fashion branches. Bloomingdale's, 1000 Third Avenue, New York. 355-5900. Open late Monday and Thursday evenings.

59

What a joy to open a newspaper and be greeted with this "JM Amusement." Polka dots...polka dots...polka dots cover every inch of this page. The art is red, blue, yellow, black and beautiful. And the message is right on target. Dots will be important now until spring. When Joseph Magnin offers a "fashion celebration," everybody celebrates.

JOSEPH MAGNIN LOOKS AHEAD

by MURIEL SINCLAIR, *JM FASHION DIRECTOR* here is a midi look that is the essence of the new romantic revival and that fulfills a desire to indulge in make-believe moods, those happy, magic pauses in our jet-paced lives. but let's separate the fact from the fiction concerning midi-length clothes. the midi has nothing to do with everyday. it is a charming, utterly feminine look, inspired in part by recent reel-life heroines and now moving into real life. it is a chance to explore an exciting new look and to add to a wardrobe of many moods. never forget, you do not have to give up one length for another. the midi is not a replacement length, but an additional special occasion fashion. we are in an era of multiple length fashion, but the mainstream remains short. the midi is an imaginative new length intended to enhance a wardrobe and a life.

A NEW SUMMER ROMANCE. indulge yourself. if you'd like to be the girl of your dreams, you may find yourself stepping out into a fragrant, sun-filled garden, picnicking on a cool, grassy slope or dancing under a warm sky full of stars in a real victorian storybook heroine dress, the enchanting midi. it's for you, the free, young romantic spirit searching for a very special dress for a very special occasion. here, it's white cotton-and-polyester, sizes 6 to 14, 26.00, from jm young connoisseur collections.

SHOP JM IN METROPOLITAN LOS ANGELES: CENTURY CITY; SHERMAN OAKS, WOODMAN AND RIVERSIDE DRIVE; GLENDALE FASHION CENTER; TORRANCE, DEL AMO SHOPPING CENTER; CANOGA PARK, TOPANGA PLAZA, VENTURA, BUENAVENTURA CENTER, SANTA BARBARA, LAS VEGAS.

The prophetic look ahead. This is 1968. No store would dare speak for the midi but Joseph Magnin. Read what Muriel Sinclair, JM's distinguished fashion director, had to say. The ad itself...the layout, the art...achieved a fantastic contrast with JM's daily fashion advertising of the time.

61

Garden party

the Denver

Spring is when you want to look soft, sweet and tender. Romantic. And this spring, fashion lingers, with sensuously soft fabrics, delicate drapings, alluring laces, frivolous ruffles, to your social occasions. Discover our enchanted garden party. Dresses Downtown, Cherry Creek, Lakeside, Cinderella City, Aurora, Northglenn and Southglenn (unless otherwise noted)

The romantic print dress by Lanvin of Blue Purple polyester crepe sizes 8 to 14. $78

Floral crepe de chine by Donna Morgan for Nan-Dorsi, V-slit with white collar, detachable crinoline Sizes 8 to 14. $90

Romantic satin dress by Cachet of New York, V-slit georgette with double skirt. Sizes 8 to 14. $80

Pin and green georgette gown two-piece by Maurices of the Mall 12 in pink floral. $80

Salvation by Jack Mulqueen floral crepe du chine, pressed in Sizes 8 to 12. $125 (Lanvin)

Tip: Romeo, sheer navy polyester with floral fashion print, pleated bodice. By Le Perrins sizes 6 to 14. $58

Sheer lilac floral print with white collar ribbon trim. By John Roberts, 8 to 16. $58 Please allow 10 days for delivery.

Floral print on white georgette, polyester georgette, by Ursula of Switzerland 6 to 14. $94

Pleats and ruffles in a delicate print, pale pink print by Le Roberts. Sizes 8 to 16. $78

Intermission-length pink silk chiffon evening gown with kerchief hem. By The Silk Farm of Denver. Sizes 8 to 14. $200 Downtown and Cherry Creek only.

Eyelet combined with a paisley print surah by Nancy Greer. White with green. Sizes 8 to 16. $72

Vicky's Fashions in semi-sheer white floral border print. Sizes 6 to 14. $80

The cover of Macy's "Body makeup" mailer has been picked up in this ad to reinforce the book and to give additional customers a chance to get expert help. Five events relating to figure shape up are announced, all taking place on the second floor, building even more traffic for underfashions.

Left:
These doublespreads by the Denver take your breath away. This is headquarters advertising, telling people that there is only one choice—the Denver.

63

SHAPE UP!

See Daily Demonstrations Downtown
on Hudson's Mezzanine Drug Department
now through November 18

See new exercisers that are fun and easy to use. **Hear** demonstrators explain new therapeutic aids to physical fitness. **Discover** how easy it can be to trim down in your own home. **Let** the experts give you tips on weight reduction. **Learn** how to firm face and throat muscles. **Find** ways to soothe, relax tired muscles. **Come** to Hudson's for tips on all-over physical improvement.

Tone and trim your entire body with this Two-way Thrift Cycle Exerciser—the spring-action handlebars move back and forth to exercise arms and torso while the pedal action trims legs and hips. This is a heavy-duty exerciser with a twin-bar tubular frame and standard adjustable saddle .... Just **19.95**

Pedal your way to physical fitness on a Walton Speed Bike from Hudson's. Fingertip control adjusts pedal tension from light to heavy. Chromed handlebars provide a swimming motion action. Two unusual features, the Speedometer and Odometer tell your daily speed and distance. Easy to assemble **89.95**

Have a year-round tan with the G.E. Sunlamp Kit that is so light and portable for easy traveling. Kit includes the bulb, holder with chromed safety guard, goggles, tanning lotion and rugged carrying case. See it in operation at Hudson's during demonstration days. The G.E. makes a great gift, too **16.95**

Help bring facial muscles to youthful resiliency with our Dynatone Isometric Facial Exerciser. Used daily, it can quickly firm-up delicate face and neck muscles that cause loose, sagging skin as well as many other facial contour problems. Dynatone is gentle and effective. Try it .... Just **69.95**

Give yourself professional-type whirlpool treatments at home with the Songrand Turbo-Jet Whirlpool Bath. Fits any bathtub and pumps 70 gallons of water per minute. Has an adjustable jet spray and automatic timer for on and off. The Songrand gives wonderful relief to muscles. UL approved. **199.95**

Let thousands of magic swirling 'fingers' of warm water gently massage tired aching feet, ankles, wrists or hands. The Songrand Thermo-Jet Footbath soothes with its turbulent whirlpool movement easing tiredness and soreness. A boon to those who must spend long hours on their feet. UL approved. **39.95**

Have a floor-model sunlamp you can set up permanently in your bedroom or office. The Sperti Monte Carlo shown here, is a full-power unit with 425 watts of Sperti® sunlight. The complete unit includes the adjustable, self-supporting stand, chrome-plated reflector and goggles. UL approved **31.99**

Give yourself salon-type facials at home with the Pollenex Facial Sauna. Just plug it in. New comfort-control design directs moisturizing 'beauty fog' to important facial areas. Pores are deep-cleaned of all hidden dirt and oil, leaving your skin clear, radiant. Has night-light base. UL approved. **19.95**

HUDSON'S

See the action in Hudson's Drugs—Downtown,
Mezzanine; Northland, Eastland, Westland, Pontiac. If
you can't come in, order by phone, call CA 3-5100

Hudson's drug department is a popular health center complete with demonstrators, information, and the latest ideas. The retailer was early to promote the health trend in 1968.

This is high-on-sex-appeal advertising and possibly that's what it takes to motivate the selling of teddies. The copy is delightfully suggestive, the models are beautiful, the photography is top grade and the layout is one of the best of the year. If this doesn't illuminate what teddies are all about nothing will. Surely the best seen and most talked-about ad of the week.

Dayton's has often been involved in programs for its community but with Minnesota Women at Home, members of its community were involved in its advertising campaigns. In September of 1974, four full-page ads featured active and attractive local women who were photographed in their homes wearing fashions from Dayton's intimate apparel. This is a basic, person-to-person approach to advertising, superbly presented by Dayton's.

The problem is how to show Joseph Magnin's use of color in our black-and-white publication. Visualize if you can each color a special ink. No usual "process" colors. The merchandise has to be shown accurately, as close to the real thing as modern newspaper printing can make it. The settings, however, the backgrounds, can be fabulously imaginative. Witness the safari behind the intimate apparel. This art deserves to be hung in a sophisticated gallery.

A SPECIAL SPECIES RARELY SEEN...THE FRAGILE FRANGIPANI THAT BLOOMS IN BRIGHT PROFUSION ON WARNER'S NYLON TRICOT BRA, 5.00, LYCRA SPANDEX PANTIE GIRDLE, 12.00, OR GIRDLE, 9.00, NYLON TRICOT HALF-SLIP, 5.00, PANTIE, 3.00, IN ALL JM FOUNDATION SALONS. JOSEPH MAGNIN

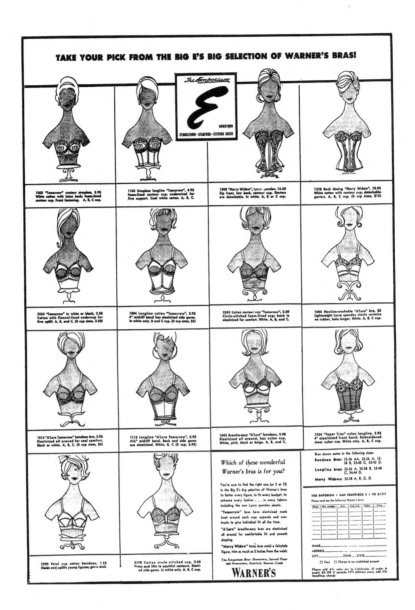

We'll probably never see the likes of this again. It's hard to believe that back in 1961, the Emporium did a selection ad of 14 bras by one resource—all at regular price. Sizes and colors are even indicated. What's more, the display torso device is an excellent one.

Right:
One of A&S's famous selection ads. This time for 11 bloomers. The art and copy are lighthearted, perfect reading—and buying—for a summer's day.

BLOOMERS

They're back! The same be-ruffled and flounced underscorers that emancipated Grandma...
and A&S has enough of them to work history-making wiles under every whirling skirt!

Under billowy bouffants...action-minded wrap skirts
...culottes...even floor sweeping formals, the
no-nonsense bloomer makes cool and comfortable fashion
news. Color-mad prints, appliqued and patch-pocket
solids, all in a breezy collection of cottons or carefree
blends proportioned for Misses' and Junior sizes.

A. Junior's ankle length white bloomers a'whirl in eyelet ruffles. S. M. $6
B. Double rows of pleated ruffles frill bright blue Dacron® polyester,
nylon and cotton blend bloomers. S. M. L. $6
C. Junior's gingham girl applique on white bloomers. S. M. $4
D. Nosegay flowered pocket bloomers in pink or blue. S. M. L. 2.99
E. Flowery border print bloomers ruffled in eyelet. Orange and white.
S. M. L. $3
F. Red 'n' white bandana bloomers knee-high in eyelet ruffles. S. M. L. $5
G. Half-and-half dot and stripe pocket bloomers. Pink or blue. S. M. L. $3
H. Flounced bloomers, five ruffled rows of white eyelet. S. M. L. $6
J. Nylon lace frilled white pocket bloomers. S. M. L. 2.99
K. Whimsical Mexican applique trims snowy white bloomers. S. M. L. $6
L. Mad money pocket accents eyelet ruffled white bloomers. S. M. L. $3

All from A&S Misses' and Junior Lingerie—
Street Floor, Second East, Fourth Floor.

SEE THE MAD AND MARVELOUS BLOOMERS AT A&S BROOKLYN,
HEMPSTEAD, GARDEN CITY, BABYLON AND HUNTINGTON STORES

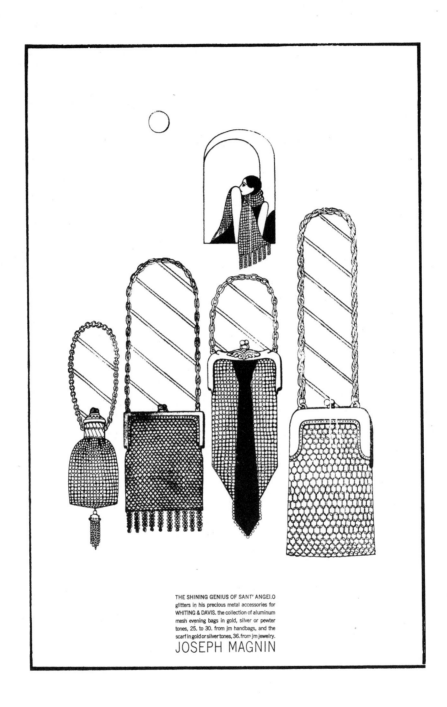

THE SHINING GENIUS OF SANT' ANGELO
glitters in his precious metal accessories for
WHITING & DAVIS. the collection of aluminum
mesh evening bags in gold, silver or pewter
tones, 25. to 30. from jm handbags, and the
scarf in gold or silver tones, 36. from jm jewelry.
JOSEPH MAGNIN

Joseph Magnin's "precious metal accessories" is printed in precious
metallic inks, gold, silver, pewter. A fantastic printing job by the
San Francisco Examiner.

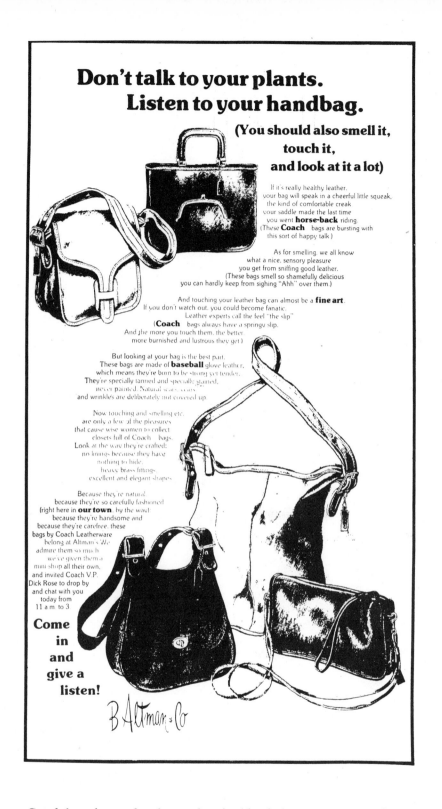

Don't talk to your plants.
Listen to your handbag.

(You should also smell it, touch it, and look at it a lot)

If it's really healthy leather,
your bag will speak in a cheerful little squeak,
the kind of comfortable creak
your saddle made the last time
you went **horse-back** riding.
(These **Coach** bags are bursting with
this sort of happy talk.)

As for smelling, we all know
what a nice, sensory pleasure
you get from sniffing good leather.
(These bags smell so shamefully delicious
you can hardly keep from sighing "Ahh" over them.)

And touching your leather bag can almost be a **fine art**.
If you don't watch out, you could become fanatic.
Leather experts call the feel "the slip".
(**Coach** bags always have a springy slip.
And the more you touch them, the better,
more burnished and lustrous they get.)

But looking at your bag is the best part.
These bags are made of **baseball** glove leather,
which means they're born to be strong yet tender.
They're specially tanned and specially stained,
never painted. Natural scars, scars
and wrinkles are deliberately not covered up.

Now touching and smelling etc.
are only a few of the pleasures
that cause wise women to collect
closets full of Coach bags.
Look at the way they're crafted:
no linings because they have
nothing to hide,
heavy brass fittings,
excellent and elegant shapes.

Because they're natural,
because they're so carefully fashioned
(right here in **our town**, by the way),
because they're handsome and
because they're carefree, these
bags by Coach Leatherware
belong at Altman's. We
admire them so much
we've given them a
mini shop all their own,
and invited Coach V.P.
Dick Rose to drop by
and chat with you
today from
11 a.m. to 3.

Come in and give a listen!

B Altman & Co

Coach bags have often been advertised lately but no store anywhere
made the merchandise mean so much. Here is the story of leather
made so exciting that nobody could resist. Students of copy should
save this Altman advertisement to study and emulate. Buyers should
too, because this is the kind of personal one to one communication
advertising should be.

The
Big Bag
Invasion

Headed up by Le Sportsac—
space-age bags of unrippable
parachute nylon, trimmed with
canvas. Portables that travel
light and fold to fit in a pocket-
sized pouch. And for
reinforcements, bold and
baggy jeans, making a big
impact everywhere they land

Saddle bag
with inside and
flap zippers
Style # 7176 $27

Sasson's 100%
cotton blue denim
jeans 4-14 $38
Contemporary
Jeans (367)

Top zip tote with
front zip pocket
Style # 7169 $20

100% cotton
blue denim jeans
by Jean St. Tropez
3-11 $30
Better Junior
Bottoms (379)

Long shoulder strap
camera case with outside
pouch and zip pocket
Style # 7168 $25

All Le Sportsac bags have a
matching pouch/carrying
bag. Handbags (170)

Trouser's Up pinwale
cords in cream or purple
cotton/polyester 5-13 $32
Junior Bottoms (360)

Short shoulder bag,
double zip with key
lock. Style # 7170 $30

Cotton corduroy jeans by
Freeway in garnet, blue,
barley, black, mahogany,
alabaster. Not all colors
in all stores. 4-14 $47
Contemporary Jeans (367)

Abraham and Straus

Brooklyn • Queens • Hempstead • Manhasset • Babylon • Huntington • Smith Haven • Massapequa • Flushing • Kings Plaza

"The big bag invasion", space-age bags of parachute nylon, plus the newest baggy jeans. Put it all together, add a little high-flying imagination, and there you have it from Abraham and Straus. This has got to be the best seen, most exciting ad in the newspaper, a fine job of photography.

The good citizens of Winnipeg had to sit up and take notice when these five shapes of sunglasses looked at them from Eaton's page. We've all seen these rhinestone symbols on display but never has the idea been presented more dramatically. It's good to know that there are places in this world where advertising imagination can be utilized to give the customers a lift. Sales will inevitably follow.

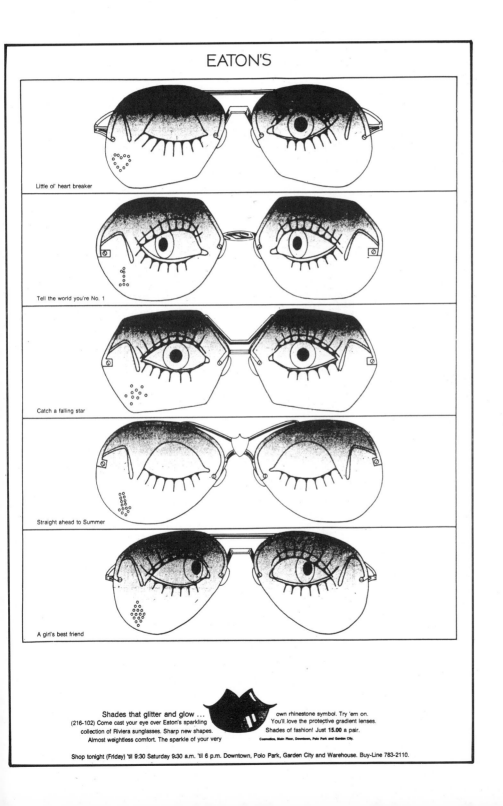

73

The Tuxedo

The newest collar, done here in poly/cotton in rich, earthy colors. Sizes 5/6 to 13/14, **24.00.** Silk foulard tie, **9.00.** Corduroy vest, **26.00.**

The Peter Pan

Simple rounded collar on a poly/cotton shirt. Tapered raglan sleeves. Sizes 5/6 to 13/14, **24.00.** Silk tie, **11.00.**

The Blazer

A traditional shape in 100% cotton. Long scooped shirttails. Sizes 5/6 to 13/14 **30.00.** Wool plaid tie, **11.00.**

The Grandfather Shirt

No collar, just a simple band on this 100% cotton shirt. S-M-L in assorted antique stripes and solids, **34.00.**

The Tie Tab

Unique button tab keeps your ties in place. This shirt is cotton/poly flannel weave. Pretty plaids. Sizes 5/6 to 13/14, **30.00.** Crochet tie, **16.00.** Corduroy vest, **26.00.**

The New Ideas

Five important collar shapes from John Henry in the Sportswear Departments Downtown, South Plains Mall

Hemphill-Wells

How does the customer learn what's new and what's right in fashion? We're in a rapidly changing fashion scene and the customer needs to know. Who is to tell her? Hemphill-Wells wins plaudits with this ad. The new trends, the new ideas are here, five of them, carefully sketched and simply described. A persuasive ad that readers will love.

Right:

Capezio's shoes, bags, belts, bodysuits, tights and jewelry all get together and become "a kaleidoscope of a shop" at Wanamaker's. And, to celebrate the occasion, along comes this kaleidoscope of an ad, done beautifully in living color with living copy and art. A joy to read and long remember.

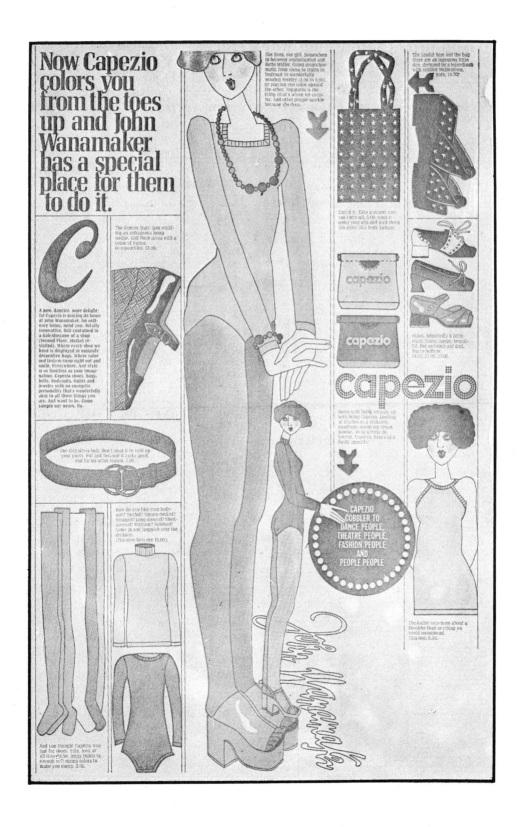

The idea of gathering all the ''anti-freeze'' merchandise into one ad may not be new but John Wanamaker does it with such aplomb that it becomes irresistible. It's a beautiful ad. The graphic concept, the chorus line of socks and the judicious use of color all add up to something the customer will see, study and remember.

This clock-look is somehow fitting and proper for a ''Round-the-Clock''
promotion. Leave it to Joseph Horne to do it with imagination and superb
good taste. The actual ad, showing a great variety of stocking shades, is
printed in three colors and black. A masterpiece of color blended with color.

JOSEPH HORNE CO.

How many times have you tried to say, in your advertising copy, that the manufacturer's brand name can't be disclosed. Leave it to Eaton's in Winnipeg to make this "we can't say" bit a big smashing event. What usually sounds like a frustrating little apology now becomes the driving force to help make sales.

Marshall Field's accomplishes a great deal in this ad. Hats, jackets, gloves, mufflers, shawls, socks, boots and shoes are all promoted in a clear, clean format.

Eaton's, Vancouver, knows just how to sell scarves, one of the most important accessories of the season. The full-page shows a multitude of prints and solids in four color inks. A column to the side shows just how the scarves can be worn, especially the important turban.

80

ONE SCARF
TWELVE WAYS

Knot it around your head, loop it on a bag, wrap it 'round your waist, chain it with a belt. Anything goes! It's sixty inches of long, lanky scarf and it's the accessory of the season. We came up with a dozen ways to wear it, but you can do better than that! Latch on to it now and let your imagination go. Shown in smashing paisley. It comes in florals, geometrics, and foulards, too. Visit our Scarf Department Friday and see a model demonstrate more inventive ways to wear it! By Glentex. Scarves, Main; and in all John Wanamaker stores. Just 3.00

John Wanamaker

How to present an item of merchandise so thousands will look again and again. The idea, the layout, the artwork, the copy, the merchandise...this is advertising at its very best.

So you have a wig salon and you don't know how to advertise it? Take a lesson from A&S—a fabulous idea beautifully done. In seven columns yet! If you have a story to tell, TELL IT, and make enough impression so customers remember it.

Right:
One of the first people as both retailer and wholesaler to promote fine art jewelry, Laura Kruger, of The Kruger Gallery, Inc., New York comments on this smashing doubletruck: "With this ad, Saks is taking a leadership position in fine art jewelry. They have gone out of their way to educate themselves about the artists and their designs and I am proud and happy to have been part of the whole process!" Kruger reps the work of artist Mark Spirito shown in the upper right.

Ornaments as Art

You see before you the new artisans of glamour: Robert Lee Morris, Rafael Sanchez, Mark Spirito, Alex and Lee and Arthur Koby. Master jewelers whose craft and interpretive powers exalt them to a higher plane in the scheme of fashion today. Seers—prophets!—creating a whole new form of art to wear. Important new jewelry that's all at once classic yet futuristic, inspired juxtapositions of exotic textures and unexpected shapes. Here then, the new artisans and their legacies. A sampling of the exquisite treasures awaiting you now, in our Fashion Jewelry Collections. Ornaments As Art—in Fashion awaiting you now, in Saks Fifth Avenue.

Right: Robert Lee Morris, and below, his bold, burnished, utterly exquisite bracelet cuffs. Their impact immediate. The appeal irresistible. The shell cuff and the strapfoil cuff, both executed in 24K gold-plated brass, $260 each.

Left: Rafael Sanchez, and below, his stunningly carved teak-wood pendant, with a double strand of tiger's eye and black obsidian beads, $375. Just one from his latest collection of shapes and textures, all vividly keyed to this bold new age of opulence and drama.

Left: Mark Spirito of the Kruger Gallery, and below, the large, cascading drop earrings in 24K gold-plated brass, $250. Intriguing dimensions that conjure up another era, another place...for they are created in the present, yet have an almost medieval enchantment to them.

Right: Alex and Lee, and their one-of-a-kind necklace of crystal and gold-plated chalcedion agates, $1200, in New York only. A fantastic fusion of fashion and art, avant-garde glamour carried to a most dramatic conclusion.

Left: Arthur Koby, and below, his five-strand collar composed of handwrought antique textured bronze beads, embroidered Chinese Raffia beads, gold coral and Asian seeds. One of a kind. $1500, New York only. Rare interminglings of natural splendours gleaned from throughout the world. Fantasy glamour that's shot with color: burnished, textured, almost sculptured.

This week, meet the artisans of Ornaments As Art. Mark Spirito, here in New York on September 30th from 12 to 4 and in White Plains on October 1st from 11 to 2. Rafael Sanchez, here on October 1st from 12 to 4. Robert Lee Morris, here on October 2nd from 12 to 4. Alex and Lee, here on October 5th from 12 to 4. Arthur Koby, here on October 6th from 12 to 4. Meet them all in Ornaments As Art, Fashion Jewelry Collections. In New York—where we are all the things you are

Saks Fifth Avenue

It's so hard for retailers to understand that advertising is most powerful when it promotes one classification and one idea at a time. This one by Fortunoff promotes Valentine's Day jewelry—hearts—priced from $5 to $15,000. It's a fabulous idea doing a super copy job nobody can resist. Especially with that smashing headline.

Hearts, from simply platonic to truly romantic to out and out lecherous.

Every year there comes a time when a man's (or a woman's) heart turns to hearts.

And this is the time.

And that's why you'll want to visit us. We're Fortunoff, the source. We have more hearts than you've probably ever seen in one place, at one time, in your life.

Here on this page are just a few. But we have hundreds more. Every kind of heart your heart desires.

I like you, you're special.

We have a 'you're very, very, very special' heart. A one-of-a-kind Victorian 15 karat gold bar pin, circa 1875, with a tiny heart of turquoises in the center. $120.

Or, a wrist Valentine. A 14 karat gold bangle bracelet with a cute little puffed heart. $195.

And a bunch of hearts for a wrist. A delicate 14 karat gold disc with 5 cutout hearts. $27.

I love you.

Eight attached rings, each with a dangling enameled heart. 8 Valentines for one finger. Red hearts, blue, green, and orange hearts. $170.

An 'I love you' you can tell time by. A watch with a little red heart at its center. And your initials (and your lover's, on the face. $30.

Or, one your grandfather might have given to your grandmother. A one-of-a-kind Victorian heart locket, 9 karat gold with pearls and rubies. Circa 1890. $100.

I adore you.

Perhaps a little pair of 'you're wonderful' hearts. 2 black onyx hearts in 14 karat gold hanging from diamonds. $180.

Consider our least expensive heart. But still very loving. A very, very, tiny 14 karat gold puffed heart for your favorite chain. $5.

And if you go in for the unusual, there's a jade heart with a hand-painted family of tigers on it. A work of art heart. $80.

And what's Valentine's Day without hearts and candies? A heart shaped candy bowl. Very old-fashioned. Very romantic. Very sterling silver. $37.

I can't live without you.

One that proves size doesn't count. It's tiny, but it says a lot. A one-of-a-kind Victorian 15 karat gold locket, circa 1865, with a red enamel heart surrounded by pearls. $180.

A diamond pavé heart pendant or pin. A big beautiful 'I adore you and I want everybody to know it' heart. $1600.

Marry me.

An engagement heart. A heart-shaped solitaire diamond ring. A little one, a medium one, a big one, or even a giant one.

A 78 pt. diamond set in white gold for $850. An 85 pt. diamond set in white gold for $950. An 89 pt. diamond set in white gold for $1190.

A 1.11 carat diamond set in yellow gold for $1850. A 2.57 carat diamond set in platinum for $6,000. Or perhaps a 4.15 carat diamond set in platinum for $15,000.

Grrrrrr.

And one for the waist you love. A 30-inch 14 karat gold bikini chain with 3 gold hearts. Very sensual. $40.

A heart of 38 diamonds, set in 14 karat white gold, is a ring we'll have to admit is slightly lecherous. But gorgeous. $700.

A sterling silver key chain with a sterling silver heart. This one could be slightly lecherous too, depending whose keys it comes with. $10.

And if you want to see more, and more, and more, and more, come see us, the source.

Happy Valentine's Day!

Fortunoff, the source.

Resolved that 1973 will be the year of exciting merchandise projected in advertising
on a smash hit basis. No small ideas. No piddling little ads that get lost. For 1973
we want dramatics, heroics. Fortunoff's seascape is right on.

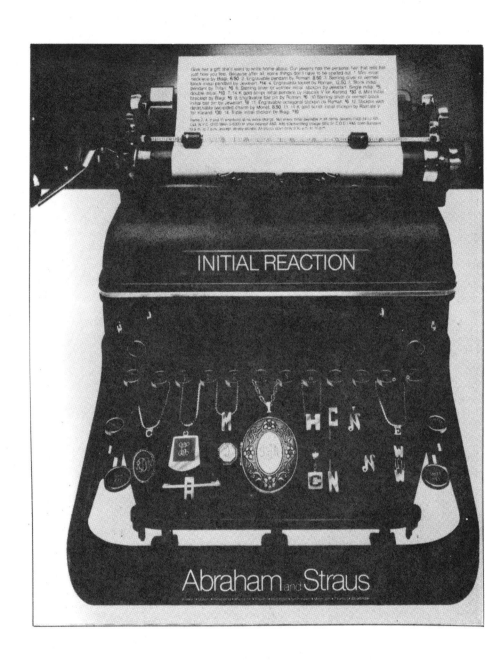

You want the spotlight? Take a familiar object...and alter it, just slightly. The reader will look long and remember well. That's why this initial jewelry ad by Abraham & Straus was so successful this past December. The second and third rows of typewriter keys have been removed and replaced with initial jewelry. Copy is set right on the sheet in the typewriter. Yes, it's small and single-spaced, but with this unique treatment, every word will be read. We wonder how many New York secretaries clipped out this New York Times page and pinned it to the wall over their typewriters.

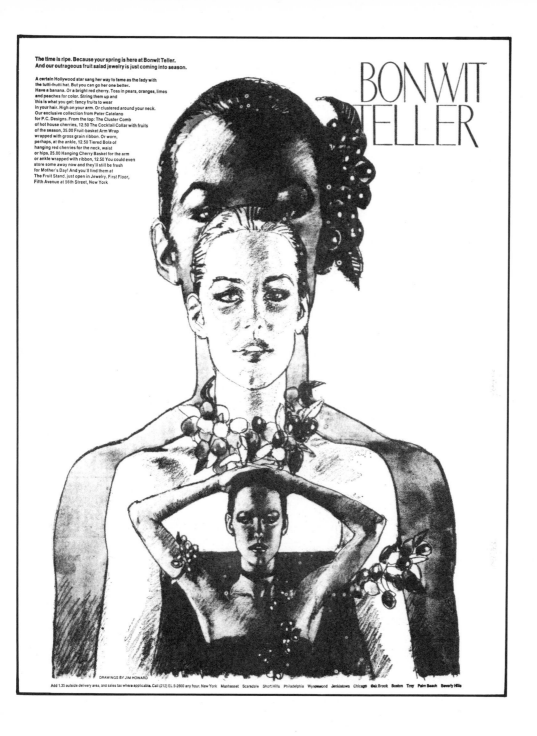

This ad on the new fruit salad jewelry has a degree of excitement that is rare to see and feel. The juxtaposition of one head over the other is breathtaking. Bonwit Teller's newspaper advertising in the late '70's achieved a new plateau of visibility and distinction and this one seems to cap the climax.

Comes a new young spirit and Joseph Magnin doesn't miss a beat.
If the pacesetter generation is wilder, JM is wilder. That's the way it is.

THE TORTOISE & THE FLAIR once upon a time, turtles were in fables, soups and children's collections. then this fall, because of fashion's predilection for calmer colors and natty neutrals, browns, greys, black and white, tortoiseshell becomes a pet accent. it's buckled, chained, buttoned, pinned, cuff-linked, stuck on to and generally a winner throughout the jm collections. but please, shed no tears for the tortoise's demise. tender-hearted jm's tortoiseshell collection is predominantly the pretend, plastic variety. we've even fondly remembered the turtle with golden-colored pins and cuff links. jmoral: long live the tortoise, it's way ahead in the fashion pace this fall. JOSEPH MAGNIN

Graduations are times for sentiment and sentimental gifts...and The Broadway takes full advantage with this Monet charmholder necklace ad. The look, the tone, the merchandise offering, every inch of this page exudes good, old-fashioned feelings. And the rebus format works beautifully to show off the little charms and their charmholders.

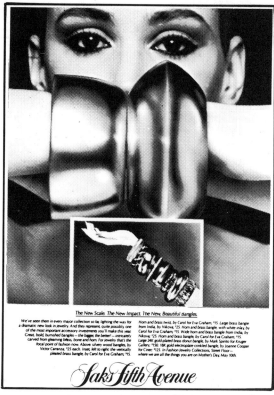

The New Scale. The New Impact. The New, Beautiful Bangles.

We've seen them in every major collection so far, lighting the way for a dramatic new look in jewelry. And they represent, quite possibly, one of the most important accessory investments you'll make this year. Great, bold, burnished bangles — the bigger, the better! — intricately carved from gleaming brass, bone and horn. For jewelry that's the focal point of fashion now. Above: silvery wood bangles, by Victor Carranza, $25 each. Inset, left to right: the vertically pleated brass bangle, by Carol for Eva Graham, $15.

Horn and brass twist, by Carol for Eva Graham, $15. Large brass bangle from India, by Nikova, $25. Horn and brass bangle, with white inlay, by Nikova, $25. Horn and brass bangle by Carol for Eva Graham, $15. Wide horn and brass bangle from India, by Carol for Eva Graham, $15. Large 24K gold-plated brass donut bangle, by Mark Spirito for Kruger Gallery, $150. 18K gold electroplate crinkled bangle, by Joanne Cooper for Ciner, $125. In Fashion Jewelry Collections, Street Floor — where we are all the things you are on Mother's Day, May 10th.

Saks Fifth Avenue

There is something disarmingly attractive about a large close-up photo and an inset of a mid-distance shot. That's just what Saks did in this accessory campaign. Shown here, ads for the concha belt and wide bangle bracelets.

Page right:
If there ever was a need to build confidence it is in the jewelry business. Rose of Detroit goes at this requirement seriously, offering a penetrating study of great interest to anyone who ever looked a pearl in the face. This is outstanding customer service.

The Concha Belt: An Enduring Art Form Of The Southwestern American Indians.

More than a new fashion accessory, more than a dazzling display of jewelry, the concha belt is a native American art form to be collected and treasured. As such, its authenticity, integrity and purity of design serve as constant reminders of the rich cultural heritage of its creators — the Navajo, Zuni and Hopi tribes of the Southwest. The belt featured above is an authentic concha made of sterling silver with turquoise stones, $1500, in New York only. The smaller photograph shows four more belts.

the top belt, also an authentic concha, is of brass and leather, $475. The other three are carefully detailed interpretations of this art. From top to bottom: the pewter and leather belt in natural, by Anne Klein for Calderon, one size, $75. The brass and ceramic beaded belt by Heaven, one size, $180. Find these, plus other authentic and replica concha belts now, in Belt Collections, Street Floor — where we are all the things you are

Saks Fifth Avenue

what you should know about Pearls before you buy them

It's likely that sometime you'll give—or receive—pearls in some form: a necklace, a ring, a pin. For the popularity of pearls has remained virtually unchanged for centuries. Yet few people know much about this most remarkable jewel: the only jewel created by a living creature. Perhaps we can help you make a better evaluation and wiser purchase by answering some of the most frequently asked questions.

What is the difference between "natural" and "cultured" pearls?

Actually, there's no difference—in the substance of the pearl. The natural (or "Oriental") pearl is simply formed and found more or less by accident, where the cultured pearl owes its existence to man's helping hand. Pearls, as you know, are formed around a foreign object inserted into an oyster: usually a grain of sand. If Nature introduces it, the pearl is "natural." If Man introduces it, the pearl is "cultured."

There is a third category of pearl: the artificial ones manufactured by chemistry (of materials like glue and fish scales). They have a superficial resemblance to genuine pearls, but their value and beauty are negligible.

How can you tell a fine pearl?

When the oyster builds the pearl, he does it by secreting layers and layers of lime crystal tears around the intruding object. These crystals—called "nacre"—give the pearl its luster, its luminescence, its color. When you hold a pearl to the light, you should see deepening rays of light reflected and refracted through these endless layers of crystals. It's a soft, warm, living glow; an inner radiance.

On the other hand, an artificial pearl simply has surface shine.

A little historical background.

Before 1907, all pearls were natural—in spite of the fact that experiments in pearl culture had begun in China in the 13th Century (where monks tucked statuettes of Buddha into oysters and were rewarded by pearl-coated Buddha statuettes). The Germans tried pearl-making in the 16th Century, using Rhine River mussels. But it was in Japan—where the finest pearl-bearing oysters are found —that naturalists pried the secret from the oyster in the late 19th Century.

Pearl-making isn't everyone's oyster.

If creating a cultured pearl were as simple as inserting a grain of sand into an oyster and waiting three or four years for a pearl to emerge, the value of cultured pearls would be considerably less. However, pearl oysters are extremely rare; only in Japan and in certain parts of the South Seas are they found—and only certain species of them yield good pearls.

The pearl-producing oysters are kept in "farms," and are floated from place to place in bamboo cages as they develop. The average pearl oyster travels 200 or 300 miles in its lifetime. But even with all the controls of modern science, the percentage of production is dishearteningly small.

For example: while over 80% of the oysters harvested for 5 millimeter pearls (the smallest usual size—with the exception of tiny "seed" pearls) yield pearls, only 5% of these are considered fine in quality. As the pearl grows, so do its chances of becoming imperfect. Blemishes appear. The oyster dies. The pearl becomes lopsided. Fewer than half of the pearl oysters can bear larger (7mm to 9mm) pearls; and of these, only 2% are of fine quality. In fact, with 9mm pearls, only 20% of the oysters provide a yield, of which 1 10th of 1% is of fine quality.

How are pearls classified?

The simplest classification is by size (Japanese pearls grow as large as 10mm, South Seas pearls as large as 15mm).

The next classification is shape; and while there are more than 15, the broadest distinction is "round" or "baroque" (irregularly shaped). "Mobe" or "blister" pearls (formed on the shell of the oyster) have a flat side, and are used primarily in pins, rings, and earrings. The third —and most important —classification is quality: the color and opalescence that are the pearl's unique qualities. Shape, cleanliness, and color are primary considerations.

In pearls—as in almost everything else—quality is more important than quantity. A small pearl of fine luster and symmetry is invariably more costly than a large pearl of indifferent quality. Unfortunately, too many people confuse size with value.

How much should you pay for pearls?

While you can buy cultured pearls at many different prices, the value of an individual pearl seldom varies (except that its value increases, as the value of any fine thing increases, with the overall economy). Any variance in the price of two cultured pearls of equal quality usually lies with the dealer: how wisely he purchased the pearls, and how large a mark-up he takes. At Rose, for example, you can buy a single strand necklace of 6mm pearls for as little as $19.95; a ring with a single pearl set in 14K gold from $20, earrings from $10, bracelets from $50, pins from $20, and pendants from $10. And you can buy them with the knowledge that you're getting the very best for your investment, whether it's large or small.

A Helpful Glossary of Terms

Millimeter: the measurement of the diameter of a pearl, equivalent to 0.03937 inch. For example, 5mm equals 3/16".
Round: the most common shape, although very few pearls are perfectly symmetrical. To the untrained eye, most pearls appear round.
Baroque: irregularly shaped pearls. These can have great beauty, and often command high prices. However, their value lies in their overall quality.
Mobe: large pearls with one flat side, usually used in pins, rings and earrings.
Uniform: a strand of pearls of equal size (or what appears to be equal size).
Graduated: a strand of pearls with the largest at the center, the smallest near the clasp.
Choker: a pearl necklace that hugs the neck.
Princess: a pearl necklace approximately 18 inches long.
Matinee: a pearl necklace approximately 24 inches long.
Opera: a pearl necklace approximately 32 inches long.

ROSE
JEWELERS

Macy's makes a statement, asks a provocative question, and gives a provocative answer. Style and comfort for feet...let the feet answer! A superlative idea that got superlative treatment in copy, layout and art. Who could pass it up?

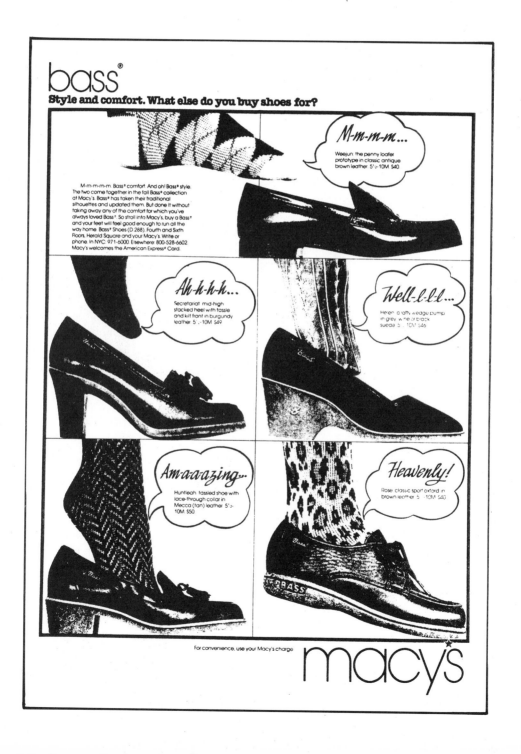

Here's how to promote shoes! A sparkling rebus layout. Four-color inks with color on the shoes, color on the type. The sandal story is short and sweet...and we doubt that even a single reader in Houston missed it. A toast to Joske's!

"Things to do in 1980" is a note tacked up on the cork board with eight resolutions starting with "lose 10 lbs" to "buy Garolini pumps". Macy's delightful approach to announcing the sling has double merit. It explains the new shoe carefully, observes the new heel (but doesn't mention the price!) and it's loaded with human appeal and memory value. The shoe is shown larger than life, a technique that increases impact.

The person behind the name is often very special news. Saks Fifth Avenue has sensed the importance of drawing a profile of such people, in this case of Ferragamo, the brilliant shoemaker of Florence. The telling of his story, his career and his craftsmanship makes his product just that much more beautiful and desirable. A joy to read.

Within the image: **norsport**

WE CARE ABOUT FIT and that's why we created norsport active sport shoes for women. all norsports come in sizes 5-12 slim as well as 3-12 medium, compared with other well-known sport shoes, norsports are made with better materials and cost less. in fact, we believe in norsports so strongly that we guarantee your complete satisfaction.

the 'ace' tennis shoe in white leather, 24.95. found exclusively in brass plum shoes, all Seattle area stores.

nordstrom nordstrom nordstrom nordstrom

Nordstrom is a winner for immediate impact...and long-range marketing concept. We love the powerful looks of this page, the giant sport shoe, the reverse "Nordsport" type, the active figures racing right off the page. The copy story is factual and believable. Fit, materials, price and Nordstrom's guarantee are stressed.

Right:
Three versions of the jelly bean—"the favorite of former movie stars and current presidents—a jazzy, transparent jacket—a spunky summer shoe—". A delightful page, printed in jelly bean colors, featuring timely classifications. With happy advertising like this The Bay captures a large audience in British Columbia. Who can resist?

jel·ly·bean
(jel'ē·bēn') n.

1. An exceptionally scrumptious *CANDY*, known at the Bay as the "jelly belly" jelly bean. A favorite with former movie stars and current presidents. In 16 surprising flavors, from the Bay's Candy department. Irresistible, and only *4.99 A POUND*. See fig. no. 1.

Fig No 1

Fig No 2

2. A jazzy, transparent *JACKET*, in brilliant shades of pink, yellow or green. Also found in clear. Presently hanging out in the Fashion Accessories department at the Bay. Comes in sizes common to all, i.e., small, medium and large. Very fond of rain and very inexpensive. *(ONLY $8)*. See fig. no. 2.

3. A spunky summer *SHOE* popular because of its clearly delicious colors, i.e., root beer, passion fruit blue, ice blue, or raspberry pink. Now hoofing it in the Fashion Accessories department at the Bay. Yours for *A MERE $10*. See fig. no. 3.

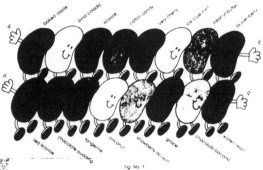

Fig No 3

THE BAY KNOWS:
There's more to a jelly bean than meets the mouth!

Hudson's Bay Company

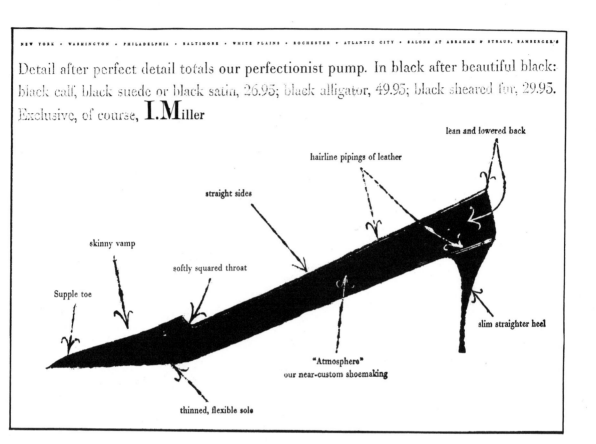

Shoe advertisers have long been aware of the unconventional I. Miller approach. Their extreme stylized shoe drawings have been praised and condemned with equal enthusiasm. The fact that the approach *works* and makes sales for I. Miller has never been questioned. Now comes this utterly fascinating advertisement in which a most dreamlike shoe drawing is combined with nine bits of factual information and style detailing. All done with pointing arrows, if you please. Blue sky nailed down to earth. A rare accomplishment.

Left:
When John Wanamaker wants to make a fashion statement for Philadelphia to remember, it pulls out all the stops. The objective here was to get customers to "read" high heels when they saw that page. A 1976 pump classic was selected and the artist was given the liberty to take the shoe to super-human proportions and the heel to higher-than heights. This was a Sunday ad and the paper was not able to mix inks, so JW decided on four color. Four color gave the single brown pump its rich body, its golden highlights. A swatch of every shoe color? That would be just too pedestrian for Wanamaker's tastes. And the background? A pure silence of white allowing the shoe to make its own statement. Now, that's unforgettable music!

Joseph Magnin has always been able to make living, breathing advertising. Now we have talking shoes.

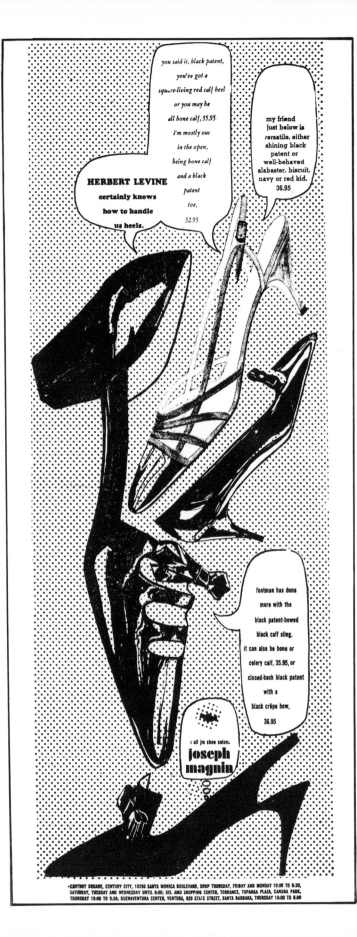

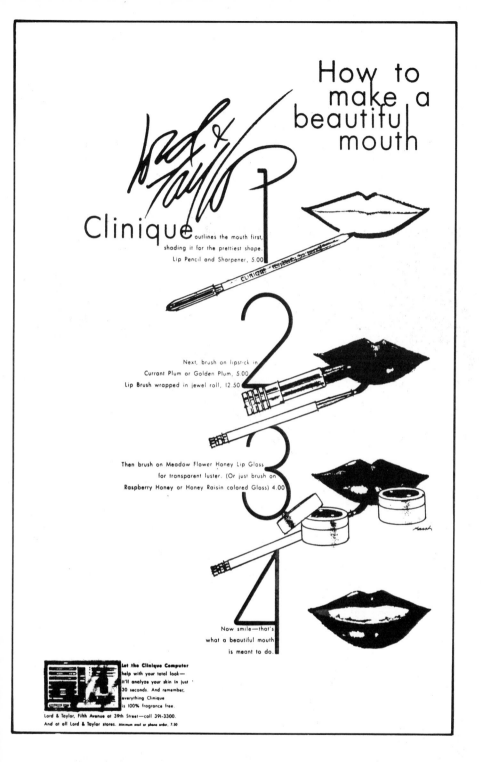

Lord & Taylor lets several Clinique cosmetic items tell "how to make a beautiful mouth." The idea is developed step by step to number 4—"now smile, that's what a beautiful mouth should do." A great idea delightfully visualized. It's the most noticed and best remembered ad of the week.

Advertising cosmetics must be one of the most elusive and difficult assignments an ad department can have. For some reason copywriters seem to get into rapturous moods and so often it comes out flaccid and meaningless. Not at Neiman-Marcus. Here we see cosmetic copy simple and practical, in direct conversation with the customer, talking to her in plain language, relating to her immediately and convincingly. Good graphics, too. A beautiful ad in all respects.

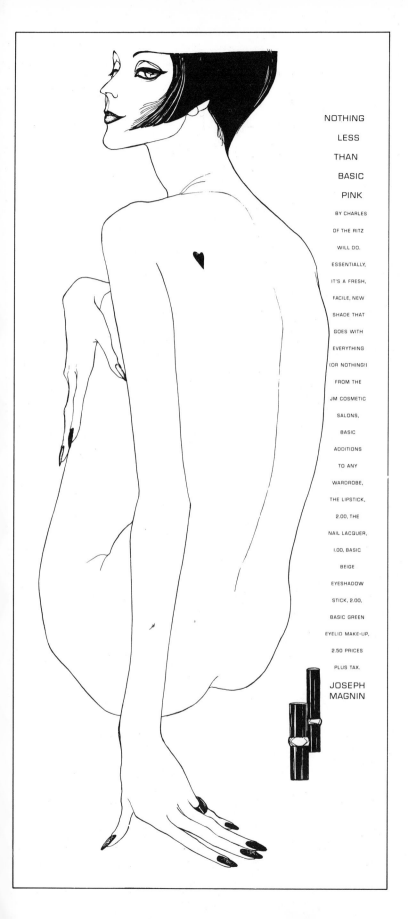

NOTHING
LESS
THAN
BASIC
PINK
BY CHARLES
OF THE RITZ
WILL DO.
ESSENTIALLY,
IT'S A FRESH,
FACILE, NEW
SHADE THAT
GOES WITH
EVERYTHING
(OR NOTHING!)
FROM THE
JM COSMETIC
SALONS,
BASIC
ADDITIONS
TO ANY
WARDROBE,
THE LIPSTICK,
2.00, THE
NAIL LACQUER,
1.00, BASIC
BEIGE
EYESHADOW
STICK, 2.00,
BASIC GREEN
EYELID MAKE-UP,
2.50 PRICES
PLUS TAX.
JOSEPH
MAGNIN

The controversial "nothing less" ad. Nudity was not yet in style when Joseph Magnin published this ad. Always the pioneer, always daring to do the young, kicky thing. So a few irate letters came in. So what. The JM customer loves it all.

"I don't have to be skinny to look trendy!"

 You are so right! Now that designers and manufacturers are turning out really smart, flattering, fun fashions for big sizes (and they are — like never before!) you can see the latest trends, every day, in Famous-Barr's Women's Editions.

But this week...this great big beautiful week...we've got very, very special plans.

Most special of all: our two fabulous Ice Cream Socials, with fashion shows and more, happening Thursday and Friday, Downtown and Clayton.

Naturally, there'll be ice cream galore (our own satiny smooth, extra-rich Famous-Barr ice cream...yum!) along with favorite toppings, syrups to nuts, even the cherry on top! Build your own sundae and enjoy, enjoy!

And you might win an attendance prize — there'll be two at each social. One lucky woman will win a free dress, another a free sportswear outfit. And each woman can choose her favorite in our Women's Editions area.

 There's more, too — you'll see makeovers (hair, cosmetics, and also fashion) on three women from the audience. And when you see the before-and-after difference, you're going to be glad that every woman attending will get her own beauty discount card! It's good for a fabulous 20% savings at any Famous Beauty Salon on any of our hair services: Just when you want a new spring hairstyle!

And, above all else at our socials, you'll be able to feast your eyes on the styles you really love, in the size you really wear. All modeled on women your size.

You'll see sportswear, such as our City Blues coordinates from Stephanie K., (shown above: wrap skirt, sizes 32-40, $30; blouse, 38-44, $23) and our Lady Devon Spring I coordinates (shown at left), all Visa® fabric of polyester (blazer shown, 38-44, $33, and pants, 32-40, $17).

 And you'll see great-looking dresses, such as Forever Young's crisp polyester linen-look shirtdress, at left, in clear red, 14½-22½, $48. And, shown at right Jacket dressing from Amy Adams, this one navy with snappy white braid, 14½-22½, $72.

See it all at our fabulous Ice Cream Socials and attend our other fashion events too — no charge for any of it, but we do ask you to RSVP for the socials.

You'll see — you really don't have to be skinny to look trendy!

MARK YOUR CALENDAR

Ice Cream Socials (sundae-making actually starts at 12:45 — please R.S.V.P. by calling 444-4185 during normal business hours.)
1 p.m., Thursday, March 22, Downtown
1 p.m., Friday, March 23, Clayton

Informal modeling
11 a.m. to 2 p.m., Monday, March 19, Stephanie K., South County
11 a.m. to 2 p.m., Tuesday, March 20, Amy Adams, St. Clair
11 a.m. to 2 p.m., Wednesday, March 21, Amy Adams, Northland
11 a.m. to 2 p.m., Saturday, March 24, Mr. Alex at Northwest and Stephanie K. at Alton (also, Alton mini show at 1 p.m.)

IT'S *Famous Barr*

One of the cries we've heard for years came from the larger women who read fashion magazines, roamed the stores, saw what they liked but "never in my size". That's changing rapidly, as we all know. Designers and manufacturers are solving this big gap in apparel sales. It's good to see how exciting the subject can be made.

Famous Barr does a series of fashion shows and events for this customer and comes up with this interesting, informative and handsome page. A great headline says it like it is.

Ivey's Florida does a fine job of targeting in on a market that has long been over-looked...the missy petite. Graphics and headline immediately identify the audience. There isn't a 4'10'' to 5'4'' woman alive that won't relate to the ''you've never been head and shoulders above the crowd...but now you can look that way...'' headline! Copy further clarifies: ''You may be tiny, but we know you've been having big problems finding updated styles that suit you...not your teenage daughter...'' Direct, clear communication wins that special customer.

CHAPTER II

MENSWEAR

Just as the women had their fashion upheavals so did their partners.
For men, the "peacock revolution" of the mid-60's was a shocker!
There were Nehru suits and neck chains, flowered shirts and ties.
And again, freedom bred two looks—that of success or total disaster.

After the smoke had cleared, the menswear retailer had a lot of
confused, dissatified customers on its hands—and it won back
confidence with well-thought-out campaigns that reinforced the
store's image as a dependable fashion authority. The reader will find
ads in this section that explain executive dressing, made-to-measure
suits, store services and value.

Innovative fashion is still news but chances are the more adventurous
items (like the urban cowboy look and leathers) are promoted for a
man's weekend.

Casual wear has taken its cue from active sportswear with the rugby
shirt, and the knit shirt (sporting tiny logos of polo ponies, alligators,
penguins or foxes) making important advertising.

You will also see a studied return to elegance. Look particularly to
Paul Stuart's "Mad dogs and Englishmen" ad on page 146,
Bloomingdale's "Chariots of Fire" campaign on page 147 and "The
gentlemen's blazer" from Neiman-Marcus on page 148.

All in all, the menswear retailer, both specialty store and department
store, has done an excellent job in restoring confidence in the
consumer. Look to the ads in this chapter as proof.

"I hate shopping around for clothes. But at Marvin Brown, it's a pleasure."

"Going one place for a suit, another for sport clothes and still another for shoes is my idea of torture. But for a long time I had no choice. Because I'm fussy. I like well-tailored, natural-shoulder clothes. And I won't buy run-of-the-mill. So when Marvin Brown opened two years ago, I finally found a home. In fact, finding what I want at Marvin Brown is easy. It's choosing that's hard."

marvin brown

Open Monday & Thursday
evenings and by appointment
(214) 369-1133

Old Town in the Village

Marvin Brown, Dallas, does a masterful job of institutional advertising. In the first place, the store knows its customer. He is a man with fine but conservative tastes. He has little time or patience for shopping around. He may even dislike it. Marvin Brown photographs him trying on a jacket and lets him talk in headline and copy. He tells readers he can find everything he wants at one store. That the clothes are well tailored and natural-shoulder. Not run-of-the-mill. And there is plenty to choose from. A direct approach that hits the target.

Everybody has a birthday! Weber & Heilbroner, New York, aims this ad at the friends and relatives of Libras (September 24-October 23) and prints it September 23. Nine pieces of fall fashion merchandise are promoted in this sure-to-be-read format. Chances are that those intelligent, intuitive, charming Libras will even buy some of this merchandise for themselves.

Sakowitz does a campaign of gutsy half-pages. Top: an institutional for the quality of merchandise. Copy reads in part: "Our buyers research every label. Not only when the name is added to Sakowitz stocks, but again every season. We expect superior quality. Our standards are high." Bottom: a promotion for a textured polyester blazer. The copy story shows how the reader can stretch his clothing dollar two ways: by the moderate price ($85) and by the new one-way stretch polyester fabric of the blazer.

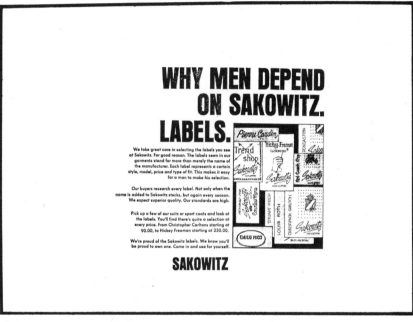

How the men who run things identify one another.

They have never stated it in so many words.

But the men in positions of authority in business, government and the professions have come to expect the men with whom they associate to dress in deference to a particular code.

Central to which, it goes almost without saying, is the natural-shoulder suit.

And if, like most men, your tastes and temperament require some subtle degree of individuality within this code, it behooves you to seek out the expertise of a men's store with a thorough understanding of the permissible variations of the dress code, and a rich enough selection to represent them all.

A men's store like Barney's.

Where you will find that what you always thought of as the "business uniform" is, in Barney's Madison Room, by no means uniform.

Depending on your build, your personal taste and even the nature of your career, a Madison Room salesman, a specialist in the subtleties of traditional styling and fit, will guide you through a selection that includes every significant interpretation of conservative business dress.

From the full, traditional cuts of such acknowledged masters of the natural shoulder as H. Freeman,

Norman Hilton and Majer to the slightly more contoured but equally traditional styling of Cricketeer and Ralph Lauren for Chaps.

Once you have made your selections, you'll be meticulously fitted for free alterations by Barney's own custom tailors. Men entirely capable of making a natural shoulder suit from scratch in their own right.

But Barney's professional obligation to you doesn't end there.

How could it, when the look of your suit depends on how well you choose its accessories.

Enter Barney's Fashion Co-ordinator. Who can, if you wish, help you select shirt and collar configurations in solids and/or patterns that not only work with the color and texture of your suits, but with the shape of your face. The shirts to be paired with precisely the right ties, from Barney's complete collections of prints, knits, club ties and regimentals.

Traditional dress requires one of the following tie motifs: paisley, club, regimental or foulard pattern.

Barney's has also added a second and entirely new shoe department devoted to the finest in traditional footwear from England and America.

As well as a new department devoted to the finest in traditional hats from England and America. Including Herbert Johnson, Dobbs and the exclusive collection of Cavanagh.

So, if you find yourself in front of the mirror one morning, facing a crisply turned-out executive you can barely identify, rest assured that the men who run things won't have that problem.

Barney's Madison Room.

The man at the top, or aspiring to the top, doesn't have time to make mistakes in his wardrobe. Barney's understands and appeals to this customer-target in a full page ad just crammed with useful information, establishing the store as THE authority in dressing "the men who run things". There is nothing wishy-washy about the advice here. Specifics are given, specific makers for natural-shoulder suits, specific shirt-collar choices according to face shape, suit style and tie, specific tie and shoe choices.

The Appointment:

Now, there's a new way to shop for men's fashions. Barney's introduces "Reserve-a-Salesman."

"Do you have an appointment, Doctor?"

The average New Yorker has 935 more things to do than the average resident of Blair, Nebraska. He also has less time to do them in. He plays The Waiting Game. He waits for trains. He waits on trains. He waits for planes to come. He waits for planes to go. He waits for lunch. He waits to pay for lunch. He waits for elevators, cabs and for telephones to ring.
The New Yorker's problem? Over wait.

Wait Not. Want Not.

On the other hand, here is Barney's. The whole world of men's fashion in just one place so the New Yorker doesn't have to go all over the world to see what's going on. Ten men's shops under one roof. Sixty thousand fashions. The Great Americans, plus The Pierre Cardins, The Hardy Amies, The Philippe Venets, The Brionis, The Gilbert Feruchs, The Christian Diors. The Gamut.

The New Yorker saves a lot of time this way. But, if he has to wait to be waited on, he begins to lose some of it. And, Barney's could begin to lose him.

The Reserved Corps.

Beginning today, no New Yorker need wait at Barney's—ever. Just call ahead to WA 9-9000 and make an appointment with one of Barney's Reserved Corps; an elite group of Barney's most experienced salesmen who can guide you quickly and effectively through all ten men's shops.

Your salesman will note the exact minute, hour and day you intend to arrive and will be waiting for you when you do.

Monday-Friday, 9:30-4:30

This service is made available every week day until 4:30 pm.

If you want to open a charge account, simply give your salesman the information over the phone and he'll have the forms all ready for signature upon your arrival.

And, to speed your arrival at Barney's, you get free parking and plenty of it. (No midtown parking or traffic jams.)

Barney's has 17 fitters for faster service. (Who wants to stand around watching other men in the mirror?) And, Barney's has 140 Old-World tailors so that when you return for your altered fashions, they're altered. Your way.

60,000 Fashions and The Time to Enjoy Them.

Barney's knows one thing about the average New Yorker. He isn't average.

It takes 60,000 fashions to cover the individual ways in which New Yorkers wish to express themselves while covering the individual sizes in which New Yorkers come.

You've always been sure Barney's has the selections. Now, you can be sure you'll have the time to select them.

Select, don't Settle® at Barney's. 7th Avenue and 17th Street. Open evenings 'till 9:30.

Barney's

Reserve a salesman this week. Call WA 9-9000.

Barney's has an idea. "Reserve a salesman" is an exciting approach and the ad is a smash. Obviously Barney's isn't going to pass up an opportunity to tell the full story of the store. Why not, as long as it can be told so interestingly.

Detroit threw its biggest party of the year (the Republican Convention) and Kosins Clothes was there with this full-page ad. In tongue-in-cheek fashion, Kosins recalls the highlights of each decade in Detroit and the obvious fact, "Kosins was there". Simons Advertising & Associates, Inc., Southfield, did the ad.

Left:
A famous couple finally break the silence of many years and tell us what they really think. A tip of the hat to Barney's and a deep bow to Grant Wood.

THERE'S A NEW SAVINGS BANK IN BOSTON.

IF YOU LIKED OUR BOOK YOU'LL LOVE OUR STORE.

Thousands of Boston men and women who've shopped from the Jos. A. Bank catalog already know our fine traditional clothing and significant savings.

But until today, you had to be in Washington, Chicago, Philadelphia, Atlanta, Baltimore, Richmond, or Charlotte to experience the pleasure of shopping in a Jos. A. Bank store. Now you can see Jos. A. Bank quality — touch it, try it on, and save, right here in Boston at 122 Newbury Street.

IF YOU'RE COMFORTABLE WITH YOURSELF, YOU'LL BE COMFORTABLE HERE.

Jos. A. Bank is for men and women who don't need prestigious store names and matching prices to tell them who they are. Our customers tell us they find our fabric choice, styling and workmanship the equal of other prominent but far more expensive labels. What's more, the people who design, craft, and present our selections are unsurpassed in their understanding of traditional clothing, and the person who prefers it. They can help you build a wardrobe of authenticity, good taste and uncompromising integrity.

IT'S NOT JUST WHAT YOU SAVE, IT'S WHAT YOU GET THAT COUNTS.

If you're accustomed to buying fine, traditional clothing, you've seen reduced prices only at end-of-season sales. At Bank you enjoy substantial savings all through the season on everything in stock. It's not a "discount" — we planned it that way.

WE DESIGN AND MANUFACTURE OUR OWN CLOTHING.

All cutting, matching, stitching, hand-pressing and fitting qualities of fine tailoring stay in. The economy comes from selling through our own stores and through our catalog. The result, we believe, is the very best value you can get.

WE INVITE YOU TO JUDGE FOR YOURSELF.

You'll find that our poplins, cords and seersuckers are $110 for men (compare at $180) and $115 for women (compare at $200). That our hopsack blazers for men and women are $115 (compare at $150). And so on for all our own make classic clothing. (There is a nominal charge for alterations).

We also carry fine silk neckwear, all-cotton button-down shirts and other traditional furnishings and sportswear for men and women at similar savings.

Year 'round tropical tailored of 100% superfine pure wool worsted. Available in our natural shoulder 3-button (shown) and 2-button models. Made to be worth $275 in other fine stores. Our price: $197.50.

You'll be pleased to note, too, that our store prices and our catalog prices are the same.

SELECT CUSTOMERS DESERVE SELECTION.

Whatever the size of person or purse, there's a quality about dressing well. So our selection is as broad and deep as our prices are modest. Thousands of garments in regular, short, long, and extra long sizes for men, and regular and tall sizes for women.

THE REST MUST BE SEEN.

Visit our new Boston store, meet our staff of professional salespeople, and pick up a free catalog. Start saving in season, every season.

Our elegantly tailored suit of 100% hand-loomed India silk. 2-button jacket, A-line skirt. Regular sizes 6-16, tall sizes 10-16. Made to be worth $325 in other fine stores. Our price: $225.

Jos. A. Bank Clothiers
Opens tomorrow at 122 Newbury Street

Open Monday thru Friday 9 to 6; Wednesday 9 to 8:30 Saturday 9 to 5:30.
Phone 536-5050 MasterCard and Visa charges are welcome.

Jos. A. Bank offers some pertinent thoughts in this store-opening gem. Please read every line of the copy. It will help you to think about your own store's communications. We particularly commend the top headline in the second column, and the reason for visiting the store just above the logo.

ARE YOU PROUD OF THE FAMOUS LABELS IN YOUR CLOTHES, BUT EMBARRASSED ABOUT THE STORE YOU BOUGHT THEM IN?

There was a time when the major names in men's clothing could only be purchased in the finest stores.

But that's not true anymore.

Today you can buy major brands almost anywhere.

If you're the kind of man who's willing to shop almost anywhere.

The men who buy their clothing at Morville are a little more selective.

It's true that they shop here because we carry only the finest quality clothing from the most famous designer and brand names available in America.

And it's also true that they shop here because we offer the kind of low prices even the discount stores are hard put to compete with.

But they also shop at Morville because they're both concerned about their image and impressed with our reliability.

And they know that a Morville label in their clothing says as much about their good taste as the clothing itself.

So the next time you go shopping for a suit, sport coat, slacks, dress shirts, neckwear, your new summer sportswear or whatever, join the men who are proud to shop at Morville.

Then, when you walk out of the store carrying your Morville package, you won't have to hide if you see someone you know coming down the street.

MORVILLE
Where you get great value without being embarrassed about it.

15th at Walnut; York Road & The Fairway; Jenkintown; Moorestown Mall; Plymouth Meeting Mall; 101 East City Line Avenue, Bala Cynwyd Shopping Center
All Stores Open Evenings till 9 PM (Walnut Street till 5:30) All Stores Open Sunday, 12 Noon till 5 PM
We honor American Express, MasterCharge, Visa   Free Parking at all stores.

Morville capitalizes on the best of both worlds—low price and image—in this page. We love the logic of the headline and copy and the charming embarrassment of the photo.

Beautiful art sold classic quality fashion for Saks Fifth
Avenue in 1975. It is art that almost any man can identify
with, detailed but just bold and crisp enough to command
attention. Poses are thoughtful, not self-conscious. Figures
reach up to the tops of the brownstones to show their power.
    The message is a one-week coat sale, and if you are Saks,
you tell it strongly but in a calm voice. No screaming. The
emphasis is on style, comfort, quality. In total: all very well-
bred and powerful.

LONDON FOG: A SMART DEFENSE

maincoats:® next
dryest idea
to staying inside

Flatter yourself, rain or shine, with the Preston: a blue-and white check with subtle burgundy over-plaid. This fashionable $55 coat, with slim-line fly front, center vent, and split-raglan shoulder is made of Clipper Mill® fabric: a rain-tight 50/50 weave of Dacron® polyester and combed cotton that's wash and wear. It has a contrasting yoke lining where rain hits hardest. Regular, 38-46; short, 36-42, long 40-46. Or, if you prefer, try the Embassy: a light $55 button-through in wash-and-wear Flite-Air® cloth, 65% polyester and 35% combed cotton. In navy or ivory with split-raglan shoulder and self-yoke lining. Regular, 36-44; short, 36-42; long, 38-46. For a dry head, unfurl 'Totes'® umbrella, $14.95. Mail order or call 421-4500. Men's Departments, all stores.

Famous-Barr, St. Louis, knows how to send the message in an exciting visual. Handleless black umbrellas float around two raincoat figures. Background is uncluttered gray screen. "LONDON FOG: A SMART DEFENSE" is a bold, active way to continue the message.

We love the one-to-one of The Sample's wonderful item headline: "a roomy golf jacket, La Paz, from Catalina, because your standards don't relax when you do". And, with its ragged-left layout, look how easy it is to read. The art is active, shows the merchandise well. Copy and phone appeal are also well designed. All this power in a small-space package at the bottom of the page of the Buffalo Courier-Express, Sunday edition.

a roomy golf jacket, La Paz, from Catalina, because your standards don't relax when you do.

A classic sportsman's jacket created because neatness is not just a nine to five phenomenon. Constructed of the hardiest fortrel and poly/cotton blend, making it so simple to care for, practically indestructible to wear! A move-with-you bi-swing back, complete with a mesh insert. Light blue or oyster. 36 to 46. 38.50 in our menswear departments at every Sample store except Boulevard, Tonawanda and Southgate.

phone 853-6270 today,
Monday 836-1234

Goldstein-Migel, Waco, knows how to sell a suit to a quality-minded customer. In three excellently-written paragraphs the store tells the story of the Hickey-Freeman $265 suit. It's all done in an easy, conversational fashion. A handsome suit sketch goes along with it. Appropriate shirt and tie are subfeatured. All in all a quality job.

What makes a suit worth $265?

You'd be surprised how often a customer browsing through our men's suits picks out a Hickey-Freeman first. When he sees the price tag, he usually starts looking again. But quality shows! It attracts the eye.

When a man pays $265 for a suit, there has to be a reason! Hickey-Freeman is constantly searching the world for unique fabrics, rich patterns and subtle shadings. Then, they hand tailor the suit because no machine is sensitive enough to achieve such superb fit. You can see and feel the difference. The lapels roll softly; the collar hugs the neck neatly. The coat gives you a sense of freedom.

A lot of men who could afford a Hickey-Freeman suit have never been inside one. But if they could see how it fits and feels, they'd know what makes a suit worth $265 and the man inside feel like a million dollars. Men's Shops, Downtown and Lake Air.

Hickey-Freeman

Short sleeve Hathaway
Finest quality and design in 65% polyester/35% cotton. Machine wash and durable press. Sizes 14 1/2 to 17 1/2. Brown and blue.
14.00

Countess Mara ties
Integrity in design and workmanship explains the appeal of Countess Mara ties. The Countess' coronet signature is on each tie.
From **10.00**

Goldstein-Migel

DOUBLE TEXAS
GOLD STAMPS MONDAY

Dayton's creates a bright new format for its designer menswear. Handsome suit photo is set against a wide frame of white. Headline is only 18 point, understated and elegant, and just right to talk about a John Weitz suit. The store logo is the largest type on the page.

John Weitz designed this all wool Palm Beach suit with both you and your budget in mind.

IT'S PURE WOOL. IN A CLASS BY ITSELF.
And it's also a natural shoulder silhouette so it's easy and most comfortable for you to wear. This one in a handsome all wool twill fabric in dark beige. And like all quality suits it carries the Woolmark label. In 36-48 regular, short, long and extra-long sizes. $135. See the entire John Weitz collection of Men's Clothing, all stores except Rochester and Fargo.

PURE WOOL

DAYTON'S

Pierre Cardin strikes again.

In the same place. Barney's, 7th Avenue and 17th Street.

Barney's, New York, introduces fall-winter fashion in a beautifully subtle manner. Suit model stands against an uncluttered ground of seamless paper. Headline is the only bold type on the page: ''Pierre Cardin strikes again.'' A single line of copy tells where: ''In the same place. Barney's, 7th Avenue and 17th Street.''

GIORGIO  ARMANI

Fluent Italian design for the American man.

IT'S MEN'S DESIGNER WEEK AT DAYTON'S

- **Tomorrow at 11:30 a.m.** attend an Aramis grooming clinic in Northbriar®, Downtown Minneapolis.
- **At noon,** see a Giorgio Armani fashion show with special appearances by Adriano Gianelli of Armani & Bob Beauchamp, fashion director of Gentlemen's Quarterly, L'homme, Downtown Minneapolis.
- **At 1 p.m.** Marshall Myles of Roots Footwear will be in Men's Shoes, Downtown Minneapolis.
- **Tuesday at 11:30 a.m.,** attend an Aramis grooming clinic in Northbriar®, Downtown Minneapolis.
- **At noon** there will be an informal modeling of men's sportswear with special appearances by Henry Grethel of Equipment, Ron Chereskin of Ron Chereskin Ltd., & Bob Beauchamp, fashion director of Gentlemen's Quarterly, Men's Better Sportswear, Downtown Minneapolis. Marshall Myles of Roots Footwear will be in Men's Shoes, Downtown Minneapolis.

Introducing the collection to Dayton's.
L'homme, Downtown Minneapolis.

DAYTON·S ⋙

Whether it was "soft shoulder" or "easy suit" or "soft suit" or "unconstructed suit" or "phantom suit"...it was what was new and important for spring and summer '71. Bloomingdale's led the way with this powerful Polo presentation.

Page left:
A dynamic introduction for Giorgio Armani to L'homme at Dayton's. The crisp starkness of this full page ad is guaranteed to be an eye-catcher. The subhead "Fluent Italian designs for the American man" says it all. The designer's name in inch-high bold letters, and the artist's sketch reiterate. This is a perfect formula for a powerful ad.

Whitehouse & Hardy, New York, turns its Yves Saint Laurent promotion into a special event. Artist, Lynn Kirkwood, is photographed with a sign tacked to her board that there is a "Free Portrait with any Yves Saint Laurent purchase." Copy ends: "...when Yves Saint Laurent has turned you into a work of art, you'll have a portrait to prove it." A powerful ad, a powerful traffic builder!

Tomorrow, Whitehouse & Hardy, with Yves Saint Laurent, will turn you into a work of art.

We're going to give you a free charcoal portrait of yourself with any Yves Saint Laurent clothing purchase.

Because we're introducing Yves Saint Laurent into Whitehouse & Hardy.

One of the largest collections of Yves Saint Laurent's contemporary styling and tailoring you'll find.

Yves Saint Laurent Suits.

Yves Saint Laurent Sportcoats. All imported from France.

Then, when Yves Saint Laurent has turned you into a work of art, you'll have a portrait to prove it.

whitehouse & hardy

Fifth Avenue and 54 Street
We honor the American Express Card.
BankAmericard. Master Charge.
Whitehouse & Hardy Charge.

Portraits by Lynn Kirkwood, (201) 356-2614.

124

A Wedding Shouldn't Be The Only Time To Wear A Tuxedo.

Try anytime. Dancing, dining, or driving to your favorite night spot. The excitement of dressing escalated to its finest... The Tuxedo, by Adolfo, Hugo Boss, and After Six. The classic in a class by itself at Rubenstein Bros.

RUBENSTEIN BROS.
It's What A Men's Store Should Be

Canal Street & The Plaza in Lake Forest

Rubenstein Bros., New Orleans, knows that dress-up fashion is an important category for fall. The popularity of disco and nightclubbing made it all happen. Here's the way to take advantage of the market change. The headline is provocative. The glamorous photo shows a young look, definitely not stuffed shirt but definitely formal. Rubenstein Bros. also lists important resources: Adolfo, Hugo Boss and After Six.

The Broadway knows the way we think...and writes to it! We Americans, both love and feel slightly intimidated by the British. So when menswear retailers headline "British" this and "British" that, there are a number of men out there that feel the "British" look just a bit too classy for them. Particularly when they are easy-living, open-collared Californians. Note how beautifully The Broadway reaches these men. Drawing a commonality between them and the British. "Refinement." Now what man could feel uneasy about that? Maybe the reader will try the "British" look, after all. Thanks to The Broadway.

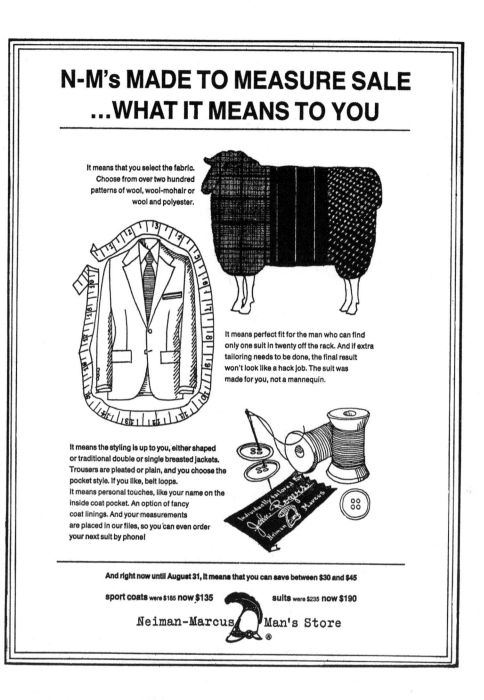
Neiman-Marcus never forgets that direct communication is the advertiser's most important tool. "N-M's Made To Measure Sale...WHAT IT MEANS TO YOU." What man could resist reading on. And he won't be disappointed. N-M tells him the facts he's looking for: 1. There are over two hundred patterns to choose from, 2. in wool, wool-mohair or wool and polyester, 3. the fit will be perfect, 4. extra tailoring will be expertly done, 5. jacket styling can be shaped or traditional, single or double breasted, 6. trousers are pleated or plain, 7. there is a selection of pocket styles, 8. belt loops and monograms, fancy coatlinings available, 9. your measurements will be kept on file.

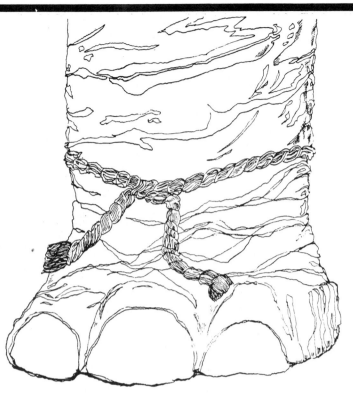

NOTHING REMEMBERS
AS WELL AS GORDON FORD'S MEMORY SUIT
OF FALL-WINTER WEIGHT DACRON WOOL

Our friend above may be known for never forgetting . . . but Gordon Ford's Memory Suit™
is one up on him. Made of men's fall-winter weight
70% Dacron* polyester and 30% wool, it remembers and maintains
original trouser crease, the fabric's smooth surface. even the shape
of the shoulders lapels, and sleeves. It also shrugs off wrinkles
. . . and that's something pachyderms will never be able to do. You have
to see this Gordon Ford of Philadelphia suit to believe.
University Shop, Second; all stores. 2 pc. suit 80.00 and vested suit 90.00

There is a thoughtful, fabulous approach to advertising
and John Wanamaker has it.
If you are shocked, surprised, or
puzzled you are the loser. This advertising penetrates
where ordinary advertising doesn't reach at all.
Get with it.

Ohrbach's talks sense to its customers...and its customers like it. Read the copy: "Do the increased costs of a date mean you can't afford to look great? You pay more to the flower lady. And car-washer. And gas-pumper. Add dinner. And movie. Or dancing. A mint! Is what's left only enough for a Leftover Look? Must you pass up a new cut, fur trims, rich leathers and tweeds? Not one bit. There's still a place where you can spend money and save money. There's Ohrbach's. (And it's where the girls are, too.)"

129

Ohrbach's talks suit-value in a most engaging, human way. What customer couldn't identify with the dapper gentleman who looks like a $2,000 raise when all he got was a pat on the back. Ohrbach's secret? The store talks to one particular, very real customer...and in doing so, talks to all customers.

Look like a $2,000 raise
when all you got was a pat on the back.

More fashion still costs less at Ohrbach's.

Today, when a man looks twice at every dollar before he spends it, he has to feel he is getting a lot for his money. Hughes & Hatcher came up with an ingenious approach. Sell four different looks and price the looks. That's really what a man buys. The knowledgeable salesman may make a point of fabric content and tailoring details but in the end he puts all the emphasis on looks. The H & H presentation is a good way to go!

The 4-piece suit.
think of it as 4 different looks at $36.25 each.

What you get is this: four items that mix up into four different outfits. First is a suit: a 2-button solid color suit with flap pockets and center vent and slightly flared trousers. It comes in shades of navy, brown, green, grey, or tan.

The next thing you get is a vest: a reversible vest that matches the suit on one side, and is checked on the other side — so you can wear it with the suit either way, depending on whether you're being dressy or sporty.

The next thing you get is an extra pair of slacks that matches the checked side of the vest — so it looks like a sport-coat-and-slacks combination when it's teamed with the suit coat. For added interest, wear it with the vest that matches the coat.

Or for an interestingly fresh look, wear the solid color coat with the checked slacks and the checked side of the vest. All in all, it adds up to four interesting new outfits (and even more, when you combine these four items with other things in your wardrobe) for the price of one: an easy-to-take $145

HUGHES & HATCHER

Roos/Atkins, San Francisco, begins a new campaign featuring real westerners photographed in Roos/Atkins' clothing. Here, a San Francisco lawyer is profiled. His work, his family, his hobbies are described. And in the last paragraph, his suit is featured. Roos/Atkins knows that showing a real customer in his Roos/Atkins' suit is indeed convincing.

Page right:
The drama of the demonstration is always the most powerful way to go. But, unfortunately with fashion, there is rarely a way to demonstrate a feature. Emporium-Capwell, San Francisco, found an exception and ran with it. If the new Haggar suit was washable then why not put the model in the shower and wash it. Here, the model sings as he soaps up.

George Carter, Jr. is going places

and dresses for it!

Meet George C. Carter, Jr., another 1973 active Westerner. He's a prime example of the West's new crop of professionals who are going places and doing things.

He's active! And he knows the importance of being well dressed at all times. George is a partner in a San Francisco law firm and obviously has to look his best.

George and his wife, Danna, and their two sons, Greg and Todd, reside in Alamo and are members of the Diablo Country Club. George is an active tennis player and skier. In fact, he and Danna recently returned from a ski holiday in Switzerland, but usually they ski the Sierras.

He's active in the performing arts, in both singing and acting. George has played musical roles in club productions and is a member of two choruses and a quartet. George also finds time in his busy life to be a member of the finance committee of the John Muir Community Hospital in Walnut Creek.

Naturally, he wears clothes that suit his active life. For example, here he is on California Street in a new multi-color plaid Ultrum™ suit from Burlington Worsteds. It's 100% Texturized Dacron™, so it travels from home to office to appointments without wrinkling. At Roos/Atkins, naturally.

Roos Atkins

132

Roos/Atkins, San Francisco, sets itself as a fashion leader with this strong "a certain style" promotion. A white summer suit is featured, accessorized to a fare-thee-well. A smartly dressed woman in the background seems to share the fashion figure's "certain style." The art, the aggressive fashion copy, the deco-feeling rule all work together to send a memorable fashion message.

Page right:
Chances are if asked to recall the wash-and-wear suit cycle, those readers of the New York Times in 1966 will recall this wonderful ad from Barney's. The shock value of seeing New York executives waiting out the wash and dry process in a laundermat, ties in place, but suitless, is enough to cause that long recall.

Poplins, seersuckers, cords and hopsack weaves. In stripes, plaids, checks and solids (Dacron polyester blends). All in the most asked-for brands. Open to 9:30 p.m. at 7th Avenue and 17th Street. Free parking.

We have 11,243 wash and wear suits. Select...don't settle, at Barney's.

What man could resist reading about Roos/Atkins' suit service
policy? ''Free replacement: If your suit should prove unsatis-
factory within one year from date of purchase due to any defect in
fabric or tailoring, or if it shows undue wear, you may choose a new
suit of equal value without charge! Free alterations: Roos/Atkins
will make any reasonable alterations due to your change of weight,
size or fit for the lifetime of the suit, without charge! Four free dry
cleanings.... Coupons are good at any Roos/Atkins and will be
provided by your salesman.''

What does it take to look great?

99.00

and a made-to-measure suit event at Eaton's

The record-breaking value that puts a man a step ahead of the rest. Expert construction. Top tailoring. The finest of Fall Fabrics. All wool patterns. The plus of incomparable fit. A price that may not happen again because of the rising wool market.

Make it the best year of your life. Get your suit and trousers for 99.00. Add a vest at 19.50. Extra trousers for 32.00. If you're size 47 or more an extra 10% will cover a good fit. Shop Thursday and Friday evening. Offer available until September 1st.

Eaton's Men's Made-to-Measure, Dept. 230, Eaton's Pacific Centre, first floor, and all suburban stores

EATON'S

Eaton's, Vancouver, attracts readers with its headline. Bold type asks "What does it take to look great?" Large type answers: "99.00." Smaller type reveals "...and a made-to-measure suit event at Eaton's." Below the headline, a neat rectangle of a suit photo. Body copy is set on either side of the photo. An outstanding job of typography.

Men! Think about that first warm day every year when your winter suit's too hot and your last-spring's suit is tired-looking. It doesn't need to happen this year. SBF's having a pre-season 20% off sale on select spring and summer suits. Monday, Tuesday and Wednesday only. Shouldn't you be there?

Stix, Baer & Fuller

This three-column ad from Stix, Baer & Fuller is packed full of power and conviction. Just read the copy: "Men! Think about that first warm day every year when your winter suit's too hot and your last-spring's suit is tired-looking. It doesn't need to happen this year. SBF's having a pre-season 20% off sale on select spring and summer suits. Monday, Tuesday and Wednesday only. Shouldn't you be there?"

The story is vested! Lightweight! Softly-colored plaids! And Hughes & Hatcher knows just how to tell it to its Pittsburgh audience. The art is dramatic. Almost a full-page of it. Tone on the suit adds to the power. The headline not only sells the vest idea but H&H as THE place to get it. A powerful presentation. One that readers will remember.

John Wanamaker, Philadelphia, gets its three-piece suit message across immediately with its giant ''3'' graphics behind a good-looking plaid suit. Sale type and price are just bold enough to cinch the deal. Copy details the suit's features. An institutional message is built in, allowing this space to sell more than just one suit, it sells the entire Men's Store.

SALE: WE OFFER YOU THE FAMOUS 3-PIECE SUIT IN FALL'S CRISPEST PLAIDS FOR JUST **109.95** Regularly 130.00

A 3-piece suit could be your best daytime investment. Handsome and masculine, the appeal remains even after you remove the jacket. Because this suit of 60% polyester/40% wool includes a matching vest. A great look, now that'll carry into Spring. And you'll find the tailoring our Men's Store is famous for. The coat: two-button single breasted with flap pockets. The vest: five buttons with watch pockets. Choose bold or subdued plaids and solid tones of gray and navy flannel. A rare opportunity to save on a fine three-piece suit. Men's Store, Second, Chestnut, Philadelphia; all JW stores.

John Wanamaker

Here was a preview of great advertising and merchandising for spring 1971! While everyone else was moderate-to-hysterical about Christmas, December, 1970, Roos/Atkins set itself apart with this welcome preview to spring fashion. The store featured half-inch herringbone stripes, light colors, two-button styling, wide lapels. The news value, the "preview" type, the light spring-look of the whites and grays...all contributed to the power of this great ad.

NEXT SPRING'S FASHION NOW IN FRESH CRISP DACRON/WOOL

New...half-inch herringbone stripes...light, bright tones of beige, brown, grey or blue...2-button styling
with wide welted lapels...button-thru pleated pockets with scalloped
flaps...straight-legged trousers with wider waistband, wider belt loops. All in comfortable,
long-wearing Dacron® polyester and wool. Another
plus, our unique suit service policy: free normal alterations, free replacement
if faulty, 4 free dry cleanings within two years. Step into Spring '71 now **125.**   **Roos/Atkins**

New Business

The look is pleated.

RUBENSTEIN BROS.
It's What A Men's Store Should Be.

Canal Street & The Plaza in Lake Forest—New Orleans, Louisiana

This quarter-page ad was a standout in the New Orleans Times Picayune. We love the "New Business" headline. It has the strength, the aggression needed to sell. We love the photo. The casual pose, the foot on one step, briefcase on the next. The message is one that will bring "New Business" right into Rubenstein Bros.

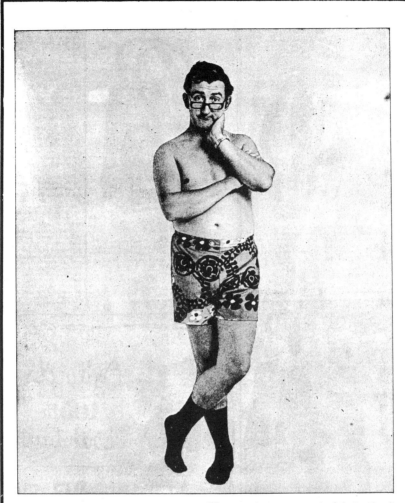

Our suits are made to order for you. You can be anyone. A rich banker? A struggling author? A famous actor? Or a first class swinger? It really makes no difference to us. We'll take your exact measurements. Show you as many as 500 really nice fabrics. And then we'll suit you up in the image of your choice. For just $69.00. Or $79.00. Or $89.00. Whoever you'd like to be. And no matter who you really are, you'll find our suits are made to order for you. **Ben Berke.**

Ben Berke, Montreal, knows how to catch the reader's attention and hold his interest. The attention-catcher: A photo of Everyman wearing jazzy shorts. The interest-holder: A copy story that's good to the last line.

One of the happiest invitations to spring fashion shopping we've seen.
Satel's, San Antonio, shows a handsome suit figure releasing a bird.
Behind him, March 21 is circled on a calendar. Headline reads ''Only 22
Shopping Days Left Till Spring.'' Copy describes a three-piece
polyester-cotton suit.

How to dress like a
financial wizard for $120.
The "I mean business" suit
for young men who
are going places. Three
pieces. Classic chalk
stripes on navy or
grey. Polyester/wool.
Robinson's
Trend Shop.

Robinson's

Robinson's, Los Angeles, does a strong fashion statement for the young business
man on a budget. The headline-copy-block tells the story with an excellent economy
of words: "How to dress like a financial wizard for $120...." (This ad ran in 1974.)
The suit model is well accessorized and posed. He wears sunglasses and a chain
bracelet (accessories that show his youth). He carries a briefcase and walks briskly
through the page (accessory and aggressive walk both mean business).

SOME SUITS INSPIRED BY MAD DOGS AND ENGLISHMEN*

(They go out in the noonday sun.)

QUITE unlike Noël Coward's Englishmen, we do not "detest a siesta." But given business realities, the daily nap has never taken hold in this country and opportunities for it are rare.

Hence, we've had to find other ways to deal with the heat of the day, calling on basic principles from before the dawn of air conditioning, with a few refinements that have come along since.

As to air conditioning, there may be some who, because of it, would question the need for specifically warm weather suits. We find, however, that energy shortages and high fuel costs have had an effect. Offices are no longer chilled to the frost point and taxis, when they can be found, cannot be counted on to be cooled. So on a hot and steamy day there very well may be no alternative to setting out in the midday sun.

Before air conditioning there was cotton, and most particularly, cotton seersucker. The seersucker suits of tribal memory have little in common with our latter day seersuckers. The one we have in mind has a two-button jacket with natural shoulders and cen-

ter vent. The body lining has been dispensed with for coolness and instead, there's something known as a French facing. The finish is so good looking that while we doubt the wearer would go so far as to toss the jacket over a chair just so the inside would show, he wouldn't mind if it did. Trousers are plain front, have belt loops. Blue, gray or tan, all with white stripes. $155.

For local heat or places even hotter we suggest a cool suit that will keep its crispness when all about it are wilting. Much of this endurance is due to the cotton and polyester poplin from which it is tailored. It has natural shoulders, two buttons, center vent and plain-front trousers with belt loops. The color is khaki. $145.

For more temperate situations—the heat wave has broken and the air conditioning is working—there's the authority of our lightweight wools, some very sophisticated suitings. These are well represented in the suits made for us by our master Canadian tailors and also in those by SOUTHWICK.

We feel very strongly that suits are best purchased in person at our store. There you have the advantage of our entire selection and we can be sure that everything is properly fitted.

Paul Stuart charge accounts, American Express and Diners Club cards accepted.

Madison Avenue at 45th Street, New York, N.Y. 10017

The headline is provocative. The 10 point subhead tells you what the ad is about. That and the mystic art just about force you to read on. To yours and Paul Stuart's benefit.

Four weeks prior to its winning performance at the Academy Awards, the movie "Chariots of Fire" began being featured in a series of full-page menswear ads by Bloomingdale's. In doing so, Bloomie's got a jump on Seventh Avenue. The English-made movie turned out to be a strong fashion influence for both men's and women's clothing for fall '82. Gordon Cooke, senior vice president for sales promotion, first brought the plan to the menswear merchants and then worked out the tie-in with Warner Brothers.

It used to be that gentlemanly art and gentlemanly copy just weren't "with it".
But times change. And now, here's N-M with the approach of the 80's.
"The Gentlemen's Blazer" headline. The Gentlemen's pose, elegant cafe dining in
a proper Lanvin blazer, white shirt, rep tie and slacks.
This is an approach to imitate.

Redwood & Ross, Madison, Wisc., knows just what a man wants from a store. Here, headline and copy tell a fashion story, but a fashion story for a man who wants to be comfortable with his peers, not a sore-thumb stand-out. It tells a service story, about salesmen, and tailors who don't pressure customers. Everything fits right in with the slogan Redwood & Ross picked out for itself: "Only our service is old-fashioned." A great job!

Hughes & Hatcher does a Johnny Carson commercial to promote Johnny Carson merchandise. We often see television commercials that are slavish copies of newspaper ads. We seldom see the reverse. And there's nothing slavish about this one. It's informative without being dull. The copy is alive, has fun, and does a selling job. Love it all.

1971 was the year of basic advertising—clear, logical, simple, believable. Dayton's does it with a headline that informs, explains the benefits, and shows a clear, square-cut photograph of the merchandise. No frills, no needless elements, and not a wasted word. Pin up this ad and study it carefully.

KNIT pants that were made for looking.
Absolutely great.
Made for sitting.
Through a long night on a plane
without ever looking like you've
slept in them. (Even if you did.)
Made for fitting. With an unflappable
combination of dress-slack swagger
and blue-jean comfort.

DOUBLE-KNIT BY HAGGAR

to keep whatever
shape you put
in them.
The new wrinkle
in pants is
no wrinkle at all.
$20.
Dayton's

Flared or straight legs. Black, tan, brown or navy or navy or brown herringbone stripes. Dacron® polyester knits in sizes 30 through 42. Men's sport furnishings, all stores. dayton's

I don't care
who's wearing
plain-front
trousers . . .
I want mine
<u>pleated</u>

You know what you like. That's why you'll find both pleated <u>and</u>
plain-front trousers at H-H-S. It's the <u>choice</u> selection.

Thin men, round men, big men, little men . . . all types of well-dressed men prefer pleated trousers. They'd stick to pleats if there wasn't another man this side of the Mississippi wearing them. And where will they find pleated trousers?—in great abundance! At HHS, naturally. We're out to please you, whatever your pleasure. And that means we carry pleated trousers in depth, season after season. For example, right now you'll find suits in 2-button and 3-button styles, with pleated trousers. You'll find slacks in pleated styles. You'll find walk shorts in pleated styles. And you'll find them in our wide selection of fabrics, colors, patterns, and proportioned sizes . . . tailored by most of the country's leading makers. (And of course, everything in plain-fronts, too.) Small wonder that most men buy their clothing at Hughes Hatcher Suffrin—where finding exactly what you want is a matter of choice, not chance.

you'll find more of everything in men's wear at

OPEN THURSDAY AND FRIDAY TO 9 P.M.
(SHELBY OPEN TO 5:45)

■ SHELBY & STATE ■ WOODWARD AT MONTCALM ■ NORTHLAND ■ EASTLAND ■ GRAND RIVER & GREENFIELD
■ MACK & MOROSS ■ WONDERLAND ■ WESTBORN ■ LINCOLN PARK ■ ARBORLAND ■ PONTIAC MALL

What is the shortest distance between the store and the customer? Hughes-Hatcher-Suffrin bridges
the gap about as well as we have ever seen.

The comic strip approach to advertising is often seen but never as charmingly and informatively as this from Hemphill-Wells. These two adorable puppies say it all and make Haggar slacks unforgettable in that marketplace. We don't often see advertising that gets seen, gets read, and gets remembered as efficiently as this. The ultimate beneficiary is the store and that's a big plus. Somebody at Hemphill's knows dogs and sketches beautifully, and the conversation is a riot.

153

Carson's has a great idea! This blue-spot-color page shows a pair of
jeans that are so cool, they're underwater. A second blue-spot-color
page appeared in a different section of the same morning Chicago
Tribune. It showed a pair of knit slacks for Father's Day, used as a
flag for a submarine. The impact of the double use of spot color
and the pants-at-sea format was quite amazing.

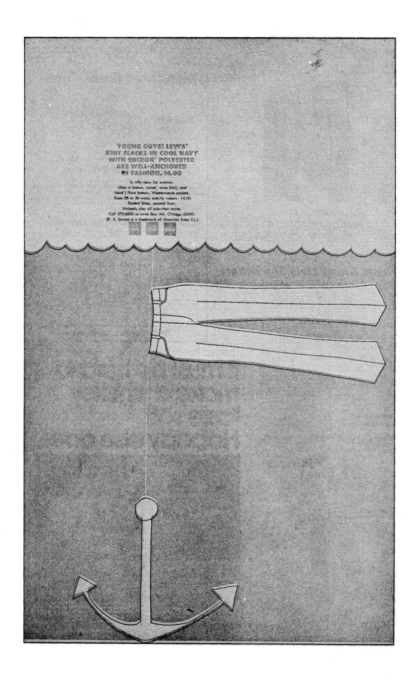

Fit captioned with feeling. Fit shown in the complete abandon to what's on the screen. You see it in the curl of the hand. If the pants fit when you sit, they'll certainly leave you free for action. It's a lovely little ad.

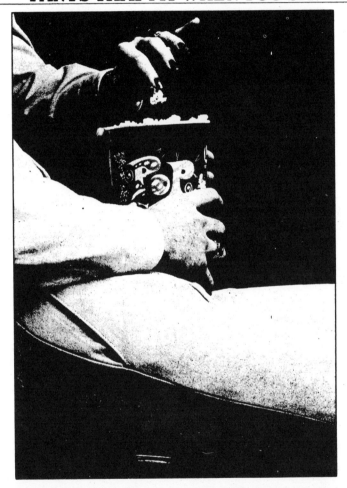

PANTS THAT FIT WHEN YOU SIT.

Levi's® Action Slacks.

Levi's® Action Slacks take you comfortably through a double-feature. **Levi's® Menswear** slacks are tailored for the man of action, from their stretch fabric and trim styling to their easy care. And there's more. For now through Sunday, March 15th, Levi's® Action Slacks in all the spring frost tones, as well as all the traditional shades, are specially priced at a low ✦19.88 a pair at all six Harry Levinson locations.

HARRY LEVINSON
FASHION SHOPS FOR MEN.

GONE WEST

a spankin' new shop deep in the heart of lex.

It's a hot little western shop tucked in the corner of our Men's Store. Where a cowboy can poke around and round-up all the extrees he needs without emptying his saddle bags. It's an in-spuration. Everything a lean, lanky man-of-the-west wears – buckles to badges. No, you haven't seen a good western, till you've done Gone West.

We'll make you a star, with your 10.00 purchase from Gone West, we'll deputize you with this shiny sheriff's badge. Gone West, Street Floor, New York. Jenkintown and all fashion stores.

SHERIFF

Bridle path, 1. brown leather with brass buckle, keeper and tip. From Dooney and Bourke. 25.00

Spaghetti westerns, our Italian leather belts from Firenze. 1" width in wine or tan, silvery buckle and studs. 21.00 1½" width in brown or tan with silvery buckle, keeper and tip. 22.50

Longhorn cufflinks, for the nine-to-five cowboy. In gold tone metal. 19.00

Lariats. Braided leather in navy, black or brown with a range of western motif slides. Here from our collection, the Thunderbird. 22.50

The western bandana, the authentic 22" cotton square in every color you can imagine. 2.00

Silvery bolos, etched with western motifs to slide over scarves or bandanas. 3.50

Western belt buckles, from our collection of silvery 1" and 1½" widths, from Firenze. 12.50. And we've a bounty of straps to fit them. Tomorrow we'll engrave your initials on the buckle you buy.

Key west, boot on a chain attaches to your belt and keeps your keys at hand. In gold tone metal. 15.00

bloomingdale's
men's store

This is just the beginning. We see the western look, not as a trend, but as a tradition that will only increase as we move into the 1980's. Here's Bloomingdale's with its new shop, "deep in the heart of lex." You'll notice that Bloomie's merchandises to all degrees of western-ness. It may be just longhorn cufflinks "for the nine-to-five cowboy", or the whole look down to a bolo for his bandana. A nice promotional touch, the store deputizes customers with a sheriff's badge when they make $10 purchases.

The lean and hungry
jeans of Calvin Klein.
All shape. All sizzle.
All...attitude!
Skinny as a stick.
Slick as a whistle.
Doing, now, for men...
what they've been doing for
women all along. And that
is, quite simply, making
American style...the, uh...
last word...in fashion today.
Calvin Klein Jeans for men.
First, now, and always...
at Saks Fifth Avenue.
Indigo blue cotton denim for
waist sizes 28 to 38 (no 35 or 37)
Westerns, shown, $37.
19" watch pocket, $37.
17" cigarette jeans, $37.
From the Calvin Klein Shop
for Men, Sixth Floor.
Calvin Klein, here Monday
with a whole crew of men
in blue. Informal modeling
from 12 to 2.

Saks
Fifth
Avenue
We are all the things you are

New York (212) PL3-4000 open Thursday until 8:30 p.m. • White Plains, Springfield and Garden City open Monday and Thursday until 9 p.m. • Bergen open Monday thru Friday until 9:30

Want to know how to sell designer-label jeans? Look to Saks Fifth Avenue. Last
month there was a powerful ad for the Calvin Klein women's jean.
This month, it's the men's turn. The same attitude is true for both ads. Clean,
simple photos zeroing in on the details, the label. To work with the almost full-
page Sunday Times ad, a 10-second TV spot on the jean. Note that only one jean
style is shown: the western. The 19-inch watch pocket style and 17-inch
cigarette jean are subfeatured.

Grodins, San Francisco, gets the attention of the young jeans customer with its "French Cut" spoof. To emphasize the new leaner cut, the store designs a green bean-type can with booted "lean jeans" crowding out of the top. For further wit, Grodins calls itself "The Jolly Jean Giant." Four jean styles float below the can. A great way to meet the heavy jeans competition in any city.

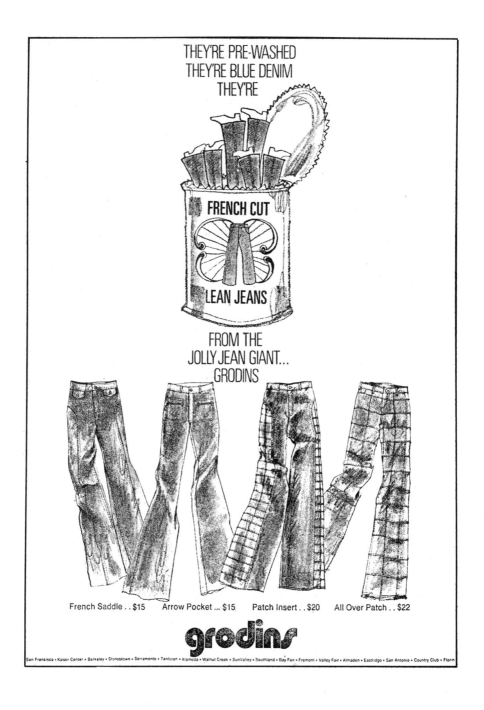

THEY'RE PRE-WASHED
THEY'RE BLUE DENIM
THEY'RE

FRENCH CUT

LEAN JEANS

FROM THE
JOLLY JEAN GIANT...
GRODINS

French Saddle . . $15   Arrow Pocket . . $15   Patch Insert . . $20   All Over Patch . . $22

grodins

If you can't interest them in the headline, you can't interest them in the merchandise. Macy's, California, knows this and writes a headline that every man can relate to. "If you remember your first pair of Levi's...You won't forget your first pair of Levi's knit jeans!"

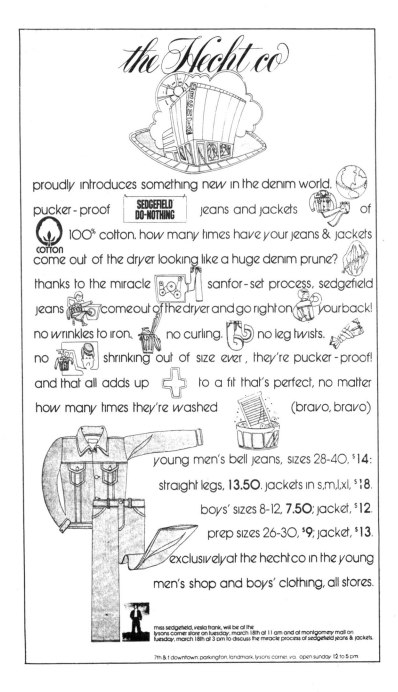

The Hecht Co., Washington D.C., has a story to tell and takes the room to tell it. It's all about Sedgefield's new "pucker-proof" denims. Everyone across the country is showing them with the denim prune symbol. But Hecht Co. makes the promotion its very own with its all-copy-and-picture display. And note how things start off smartly with a big sketch of the store standing happily on the corner in the sunshine. A grand bit of store-building. Hecht's even was able to incorporate mention of a Miss Sedgefield personal appearance with a tiny postage-stamp picture of her at the bottom of the page. It's all a joy to read.

How to acquire the rugby look without rerouting your nose.

To attain the manly élan so characteristic of British footballers, it is no longer necessary to hurl yourself into the scrum.

Simply saunter into Juster's and ask to see the new Merona rugby sweater. This is the featured component of a rugged (but civilized) new look for fall. We call it rugby without pain.

Actually, it's a good deal more than that. The Merona rugby sweater may well be the first interesting idea in woolen goods since the seventh Earl of Cardigan was charging about.

It's 100% worsted wool with all the qualities of a fine v-neck or crew neck. With one striking exception: the dashing twill collar which sets this sweater apart from all other sweaters you'll see this season.

You can see it in a choice of colors ranging from merely handsome to brilliant. But we suggest you see it soon; this will be a brisk seller. At $55, it's one of those rare items which can single-handedly rejuvenate a wardrobe, not to mention a self-image.

If you're only going to purchase one new item for fall—and we fervently hope such is not the case—this would be it.

The Merona rugby sweater. Put it on and suddenly sixty thousand people are screaming your name. Ignore them; a person could get hurt that way.

Juster's

Nicollet Mall • Southdale • Brookdale
Ridgedale • Maplewood • Rosedale • Highland Village

Lovely tongue-in-cheek copy about another part of the face.
Oh yes, about some sweaters too.

Every once in a moon almost every store has the opportunity to print in color. And so it is good to study effective color use, to be prepared when your moment comes. Stix, St. Louis, is promoting two styles of knit shirts, one style in four colors, the other in seven colors. The store could have shown the two styles of shirts on full figures, subfeaturing lines of folded shirts to display the full color story. But instead, the imaginative Stix chose to dress up a line of black-and-white penguins.

One of New York's most innovative young designers, Kolodzie, takes out a full-page in Manhattan Catalogue (a tabloid publication) for the mail order of one great cotton batiste shirt. We love the contact sheet format with its rough edges. The order form itself is just as rough-edged. The words "Mail Order" come up loud and clear.

Hudson's Men's Store, Detroit, opens the fall fashion season '74 with its dramatic "projection" graphics. "Projection" is printed in reverse against screened gray. A beam of light projects from the end of the word to spotlight the way for the fashion message. In this case, it is "Continental Concept" for shirts with a new silky texture. Directions on how to accessorize are handwritten near each shirt. The "Projection" format was also used to forecast women's fashions for the new season.

Argyle Over Easy

Exclusively at Hastings, our versatile and very fashionable Argyle pattern sleeveless sweater. Soft Orlon® acrylic that can be washed and dried by machine. In coffee/camel, navy/burgundy or forest green/camel, on natural grounds. **$16**

Underneath: Hastings color coordinated Country Twill sportshirt in natural color only **$12**

HASTINGS

IN SAN FRANCISCO · STONESTOWN · OAKLAND · SAN MATEO · PALO ALTO · SAN LEANDRO · SACRAMENTO · MARIN · MONTEREY · CONCORD · SAN JOSE · BERKELEY

Hastings, San Francisco, knows the appeal of real-to-life art. Its three-quarter-length figure looks out at the reader with easy confidence. Hands are in the slack pockets for a graceful pose. The featured argyle sweater is coordinated with solid slacks and solid shirt for an ungimmicked look that even the most conservative man would like to emulate.

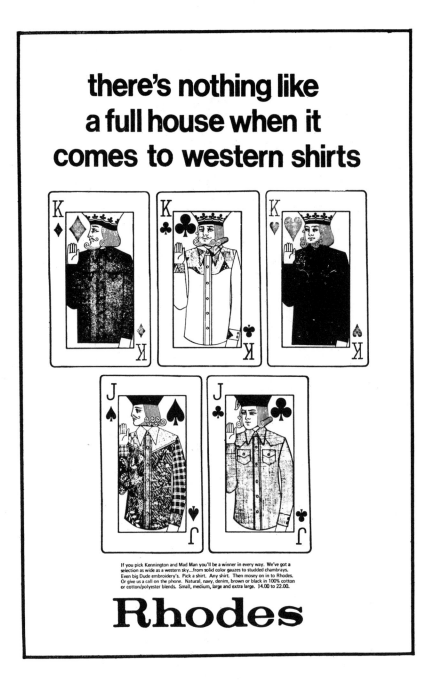

Rhodes, San Antonio, is a winner in readers' eyes with this western shirt promotion. First, the eye stops at this attractive shirt-within-a-card layout. Second, "full house" cards, headline and copy suggests that the customer will be a winner. All in all, an attractive frame for wanted merchandise.

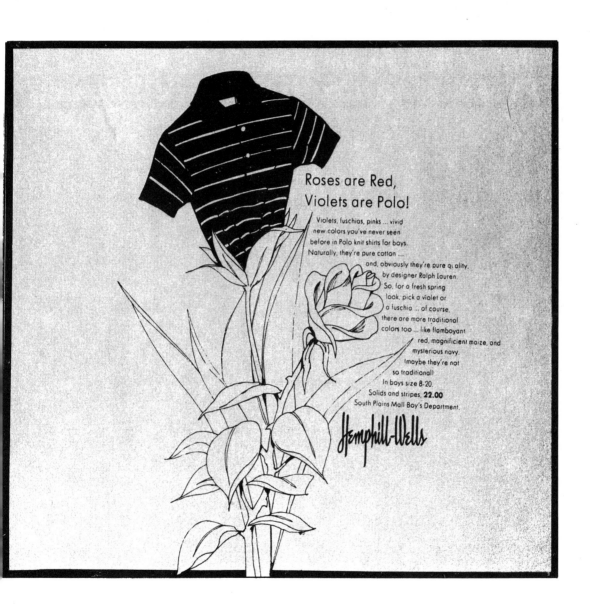

Roses are Red, Violets are Polo!

Violets, fuschias, pinks ... vivid new colors you've never seen before in Polo knit shirts for boys. Naturally, they're pure cotton .... and, obviously they're pure quality, by designer Ralph Lauren. So, for a fresh spring look, pick a violet or a fuschia ... of course, there are more traditional colors too ... like flamboyant red, magnificient maize, and mysterious navy. (maybe they're not so traditional) In boys size 8-20. Solids and stripes, **22.00** South Plains Mall Boy's Department.

Hemphill-Wells

All the world longs for spring, Hemphill-Wells decides to give its little corner an early dose. And how welcome it is! Blooming right in the Lubbock Avalanche-Journal. An outline bouquet of roses blossoms into a ''roses are red, violets are Polo!'' celebration with a striped violet shirt blossoming right out of the top stem. This ad was for boys' shirts which these days are being worn by women, as well. But we feel that an earlier, stronger declaration of men's or boys' would have perhaps helped avoid confusion.

Below:

Neusteters knew that everyone loves the story of the determined turtle
who won over the foolish hare. But the store takes the tale one step further and
shows that "This year the turtle is winning over the Men!" A total of 12 turtles are
shown in two lines. Only a general description is given for Neusteters' collection of
the legendary turtle: "This time around is versatile as its fabled counterpart. Creating
fashion looks running with distracting variety from very casual to very dressy.
In wools, acrylics, cashmeres, velours. Flat knitted, cabled, ribbed, crocheted. Figured,
argyled, checkered, striped and solidly in front in a tremendous collection from $14 to $85."

Right:

There is a lot of excitement in Vancouver these days (1967), not a little of which comes
from Eaton's. This store has taken an approach to advertising that is different and
dazzling. This is a good example, printed in the hottest colors imaginable. A smash hit.

mexican HOT tones

status tees

bring out the animal in you. answer the call of the wild in Izod*, Jordache, Hush Puppies*, Le Tigre, Polo and the Armadillo

170

Often we wonder how to sell the idea of color choice when the advertisement is in black and white. Parisian does it here with some tones of gray but mainly by words...words out of the mouths of Izod's famous alligators. What an original, delightful, attractive advertisement! Burns down City Hall!

Left:
The animal kingdom is alive and well and making quite a showing at Foley's. This rash of emblems on Tee shirts is reaching the point of being ludicrous, don't you think? Be that as it may, Foley's makes the most of it, featuring six beasts in strong colors within a neat layout. The copy up top is good—"answer the call of the wild". What else can you say? This has to be the best seen ad of the week.

Munsingwear's penguin is a lovable emblem, and look what happens! It makes a lovable ad the way The Denver does it! Rendered in suitable colors this has to be the most seen and best read ad of the week.

Pizitz, Birmingham, makes the Arrow Cotton-Ease story understandable with this delightful rebus format. We've seen the success story of Cotton-Ease, from Father's Day right through to Christmas. Although this ad ran for FD, there's no reason why Pizitz couldn't adapt the copy, show a long sleeve shirt and do the same ad right now for Christmas selling. A good idea is a good idea!

Hess's, Allentown, does a shirt promotion that is just brimming over with life. The store offers customers to take a chance on a game with giant dice in the main floor shirt department. If they throw a matching combination, they win a Manhattan ''Nature Knit'' shirt; if they throw the dice and spell the word ''natural'', they win a shirt and a tie. Shirt is shown in a rich burgundy spot color.

174

Caplan's, Alexandria, La., tells its fashion story in a big way. Headline is bold, screened type. The "fashion innovation," a button, is sketched next. The Arrow logo and shirt appear in blue spot color. A smart ad that sold a fashion idea...and a store.

THE BIGGEST FASHION INNOVATION OF 1973.

The Button

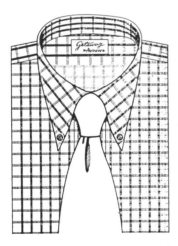

Arrow has taken the button and done something very fashionable with it. Buttoned the collar. Yes, the button down is back...but not just an ordinary button down. The famous Arrow Collar that's especially designed to accomodate today's wider ties. Decton Perma-Iron in solids, checks and stripes. See the entire Arrow collection now at Caplan's

Arrow Button Down, $10.
Other Arrow Dress Shirts, from $6.50.

➤Arrow➤
Button-Downs

CAPLAN'S
the menswear people

DOWNTOWN • MacARTHUR VILLAGE

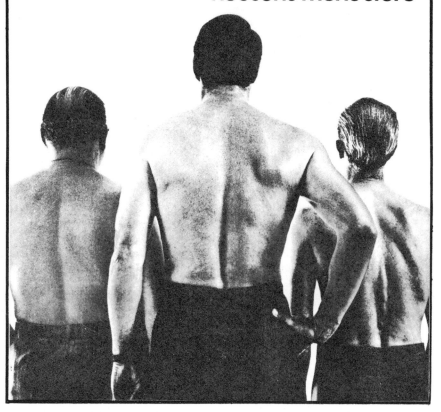

When the big three shirt makers offered us the shirts off their backs, the least we could do was accept. We did. All 23,146 of them. So now we can bring you **permanent press dress shirts,** made to sell for dollars more, **sale-priced** at a low, low **4.99.** An outstanding value in Hudson's Men's Shirts. Dress shirts of every description in solid colors and stripes. All long-sleeved with French or button cuffs, spread or long pointed collar. Your choice, just **4.99.** Fashion ties too. **SALE 2.99** each or **2** for **4.99.**

hudson's men's store

A shirt sale like no other! Hudson's, Detroit, says: "When the big three shirt makers offered us the shirts off their backs, the least we could do was accept. We did. All 23,146 of them. So now we can bring you permanent press dress shirts, made to sell for dollars more, sale-priced at a low, low 4.99. An outstanding value in Hudson's Men's Shirts." And with this declaration, a photo of the bare backs of models representing those big three shirt-less makers. A shirt sale like no other gets read and noted.

Right:
Horne's ad is pure salesmanship because it is eminently readable, informative, simple, and as inviting as a personal letter. The shirts you see, stacked up in the Van (Van Heusen!) are printed in color, and very beautifully. The copy is written with disarming simplicity, and oh so emphatic. Who could resist an ad like this.

176

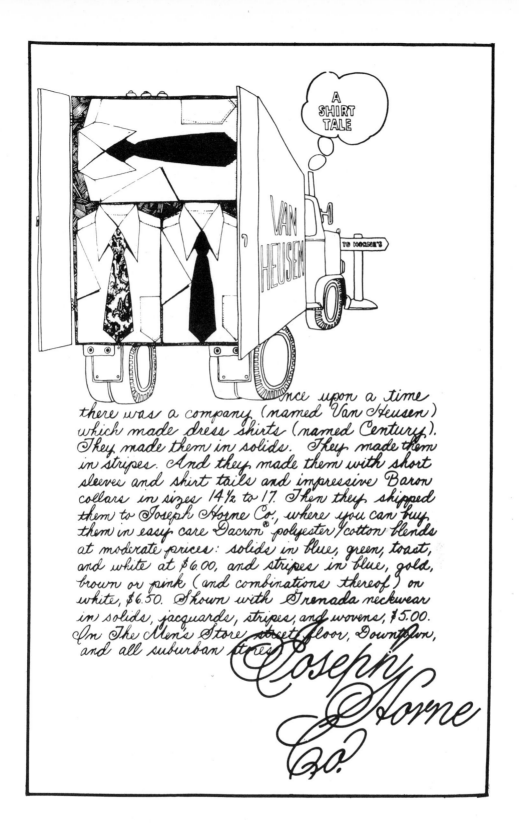

Once upon a time
there was a company (named Van Heusen)
which made dress shirts (named Century).
They made them in solids. They made them
in stripes. And they made them with short
sleeves and shirt tails and impressive Baron
collars in sizes 14½ to 17. Then they shipped
them to Joseph Horne Co., where you can buy
them in easy care Dacron® polyester/cotton blends
at moderate prices: solids in blue, green, toast,
and white at $6.00, and stripes in blue, gold,
brown or pink (and combinations thereof) on
white, $6.50. Shown with Grenada neckwear
in solids, jacquards, stripes, and wovens, $5.00.
In The Men's Store, street floor, Downtown,
and all suburban stores. Joseph Horne Co.

177

Selber Bros. Mens Shops, Shreveport, know just how to attract attention. 1. A theme with just enough wit to stop the reader. In this campaign, Arrow shirts were drawn on animals. 2. Spot color for added stop value. The color accentuated the pattern in these shirts. We're showing just two half-page horizontals from the series.

Right:

Hemphill-Wells creates pure excitement with this page, a page that Lubbock men won't forget. Design features, size and color specifications are all laid out in blueprint fashion, blue ink against white. A single shoe is shown below in brown ink. Congratulations to the store's creative staff...and to the merchants who believed so strongly in a single shoe that it all could happen.

DESIGN SPECIFICATIONS FOR NETTLETON'S CORDO-TAN

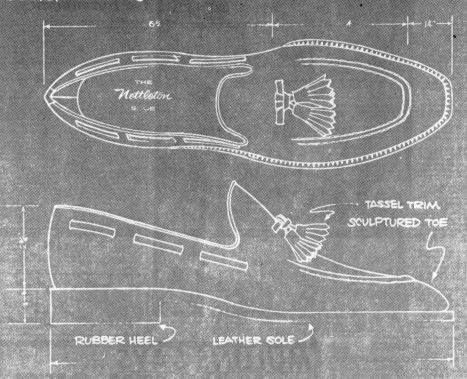

THE
Nettleton

TASSEL TRIM.
SCULPTURED TOE

RUBBER HEEL   LEATHER SOLE

DESIGN FEATURES

- ✓ RAISED SEAM MOC TOE
- ✓ LEATHER QUARTER LACING
- ✓ LEATHER QUARTER LININGS
- ✓ GOODYEAR WELT CONSTRUCTION
- ✓ WARWICK LAST
- ✓ CLASSIC LOAFER

SIZE SPECIFICATIONS

	6	6½	7	7½	8	8½	9	9½	10	10½	11	11½	12	13	14
AAA								○	○	○	○	○	○	○	○
AA					○	○	○	○	○	○	○	○	○	○	○
A					○	○	○	○	○	○	○	○	○	○	○
B			○	○	○	○	○	○	○	○	○	○	○	○	○
C			○	○	○	○	○	○	○	○	○	○	○	○	○
D	○	○	○	○	○	○	○	○	○	○	○	○	○		

COLOR SPECIFICATIONS

 CORDO-TANNED (RICH BROWN WITH CORDOVAN HIGHLIGHTS)

 EBONY BLACK (DEEP BLACK TANNED TO A HIGH GLOSS)

Just off the drawing
board...exclusively
at Hemphill's 60.00

Men's Shoes Downtown, South Plains Mall

Hemphill-Wells

Eaton's, Toronto, knows that a beautiful sense of design helps get a page read. Here, "Try A Pair On For Size At Eaton's" headline is stacked up to the left of the framed copy and merchandise. The rectangular frame contains two merchandise stories: Nunn Bush Height Increasers and Extra Large Shoes. A cut-out of the Height Increaser helps tell its story; a size chart works for the Extra Large shoes.

This has got to be the most exciting price-appeal advertisement of the year. The Treasury, with great restraint combined with unbelievable impact, refers to another man's sneaker—and pow! It happens!
Did this ad sell sneakers? Did the sales justify the cost of a full page? What do you think?

Our version 5.98

Snug-grip hand-washable vinyl upper. Sanitized. Cushioned insole. Injection molded boat sole. Black with white stripes or white with black stripes. Men's sizes 6½ to 11, 12D. Boys' sizes 2½ to 6D.

We're here to serve you better with shoes for the whole family. All first quality, excellent quality, at low prices every day.

the Treasury
family store and food center

Make someone happy. One sure way is to tuck socks in Interwoven's® exclusive Argylon® patterns into a Christmas stocking. Give ankle length, 2.00, or over the calf, 2.50. Choose dark brown, dark oxford, navy, light brown, green or black. Orlon® acrylic-polyester-nylon. Add socks of high-bulk Orlon® acrylic-nylon to your gift package. The ankle socks come in light brown, gray, dark brown or navy, 2.50. Over the calf lengths in gray, brown, navy or green, 3.50. One size fits 10 to 13. Men's Furnishings, on Main, Market, Center City Philadelphia, and all JW stores.

A full page of men's socks is not ordinary and when it is printed in soft, elegant color it becomes something sensational. John Wanamaker's advertising for Christmas was consistently sensational but advertising like this should not be confined simply to gift giving. Studies in assortments is a year 'round thing. When a store does this, for all areas of merchandise, it gains a great advantage. It says, to the customer, we have it—no matter what you want, we have it. Wanamaker does it beautifully.

This bouncing page has to be the best seen, most talked about ad of this or any week. Such imagination! Such action! Absolutely delightful. The citizens of Vancouver ate it up and we hear that Eaton's did well in sales. Why not? Not only enormously attractive and visible but hard-sell, too, with all colors and patterns showing. The printing in full color is especially well done, thanks to the Sun's cooperative staff. How can you beat it? McGregor socks never had it so good.

Orbach's, Tulsa, knows the drama of a demonstration. A photo is taken of a model wearing clumped-down-around-the-ankle socks, and another wearing Orbach's Royce socks. Models' legs are crossed for an even more dramatic contrast. The headline is as direct as you can get: "Bare ankles are not fashionable." Three columns of well-written copy sell the socks that stay up. A strong, convincing job!

Left:
It is gratifying to see a store showing its assortments so beautifully. Eaton's has created a remarkable degree of excitement by repeating the same visual form in a lively arrangement. What an eye-stopper! Here, by the way, is a Christmas approach for the consideration of any store with enough selection and the guts to do it.

185

How can you make a summer sock ad appealing? If you have the talent of Hudson's Budget Stores, Detroit, you can come up with graphics like these. Legs swing in the old hammock. A frosty tall glass of something to the left. A "Great Sport" headline in attractive screened type. Copy set in two columns with lots of white space for interest. A neat store logo stacked up in the lower right hand corner. The page borders sweep all around the four sides to end just before the logo.

Eaton's, Montreal, captures its audience with a smile. Here,
Burlington socks are suggested to prevent "Cold Feet" on the
wedding day. An almost-full-page photo of the bridal party shows an
uncomfortable groom with bare feet. Copy begins: "For any
important moment in your life you deserve to feel and look your best.
With Burlington's Endostat-treated, antistatic, no lint socks, you can
be sure that your socks will neither stick to your slacks nor fall down
in rolls around your ankles...."

The Denver makes the most of colored inks in this wonderful page of
"Munsingwear Underfeathers." The temptation, of course, would
be to feature the shirts and shorts in brilliant golds, reds and blues.
But who wants to see sketches of three men standing around trying
to look comfortable in their underwear? Instead, The Denver invents
a beautiful bird. Small sketches of the underwear are displayed to his
left. The headline and copy are just as delightful as the visual: "Are
you a secret bird of plumage? Get into Munsingwear underwear.
Even if you're the most conservative guy in the world . . . inside you,
there's a brilliant bird of paradise, beating its wings against your
grey flannel suit . . . ."

Higbee's, Cleveland, ran this smart mail order appeal for its Youngstown customers in the Vindicator. Box sale items seem to pop out of a mailing envelope. Headline on the envelope urges phone or "mail this page" orders. Copy has check boxes and a mail order form. The message couldn't be stronger or more memorable!

189

We're featuring just one ad from the Hemphill-Wells ''con-grad-ulations'' campaign. The neat looks of this omnibus layout are worth remembering for your Christmas planning. Four gift items are beautifully shown. The banner type and flow of art hold the whole thing together. The graduation gift campaign appeared in the Lubbock Avalanche-Journal.

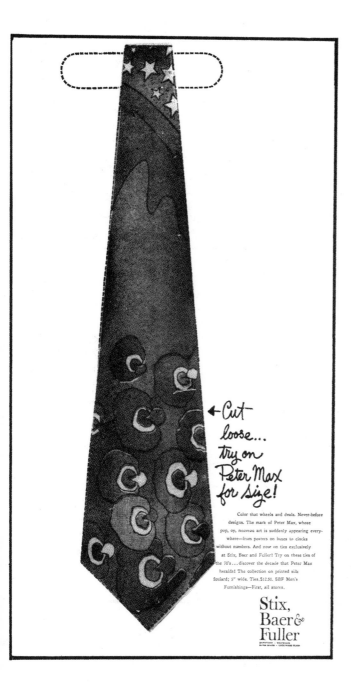

Cut loose... try on Peter Max for size!

Color that wheels and deals. Never-before designs. The mark of Peter Max, whose pop, op, nouveau art is suddenly appearing everywhere—from posters on buses to clocks without numbers. And now on ties exclusively at Stix, Baer and Fuller! Try on these ties of the 70's...discover the decade that Peter Max heralds! The collection on printed silk foulard; 5" wide. Ties, $12.50. SBF Men's Furnishings—First, all stores.

Stix, Baer & Fuller

How can you tell the Peter Max story? By showing Peter Max merchandise in exact size and full color. Stix, Baer & Fuller does more. They make an audience-participation idea out of it and it's great.

BASKIN

Fashion finds a new bow

It's a little bigger than before, but perfectly proportioned for the new button-down collar shirts so popular this season. Choose from a variety of patterns in clip-on style, or, for the more adventurous the tie-it-yourself style. We will include free instructions with every purchase. **$4.50** and **$6.50**

Baskin, Chicago, does a handsome small-space ad for the new bow. Wide-grained screen on the photo, artfully-set type work to create a clear, strong impression.

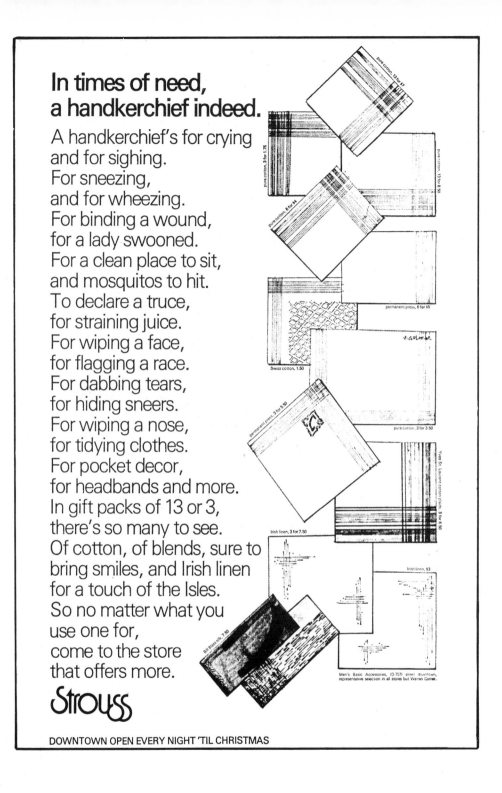

In times of need, a handkerchief indeed.

A handkerchief's for crying
and for sighing.
For sneezing,
and for wheezing.
For binding a wound,
for a lady swooned.
For a clean place to sit,
and mosquitos to hit.
To declare a truce,
for straining juice.
For wiping a face,
for flagging a race.
For dabbing tears,
for hiding sneers.
For wiping a nose,
for tidying clothes.
For pocket decor,
for headbands and more.
In gift packs of 13 or 3,
there's so many to see.
Of cotton, of blends, sure to
bring smiles, and Irish linen
for a touch of the Isles.
So no matter what you
use one for,
come to the store
that offers more.

Strouss

DOWNTOWN OPEN EVERY NIGHT 'TIL CHRISTMAS

All of Youngstown delighted in this page from Strouss. In fact they read it through a second time to themselves, and a third time over the phone to Aunt Maude.
The line-ending rhyme tickled the imagination. The subject matter evoked a common emotional response. The message that Strouss is "...the store that offers more..." has never been clearer. A powerful institutional ad, indeed.

Stores all across the country tied-into the national search for the Lagerfeld man—but we particularly like Horne's silhouette. It's something you rarely see in an ad. And it certainly gets attention.

HORNE'S IS LOOKING FOR PITTSBURGH'S LAGERFELD MAN. AND HE SOUNDS LIKE YOU.

The Lagerfeld Man is sure of his style, and puts it together with ease and wit. He knows what he wants, cares how he looks, and keeps his interests growing. Isn't that you? Aren't you the man Horne's is looking for? (Or perhaps the real Mr. Lagerfeld is someone you know. Or the man whose music makes you dance.) Who is Pittsburgh's Lagerfeld Man? Clear up the mystery now. Come to the men's fragrance bar at your nearest Horne's and pick up an entry form for our Lagerfeld Man contest. Return your entry form—along with a photograph—by June 1, and challenge the competition. If you're our winner, you'll have a chance to compete in the national Lagerfeld Man contest. As Pittsburgh's Lagerfeld Man, you can also look forward to a round of pleasures. You'll win a wardrobe of Lagerfeld fragrance, body bracers and good groomers for you, and elegant Chloe fragrance for her. You'll get a healthy tune-up at the City Club, downtown Pittsburgh's new total recreation complex. Refreshed from your tune-up, you'll have something new to change into: sports slacks, sweater and shirt from Horne's. You'll also enjoy dinner for two at LeMont restaurant, and receive a pair of tickets for "Mame" at the Civic Light Opera. Pick up the challenge and go for it all. Enter our Lagerfeld Man contest at Horne's. Pick up your entry form now at our Men's Fragrance Bar, first floor Downtown and all stores

horne's

194

It's a match! The promotional talents of John Wanamaker and Aramis.
The occasion was the U.S. Tennis Open in Philadelphia. Wanamaker's
responded with this full-page newspaper ad. The same ad appeared in the
Tennis Open program. The four-color photo of tennis racket, balls and
products immediately zaps our interest. And there are three attractive
offers: an entry-blank contest for an all-expenses-paid week for two at a
tennis academy; a gift with Aramis purchase; a practice session in the
auditorium clinic. (Wanamaker's men's division merchandise manager just
happens to be an all-American tennis champion, and took on customers.
Sessions were videotaped for the player's benefit.)

Christmas means loving and giving and what could be a better example of both than this 1974 ad from May Co., Calif. The modern pair is photographed against a dramatic black ground; the toiletries against white. All to highlight "what they have in common." "He likes to ski. 'Too cold' she says. Opera's her thing, but he likes the Stones. They never agree on movies...she's crazy for the French...but the subtitles make him dizzy. An unlikely pair? Perhaps. So what is it that makes him so attractive? Could it be the peppery blend of his Aramis? From the Merry Christmas Store."

Kennedy's, Boston, builds a "B.L.T. on 4" for extra size apparel. It's a lively idea, much more exciting to the customer than merely visiting the "big, large and tall shop." And Kennedy's announces it with a special sandwich, filled with shirts, pants, jackets, accessories. Atop the B.L.T., on either side of the olive, is a tall man and a big man. Both on sandwich picks.

men come in all shapes and sizes . . .

and mercifully, so do our summer clothes

Which is not to say we lack in regular sizes—on the contrary. Our point, however, is that we have such a wide selection of sizes that your chances of getting fitted *properly* at H-H-S are probably better than anywhere we can think of. Consider: regulars from 34 to 52, shorts from 34 to 46 and extra shorts from 36 to 42. On the other hand, you'll find longs from 36 to 52, extra longs from 38 to 52. Portlies? We have them from 39 to 52, portly shorts from 38 to 48 and portly longs from 40 to 52. ◀ But size isn't the only endearing aspect of our summer suit collection. Fabrics? You name it: wash'n'wear, all-wool tropicals, Dacron-wool blends, mohair, mohair blends, silks, silk blends and so on. ◀ And more famous makers than you can imagine. We'll list a few: GGG, Petrocelli, Eagle, Hart Schaffner & Marx, Hammonton Park, Botany '500', Palm Beach, Haspel—but why go on? And in just about every kind of pattern, shade, style you'd be interested in. ◀ As for prices, we think you'll find our price range will accommodate almost any budget, from $39.95 to $165. Honestly, can you think of a better place to shop for *your* summer suit(s)?

P.S. This same happy situation in out-sizes
applies to sportswear and furnishings too.

A store has many ways to say we have more and we can fit you right. Hughes-Hatcher-Suffrin says it in a way few will miss and many will long remember.

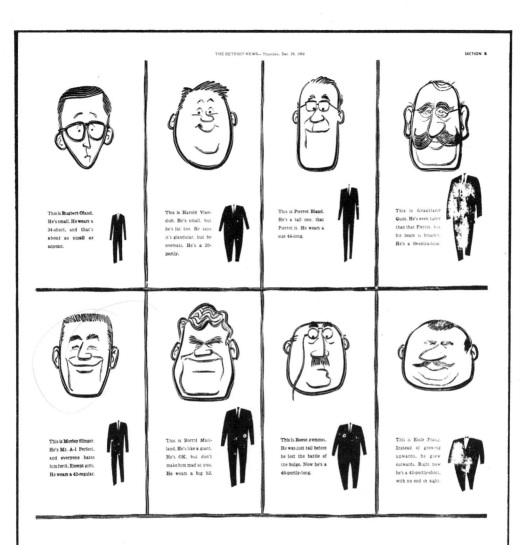

where will they all go to buy a suit?

where they can choose it right out of stock, from the largest selection of famous maker clothing ever assembled under one roof, anywhere—at HHS. It's the store where the question of size is never out of the question. For you'll find short sizes from 34 to 48, extra-shorts from 36 to 42, longs from 36 to 42, extra-longs from 38 to 52, portlies from 39 to 52, portly-shorts from 38 to 48, portly-longs from 40 to 52, and regulars from 34 to 52. (Pause for breath.) And there's a full range of sizes in shirts, hats, sportswear and furnishings. And a full range of sizes for the chips-off-the-old blocks, in our abundant Boys and Students Shops.

ALL STORES OPEN EVERY EVENING THIS WEEK TO 9 P.M.

Hughes-Hatcher-Suffrin has clothing to fit EVERY MAN, from 34-short Rugbert Oland to 52-big Borrel Maitland. This page made readers stop, look, and remember.

For excitement and story-telling action this one by Barney's is hard to beat. The headline completes the message. A convincing advertisement in every way.

At a suit a minute it would take you all day to try on every summer suit we have in your size.

We are open from 9 to 9. But if you wear a 40 regular, for example, the day isn't long enough to slip on every style and model of every famous–brand suit we have in your size: 947 at last count. Other sizes, from 32 extra short to 56 long to 60 portly (longs, shorts, extra longs, extra shorts, short portlies, extra short portlies, long portlies) abound in proportionate profusion. Which is why, at Barney's, it doesn't take all day to find just what you want. Did you <u>select</u> your last suit or <u>settle</u> for it? **BARNEY'S**

7th AVENUE, 17th STREET / OPEN EVENINGS / FREE PARKING

Eaton's says men come in assorted ages, sizes, shapes and weird poses. This is an ad that men will talk about and long enjoy.

Men come in assorted ages, sizes, shapes, and their clothing needs, desires and tastes range tremendous importance to big things of little this in mind now that the need for your new EATON'S fit you all ... short or tall ... or portly president ... thin or small.

temperaments ... from little things of importance. Keep Fall suit is pending. young executive

Keep in mind you have the choice from our galleries of Ready-To-Wear Suits ... our Made-To-Measure Service ... or for the ultimate, our Custom Made Clothes'. Colours run to every hue ... the weaves, the woofs and the warps do too ... especially what's new and right this Fall for YOU. May we fit you SOON?

*Custom Made Clothes · Downtown only

EATON'S MEN'S CLOTHES DEPARTMENTS

Downtown • Park Royal • New Westminster • Brentwood

CHAPTER III

CHILDREN

The research and marketing director of Working Mother magazine, Peter Onorati, is very happy with his statistics! He reports that in 1982, 20.8 percent of all American women are now mothers and that 54 percent of all these women are working. Not only is his market increasing but it is gaining in buying power; one half of all working mothers live in households earning $25,000 or more!

We also know that we are in a "baby boomlet" period. A Time magazine cover story, February 22, 1982, spotlights the 15.2 percent increase in the U.S. birthrate.

Marty Kramer, president of the Children's Manufacturers Assn., confirms how these statistics have effected the market he represents: "In this economic period, department and specialty stores have been sluggish in other areas, but they have expanded their square footage in children's areas and also expanded their open to buy".

Without a doubt, we can expect more volume, more excitement in children's marketing and advertising in the years to come. But how should the retailer theme those ads? Sam Kantor, president of the Florida Children's Wear Guild, gives us some guidance: "Today, the child is more independent and decides what he or she wants to wear. Retailers should go for eye-appeal, bright colors and designs that interest children. It used to be that mother and grandmother bought children's wear for durability and easy-care but that's not of prime importance anymore."

To discover how to reach the growing ranks of working mothers who have more money to spend and less time to spend it in—and to relate to their independent, TV-educated children—look to the ads in this section.

Higbee's editorial on Buster Brown's Miracle Machine is sheer joy.
The copy is all fact and fun; the art is heavenly, and what a smashing layout!
This is advertising that gets talked about.

West County Center, St. Louis, announced the end of summer and the beginning of the back-to-school shopping season with this appealing full-page ad. Little John Paul is told to cheer up because there is lots of fun in getting new clothes and being present for H.R. Pufnstuf's show. West County Center stores are listed in a screened rectangle at the bottom of the page. Center Promotions Agency created the ad.

cheer up, John Paul...

summer's almost over, but there's still lots of summer fun at West County Center. Fun like getting brand new shoes or shirts or other stuff for back-to-school...and special kinds of fun... like **H. R. Pufnstuf** *and his friends. That's right! Six Flags' own mayor will put on a crazy show with* **Cling & Clang,** *the wacky keystone cops, and that confused* **Ludicrous Lion.** *Meet T.V.'s* **Mr. Patches,** *too. See them all, Friday, August 18 from 6 to 9:00 pm. See the Six Flag's crew, Saturday, August 19, from 1 to 4:00 pm. Join all the fun... and don't worry about Mom, she'll be busy shopping the bright ideas and great back-to-school values at West County Center.*

WEST COUNTY CENTER

have a nice "back to school" shopping day...Interstate 244 at Manchester Rd.

This has to be the best seen, most talked-about, and most action-producing ad of the week. We have no idea how much response Eaton's in Toronto got and how many children participated but how could it miss? The contest is carefully planned for four-age categories and the judging is based on humor. What fun! What a smashing idea. Eaton's should publish a book.

I've been around for a long time and I know a good bunch of toys when I see them. This year I've got a new circle of friends, but they leave almost as soon as they arrive! You'll just have to meet us in person in Eaton's Toyville. Then you can choose one of my toy friends. Or take me home... I walk! It's no "Mickey Mouse" stunt.

EATON
Christmas is the light
Eaton Eaton
Your gift box is delight!

Our "Mickey" Toy, 19.99

M for Mickey. M for Montreal. M for mighty good advertising. Eaton's uses beloved Mickey as the spokesmouse for its Toyville opening. The art, the copy have immediacy, information, and much charm. Mickey sells the department and sells a specific toy, a walking Mickey for 19.99. Eaton's delightful ad is well thought out, it's no "Mickey Mouse" stunt.

An interest in being neat and well dressed can begin at any age. And Jordan Marsh, Boston, has the good business sense to foster that interest with its Young Designer contest for girls 5 to 12 years of age. The girls were invited to pick up entry blanks in the girls' departments and asked to design an outfit they would like to wear to school. The contest idea is appealing. So is JM's ad. We like the clarity of the copy with its contest rules. And the unsophisticated fashion design pinned to the wall behind the little model. It would prompt any child to think she could do better. As a matter of fact, 1,450 little girls did think that and presented their designs to JM. The winner received interest on a million dollars for a day and a wardrobe prize. The 10 finalists are having their outfits made by the store and modelled them in an August fashion show.

THE OWL PLEDGE
(to be taken only by youngsters who are earnest and wise. Repeat after Mom.)

To whom it may concern. I am an owl. I am earnest and wise. I am also important. I am going to school, and nothing is more important than that. I am going to learn about the moon and about the world. About what happened long ago and what happens far away. I am going to read good stories and learn the magic of numbers. I am going to learn so much that my parents will be amazed. I have a secret. I keep my eyes open. And I listen. No one in the world can listen harder than I can. I'll listen to my teacher because she can explain things that an owl should know. I'll be quiet so that she can talk and I can listen. I'll know more and more and more, because I listen, and because I'm an owl. Owls become good scientists, doctors, nurses, teachers, astronauts, pitchers, catchers, and quarterbacks. Owls paint the best pictures, play the best music, and write the best stories. And guess who's an owl. Who? Who? *Who?* Me. That's who.

(Mom: We have an owl poster for your owls to hang in their bedroom. $2.00 in the Young World, third floor, JOSEPH HORNE CO.)

This has to go down in history as one of the great ads of all time. This is unforgettable advertising, the kind that makes eternal friends in the community. Please note that Horne's, wisely, is offering this Owl Pledge as a poster to hang up in a child's room. $2.00. May they sell a million.

Right:
Once in a blue moon an advertisement reaches the pinnacle and this is it. Hudson's touches the human heart.

HAPPINESS IS
A PAIR OF
SHINY RED SHOES

They're Stride-Rites from Hudson's . . .
and we think they're just about the finest shoes
a little girl can wear. But to your little girl,
they're even more than that!
They're that special feeling every child
has for a pair of new shoes,
made even more thrilling because they're
shiny red ones. So go ahead, if her heart's set
on Spring's new red patents, bring her to Hudson's
where we'll fit her to the right ones.
Stride-Rite patents that give toe-wriggling room
to grow in; long wear with durable construction inside
and out. This Easter pump is just one pair
of happiness from our wide collection for sizes
12½-3, 8.99; 4-8, 9.99. Children's Shoes,
Downtown 4, Northland 3, Eastland 2.

HUDSON'S

Six appealing kids reacting to six important children's books. The "Shhh . . . children reading!" headline is a wonderful stopper. Shillito's provides marvelous service to customers with this page. This year, instead of picking up any old books for the kids, Cincinnati parents and grandparents and Aunt Minnies are going with winners, books that will help build lifetime habits of book buying for the recipients.

210

NAME YOUR FAVORITE GIRL AND WE'LL MONOGRAM SOMETHING SPECIAL FOR HER

ALISON
In a warm-up suit with bronze-tone trim. Personalized with her name in matching bronze lettering. Pullover sweatshirt top with ribbed crew neck, cuffs and bottom. Name up to 9 letters. Matching pants with ribbed cuffs, bronze trim. In olive green, fuchsia or blue Acrilan® acrylic. 4-6x, 27.00, 7-14, 31.00. Washable. By Up for Grabs.

BARBARA
Keep her warm in this bulky Orlon® acrylic knit hat with turnback cuff. Large pom pon. Embroidered name up to 9 letters. Lilac, red, royal or white. 4-6x, 5.50. 7-14, 6.00. Matching knit scarf. Self fringe trim. 4-6x, 7.50. 7-14, 8.00. Unisex.

CARLA
She'll look darling in a dress-up corduroy jumper. Polyester/cotton pinwale corduroy with bib front, side ties. Rose or lilac. 4-6x, 16.00. 7-14, 20.00. Embroidered name in white up to 9 letters. Ruffle lace collar blouse. Soft voile in polyester/cotton. 4-6x, 13.00. 7-14, 14.00. Both by Sparkle.

DANIELLE
Soft in a brushed Fair-Isle style sweater.® Luxuriously soft and washable Orlon® acrylic with ribbed boat neck. Soft pink, blue or lilac. 4-6x, 21.00, 7-14, 22.00. By Knitwaves.

ENID
In a classic crew neck sweater.® Orlon® acrylic in cream, yellow, lilac, red, soft pink, navy or light blue. 4-6x, 15.50. 7-14, 16.50. By Knitwaves.

FRANCINE
In a turtle neck sweater.® Ribbed ruffle turtle neck and cuffs in Orlon® acrylic. Light blue, lilac, pink, white or red. 4-6x, 17.00. 7-14, 18.00. By Knitwaves.

GAIL
Stylish in a prairie blouse embroidered with her name on white polyester/cotton rib. Ruffle yoke front and stand-up collar. 4-6x, 16.00. 7-14, 17.00. By Sparkle.

HEIDI
In a hand-embroidered pullover.® Colorful embroidered flowers on cream, red, navy or kelly Orlon® acrylic. 4-6x, 17.50. 7-14, 18.50. By Knitwaves.

JENNY
Great looking in our shetland-look cardigan.® Embroidered name with last initial. Orlon® acrylic in red, white, navy. 4-6x, 16.50. 7-14, 17.50. By Knitwaves.

KARYN
Keep her hands toasty in personalized storm mittens. Name up to 9 letters in white, red, or navy. Leather-look vinyl with nylon. Gold, navy, brown, red, peacock blue or hunter green. His/hers. One size fits all. 4-6x, 6.00, 7-14, 6.50.

*Embroidered name up to 9 letters or 3 initials. Underline last initial. White, red, navy, berry, gold, rust, purple, green or lilac. Allow 3 weeks for delivery.

Shops for Girls, second floor. Fifth Avenue (212) MU9-7000 and branches. Out of town call Toll Free (800) 228-5444. In Nebraska (800) 642-8777.

B. Altman & Co
It's always a pleasure

SHOP EVENINGS AT ALL ALTMAN STORES...FIFTH AVENUE, THURSDAY TILL 8...DAILY, 10 TO 6

Christmas marches on and monogramming becomes an advertising problem. Altman's approach is one of the most charming we've ever seen. "Name your favorite girl" and the ad names ten, shows ten dainty apparel items, gives credit lines to four or five suppliers and comes up with a smash hit. The simplicity of layout is an example worthy of emulating, especially the juxtaposition of black type and white space. Great copy. Beautiful ad.

Some advertisements are destined to drive straight home without a bend in the road.
The pantie ad by Hudson's is one of those rare ones.
Lives there a mother who can resist?

WITH 19 DIFFERENT STYLES of famous Kleinert waterproof panties to choose from how can any little tike be anything else? There are snap-ons, pull-ons, tailored, lace-trimmed. Ruffled, embroidered, eyelet, terry lined. There are checks, plaids, solids, too. There's Silk Softex, clear plastic, rayon, plain and fancy nylon. There's snowy white, pale pink, blue, maize, even navy blue and red . . . and Hudson's has them all. Hudson's Baby's Own Shop, Downtown, 4th; Northland, 3rd; Eastland, 2nd.

How
dry
I
am

1. Silk Softex snap-on, white Layette, S, M, L and XL........1.25
2. Silk Softex toddler pull-on, white, sizes S, M, L.........1.25
3. Pink, blue, emb., S, M, L, XL..$2
4. Nylon over plastic snap-on, white, sizes S, M, L and XL..1.50
5. Nylon over plastic pull-on, white, sizes S, M, L and XL........1.50
6. Nylon lace froufrou pull-on in white, sizes S, M, L, XL.....1.79

7. Silk Softex, white, pink, blue, maize, Layette, S, M, L, XL....$1
8. White snap-on, S, M, L, XL 1.79
9. Eyelet froufrou pull-on in white, sizes S, M, L and XL........$2
10. White rayon, S, M, L, XL 79c
11. K-Lure, white, S, M, L, XL 49c
12. K-Lure, white, S, M, L,XL 79c
13. White, rayon, toddler, S, M, L $1
14. Nylon froufrou pull-on in white or pink; S, M, L, XL.........$2

15. Rayon disposable diaper pant, white, S, M, L, XL..........1.50
16. Nylon over plastic toddler pull-on in white, S, M, L...........$2
17. Nylon cottontail with pert white or pink pompom on white pants in sizes S, M, L, XL.....$2
18. Terry lined rayon pull-on, white, sizes 1, 1½, 2, 3, 4....1.39
19. Snap-on, navy, red, blue plaid or white; S, M, L, XL.......1.79

HUDSON'S

Abraham & Straus tells the story of bears and it's no fairy tale. It's a great piece of copy and the photograph is a smash hit.

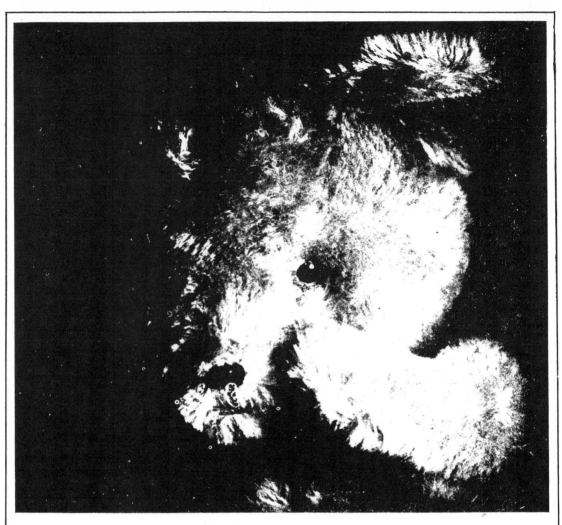

every toy should have a child

We're looking for good homes for lonesome teddy bears. As little as six ninety-five will take care of one for life. And these orphan animals are made of real fur which makes them the nicest things to hug. We seem to have more of them — kittens, dogs, lions — than anyone else. So please, the next time you're in Chicago, come to our Toy Center, Fourth Floor. There's nothing like it back home.

Marshall Field & Company

Left:
Every toy should have Marshall Field's because Marshall Field's has a way with toys and a way with children.

This is one of those rare advertisements that visualizes merchandise not shown. Does it with joy and impact. Makes an unforgettable impression for the store and what it stands for. If only more retailers would realize how much long-range influence this kind of impression can make! A loud ring of the bell for Hess Brothers.

Have Baby...Will Travel

Now there's a brand new Baby Travel Centre at Macy's, full of wonderful ways to take the worry out of taking the baby. We've made discoveries that will make your trip together a delightful voyage of adventure; safer, easier and more economical than you'd have imagined. Find out what to take, where to stay; get help from Holiday Inns, where your baby always sleeps in his own bed. And more. Drop in and consult with us before you study a single road map.

HAVE BABY...WILL TRAVEL

Johnson & Johnson Travel Kit. A durable case complete with dual-purpose hand and shoulder strap and completely fitted with little things you'll need: Johnson's Baby powder, large size; Baby lotion, medium; Baby oil, medium; Baby cream, small; Buds, small; Coets Quilted Squares; Chux Disposable Diapers. Later, use the case for a handy carry-all. #3427. Regularly 7.95.....**4**

Macy's-Own Brand Baby Kempton Deluxe Swivel-Wheel Stroller. 4-position reclining seat for sitting or sleeping; converts easily to a walker, folds flat in seconds. Heavy duty chrome-plated steel construction; tiptoe brake. Large shopping basket. Front bumper for extra safety, #5BL, **24.99.** Drop in and inspect our complete selection of folding strollers ranging from **11.99-49.99**

Babygro® by Kapart® Stretch Baseball Coverall. This seasoned traveler keeps a baby comfy sleeping or playing, in terry stretch of cotton and stretch nylon, in blue and white stripes with little slugger applique. Sizes: birth to 20 lbs., #9164; 21-30 lbs., #9165.....**4**

Not shown:

Auto-Plug In Bottle Warmer. Here's the what-to-do for warm bottles on the road: operates on 12 volts from any automobile cigarette lighter. #365....**1.99**

Playtex Nurser Kit. Contains 65 8-oz. disposable bottles, 6 nipples, 6 bottle holders and caps, automatic expander, **7.99**

Playtex Rubber Pants. A full assortment from pull-on to snap-on in various prices and qualities.........**69c** to **1.98**

Diaper-Bag Carryall. Scuffproof, fully insulated tote with a hardy spring steel frame and snap-open top. Lightweight and roomy (17x11") it wipes clean in a flash. Blue floral print #TB1857.............**5.99**

Kantwet's Fitz-All® Trav-L-Seat. Keeps the baby safely in the front or back seat; fits between split-front seats, bucket seats and console model seats of practically any car, in blue or black, #F107, **11.99.** Come and see our complete assortment of car seats for baby from **5.99-13.99.**

Kantwet's Fitz-All® Trav-L Bed. Safely snoozing in the back seat, baby travels comfortably without disturbing other passengers. Fits the back seats of all cars, the front seats of most—and locks solidly into place. Out of the car, Trav-L-Bed becomes a bassinet. In blue, #F44, **14.99.** We have many more car beds from **9.99** to **14.99.** Come in and look them over

Kantwet's® Feed-n-Play Table Chair. Allows the baby to eat and play at almost any table—in restaurants, motels and the homes of friends. Simple to set up, you can do it with one hand. In beige, #F99, **7.99.** Also, see our complete assortment of folding hi-chairs from **15.99** to **28.99.**

New Rock or Sit Infanseat® Baby Carrier. Designed by a famous physician to provide good head and back support for infants from birth to one year. Quilted cushions are electrically sealed so water can't get in. Seat switches quickly from rocker to steady, 4-way adjustable seat, to flat for carrying or storing. Guaranteed for one full year. In white, pink, blue or yellow, #600.........**7.95**

Depend on Holiday Inns for comfortable, convenient accommodations enroute; you'll like the clean, modern facilities, the ample, free parking space, swimming pools, and the considerate attention you get when you come with the baby. Complete folders of Holiday Inns are yours to pick up at our Baby Travel Centre.

Gulf

Drop in at Gulf Stations everywhere and enjoy their friendly, competent service; refresh yourselves and the baby in clean, modern rest rooms; let them assist you in finding the best routes; pick up the latest road maps.

For extra safety drop in and pick up your Safety Sticker. "Have Baby—Will Travel" bumper sticker, created by Kantwet®, has big letters that are clearly visible even at night to get you special courtesy from other drivers. It's our gift to you, available at the Baby Travel Centre near you.

Come in, write or phone LA 4-6000 or the Macy number near you. Complete Baby Travel Centres and Travel-with-Baby Booths at Macy's Herald Square, Roosevelt Field, New Haven, White Plains, Queens, and your new Macy's in Colonie. A selection at the Macy's near you.

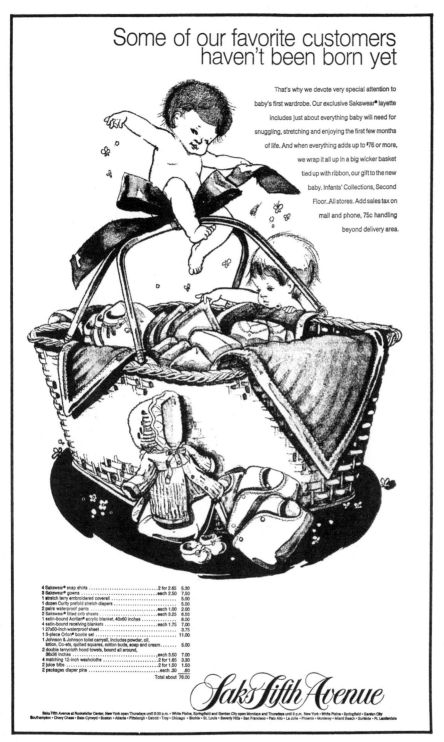

Some of our favorite customers haven't been born yet

That's why we devote very special attention to baby's first wardrobe. Our exclusive Sakswear® layette includes just about everything baby will need for snuggling, stretching and enjoying the first few months of life. And when everything adds up to $76 or more, we wrap it all up in a big wicker basket tied up with ribbon, our gift to the new baby. Infants' Collections, Second Floor. All stores. Add sales tax on mail and phone, 75¢ handling beyond delivery area.

4 Sakswear® snap shirts	2 for 2.65	5.30
3 Sakswear® gowns	each 2.50	7.50
1 stretch terry embroidered coverall		5.00
1 dozen Curity prefold stretch diapers		5.00
2 pairs waterproof pants	each 1.00	2.00
2 Sakswear® fitted crib sheets	each 3.25	6.50
1 satin-bound Acrilan® acrylic blanket, 40x50 inches		8.00
4 satin-bound receiving blankets	each 1.75	7.00
1 27x50-inch waterproof sheet		3.75
1 3-piece Orlon® bootie set		11.00
1 Johnson & Johnson toilet carryall, includes powder, oil, lotion, Co-ets, quilted squares, cotton buds, soap and cream		5.00
2 double terrycloth hood towels, bound all around, 36x36 inches	each 3.50	7.00
4 matching 12-inch washcloths	2 for 1.65	3.30
2 juice bibs	2 for 1.50	1.50
2 packages diaper pins	each .30	.60
	Total about	76.00

Saks Fifth Avenue

This has to be the most provocative headline of the season. It offers a provocative merchandise idea, too. The subject is Sakswear Layette and the copy says, "and when everything adds up to $76 or more, we wrap it all up in a big wicker basket tied up with ribbon." A beautiful proposition beautifully presented.

Left:

Macy's opens a new shop ... Baby Travel Centre. It is designed "to take the worry out of taking baby." The shop offers many items and services and this interesting page is must reading for every young family.

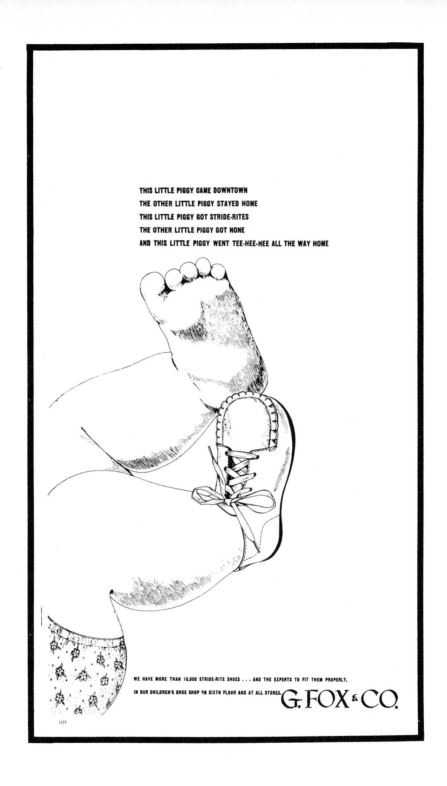

THIS LITTLE PIGGY CAME DOWNTOWN
THE OTHER LITTLE PIGGY STAYED HOME
THIS LITTLE PIGGY GOT STRIDE-RITES
THE OTHER LITTLE PIGGY GOT NONE
AND THIS LITTLE PIGGY WENT TEE-HEE-HEE ALL THE WAY HOME

WE HAVE MORE THAN 10,000 STRIDE-RITE SHOES . . . AND THE EXPERTS TO FIT THEM PROPERLY,
IN OUR CHILDREN'S SHOE SHOP ON SIXTH FLOOR AND AT ALL STORES. G. FOX & CO.

We all have to admit that this advertisement by G. Fox is one of the most appealing in a decade. Where is the mother who can pass this by, or fail to get the message?

Snoopy belongs on Broadway—and that's just where he was for his big Saturday event at Macy's. Children who came up to the fifth floor toy department got an autopaw from Snoopy and, of course, got to view stuffed Snoopies, Spikes, Belles and Woodstocks for sale. For the New York Times ad, Snoopy and his friends do a Broadway dance routine.

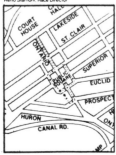

The Diaper Derby at Millers has become an annual affair and we elect it to be one of the most important races in the land. We hear these dauntless crawlers develop record-shattering speed and there is rumor of a new slot in the upcoming Olympics. What a way to put the infant department up front in the hearts and minds of parents! It's a splendid ad, typographically good and great sketches.

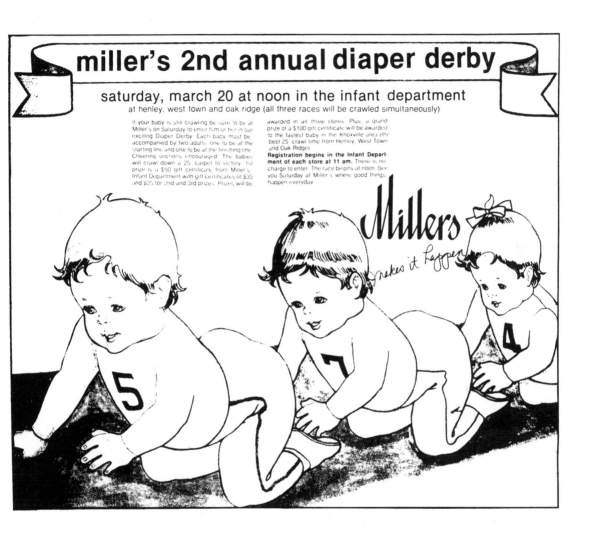

miller's 2nd annual diaper derby

saturday, march 20 at noon in the infant department

at henley, west town and oak ridge (all three races will be crawled simultaneously)

If your baby is still crawling be sure to be at Miller's on Saturday to enter him or her in our exciting Diaper Derby. Each baby must be accompanied by two adults, one to be at the starting line and one to be at the finishing line. Cheering sections encouraged. The babies will crawl down a 25' carpet to victory. 1st prize is a $50 gift certificate from Miller's Infant Department with gift certificates of $35 and $25 for 2nd and 3rd prizes. Prizes will be awarded in all three stores. Plus, a grand prize of a $100 gift certificate will be awarded to the fastest baby in the Knoxville area (the best 25' crawl time from Henley, West Town and Oak Ridge).

Registration begins in the Infant Department of each store at 11 am. There is no charge to enter. The race begins at noon. See you Saturday at Miller's where good things happen everyday.

Millers makes it happen

Left:

We can't think of a better way to get back-to-school off to a roaring start! Higbee's arranges for a one mile running race around Public Square and right through the store's main floor. Kids from 6 to 12 are eligible with a special Toddler Trot for kids 3 to 5. The ad includes an entry blank and requests a $2.50 entry fee, $3.50 the day of the race. (Copy indicates that the complete entry fee will go to benefit the Cuyahoga County Special Olympics.) The Cleveland Plain Dealer and WEWS-TV are co-presenters of the event with Farah and Fisher-Price Toys as sponsors.

Marshall Field's introduces, with imagination and excitement, a new wash-and-wear item. A lot of people will stop here.

This is
an eight-year old.
He doesn't care
how he looks.
He cares about
running, climbing
and having fun.
But when he comes down
from that tree, his
trousers will still look neat.
He's wearing new
Levi's Sta-Prest slacks
from Field's.

This is a 16-year-old.
He does care how he looks.
His slacks have been washed 10
times, never ironed. They're as
trim and good looking as he is.
Because they're new Levi's
Sta-Prest cotton trousers
from Field's.

This is a proud mother
of growing boys.
She looks happy.
She is wearing a dress
she made with the time
saved not ironing
these new Levi's
from Field's.

The crease stays in these new wash and wear Levi's

Announcing the news every busy mother has waited for. Cotton trousers with a crease that
stays in, and in, and in through repeated washings. A new process called Sta-Prest keeps these
trousers looking neater, more wrinkle-free no matter how you wash and dry them. Pants stretchers
and drip-drying can become a thing of the past. You may decide to skip ironing touch-ups altogether.
These new Levi's are only at Fields in Boys' Clothing and in Student Shop—Fourth Floor, South
State; also in Evanston, Oak Park, Lake Forest, Park Forest, Old Orchard and Oakbrook

1. Student sizes in black, sand, burnt olive; ivy belt loop style, waist sizes 29-34. Pair, $6.98

2. Boys' sizes, ivy belt loop style in sand, black, pewter, burnt olive; continental style in burnt olive, sand or black; regular and slim
sizes 6-12, pair, $4.98. 26-30 waist, pair, $5.98; ivy belt loop style also 26-36 husky, pair, $5.98

Our Brittania® jeans for boys have the hippest hip pockets in the business.

Embroidery, pintucks, piping... we've got five dynamite ways to dress up his derriere. All five are all cotton in Brittania blue. Sizes 8-12 reg. and 8-14 slim. **$13-16.50** Boy's Clothing, 98.

The Broadway
Your neighborhood store

What does it take to sell jeans to boys? The Broadway puts the focus on hip pockets, "...five dynamite ways to dress up his derriere."
The result is pure drama and pure salesmanship. The hip pockets are shown full size and each is energized with something significant.
A delightful fashion approach to jean advertising.

It's the 25th birthday party of you know who and if you don't know who this advertisement tells you all about it and a lot more. It's all joy and that's what advertising should be. Pogue's has tied in a wide variety of special events, prizes, entertainment, a six foot Snoopy (not a good likeness . . . no charm, no class) and live animals via the S.P.C.A. Surely the best seen, most talked about ad of the week.

Superman may or may not be news come August when stores get into back-to-school but something else will have arrived to give vitality to the promotion. Look for news! Your buyers in the market should forever be on the alert. Hudson's took the Superman idea and made it super-exciting. Sure, kids don't read newspapers but a comic page like this? Who knows! Mainly this is for fond parents and it works. Who can resist it!

CHAPTER IV

TEENS

As one marketer put it: ''Once they have hit 12 to 14, they're grown up!'' Today's teen customers are sophisticated, affluent and under peer-group pressure to keep up to the minute with the lastest trends.

Because they are living at home, teens from mainstream middle-income families seem to have the where-with-all to buy more expensive clothing than mom and dad wear. Their entire allowances or after-school salaries often go into wardrobes and hobby equipment. And of course, there is often free access to the family's charge cards as well.

The expensive athletic shoe, designer jean and jacket has become a basic school uniform with well-bred preppy looks, Norma Kamali sweats and post-Punk varying according to school and region.

Shopping the malls is often the major social activity for the teenage girl. And although teen boys may shop less frequently, they are just as aware of fashion--and their wardrobes are just as extensive.

This generation has no qualms about both sexes shopping in the same departments and, in fact, seems to prefer advertising and special events that speak to boys and girls alike.

The older teen has also changed with wardrobes that reflect a new serious attention to career goals. Wanda Bolton, career and college competition editor for Glamour magazine, explains: ''This year, we asked our college competition winners to select their own clothing for photos to be taken on campus. Out of the 10 women photographed for the August 1982 college issue, three or four of them were wearing business suits'', reports Ms. Bolton.

So, the college board ads from the mid-60's shown in this teen review are right in keeping with the trend. The emphasis on advice and service is exactly what this decade's college-bound teen is asking for.

Love this ad. Thalhimers comes out frankly and says, "this is our teen fashion show ad." It shows a little green plant ("we're planting new fashion ideas from our Greenhouse") and toward the end the copy says, "Plant one for a better world . . . one of the philodendron plants we'll give you." The simple hand-letter copy is good to read and there is something young and happy about it all.

Thalhimers
THE FASHION STORES

**This is
our teen
fashion
show
ad...**

So why the plant? We're planting new fashion ideas in our Greenhouse (Junior Center, Third Floor). See our teen council model sprightly fresh as dew fashions Saturday, March 11 in Thalhimers Auditorium, Fifth Floor at 3:30. They will be wearing Love Cosmetics.....there'll be Love's Lemon Hand and Body Lotion gift for you, too! Come join the fun and excitement and "Plant One" for a better world... one of the philodendron plants we'll give to you from the Greenhouse. Glen Allen.

Ohrbach's College Shop does a quiz, asks nine questions; gives nine answers and gives thousands of young people something to think about. This is advertising to win confidence and influence customers.

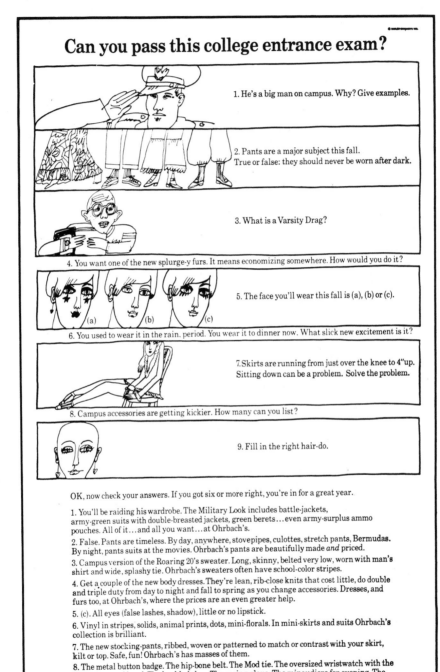

Can you pass this college entrance exam?

1. He's a big man on campus. Why? Give examples.

2. Pants are a major subject this fall. True or false: they should never be worn after dark.

3. What is a Varsity Drag?

4. You want one of the new splurge-y furs. It means economizing somewhere. How would you do it?

5. The face you'll wear this fall is (a), (b) or (c).

(a) (b) (c)

6. You used to wear it in the rain. period. You wear it to dinner now. What slick new excitement is it?

7. Skirts are running from just over the knee to 4"up. Sitting down can be a problem. Solve the problem.

8. Campus accessories are getting kickier. How many can you list?

9. Fill in the right hair-do.

OK, now check your answers. If you got six or more right, you're in for a great year.

1. You'll be raiding his wardrobe. The Military Look includes battle-jackets, army-green suits with double-breasted jackets, green berets...even army-surplus ammo pouches. All of it...and all you want...at Ohrbach's.

2. False. Pants are timeless. By day, anywhere, stovepipes, culottes, stretch pants, Bermudas. By night, pants suits at the movies. Ohrbach's pants are beautifully made *and* priced.

3. Campus version of the Roaring 20's sweater. Long, skinny, belted very low, worn with man's shirt and wide, splashy tie. Ohrbach's sweaters often have school-color stripes.

4. Get a couple of the new body dresses. They're lean, rib-close knits that cost little, do double and triple duty from day to night and fall to spring as you change accessories. Dresses, and furs too, at Ohrbach's, where the prices are an even greater help.

5. (c). All eyes (false lashes, shadow), little or no lipstick.

6. Vinyl in stripes, solids, animal prints, dots, mini-florals. In mini-skirts and suits Ohrbach's collection is brilliant.

7. The new stocking-pants, ribbed, woven or patterned to match or contrast with your skirt, kilt or top. Safe, fun! Ohrbach's has masses of them.

8. The metal button badge. The hip-bone belt. The Mod tie. The oversized wristwatch with the wide patterned band. The buckled shoe. The racing glove. The minaudiere for evening. The glittery dangly earring. The tall boot. The poncho. The buttondown dicky.

9. There isn't any "right." The rule is change. Your hair can be cap-short or long. You can even follow your mood with a tiny switch or the gorgeous fall that's so important on campus.

get <u>all</u> the answers in Ohrbach's College Shops

New York: 34th St. Mon., Thurs., Fri. till 9. Newark: Market & Halsey. Mon., Wed., Fri. till 9. Westbury L. I.: at the Raceway. Mon. through Fri. till 9:30.

228

Rich's had red telephones all over the store in 1964. Pick up a receiver and a college board member comes on the line to answer questions and help you shop. Great idea.

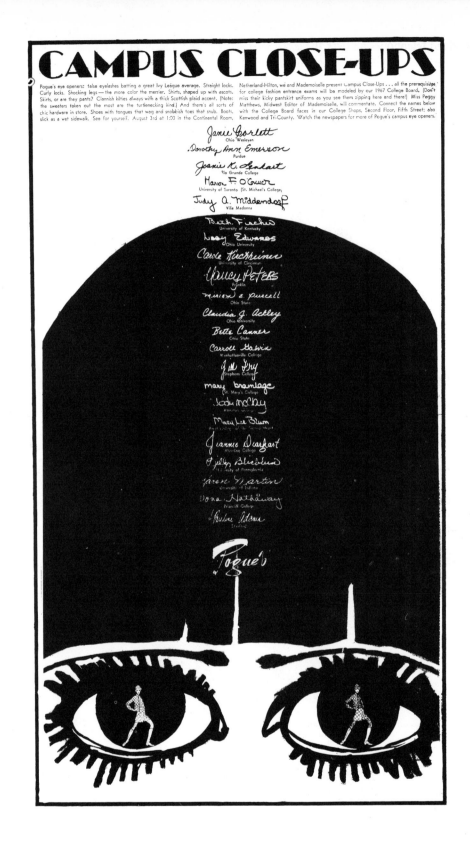

Pogue's took a new approach to the College Board announcement in 1967.
Instead of portraits the signatures are given. The layout is a smash and
there is excitement everywhere.

Sue Drake
goes to Mound High

Where casual clothes are "choice"
this fall, where bulkies, suspender skirts
and a lot of suede are seen . . . and where the
class pin is the leading accessory.

Sue agrees heartily with the casual look, almost always picks skirts and sweaters for school; suits for dress. "Nothing fancy, just plain." Now a 17-year old senior, Sue hopes to go to college and then into fashion designing. She loves to work with her sketch book, "just about anywhere . . . especially drawing faces"; is active in the Art Club.

M - M - M - M GOOD! That's what Greg Smith, Minnehaha Academy senior, says about Sue's latest gourmet accomplishment. She enjoys cooking, but usually sticks to that all-time favorite, hot dogs! Sue considers pizza her specialty. "Last year I made a whole lot of pizza!" For midnight snacking at home in the kitchen Sue chooses a plaid shift jumper and blouse, 25.98.

SUE KEEPS RIGHT UP WITH THE STYLES when she takes her turn selling. She enjoys the work and thinks it will be good experience for a career in fashion designing. Her Teen Board outfit: pleated knee tickler with suspenders.

READY FOR THE SET! Sue plays a lot of tennis in the court next to her home. Tennis and water skiing are her favorite sports for summer; she chooses skiing in the winter. Here Sue wears a classic wool tennis sweater, 13.98.

HALF-TIME CONFERENCE between Greg and Sue . . . the team looks good! And, so does Sue; in her car coat, 35.98; striped sweater, 9.98; bright red leather boots, 19.95. Sue cheers the team with the Mound Pep Club.

Girls on the GO . . . go to

Real girls and boys in real candid-camera situations in 1962. Dayton's has launched a refreshing, newsy approach to school apparel.

Left:
The year was 1961 and it was delightful to see hot music, cool refreshments and teen fashions in a gay ninety's setting. As it says in the base of the page, "WOW."

Below:
How can a store relate to people? Especially young people? Meier & Frank has a fantastic promotion going, a talent contest. Top high school talent in three cities. Complete with applause-o-meters, fashion shows and cash prizes. Great idea, great ad.

232

TEENS

TOMORROW!

See the most unusual fashion show ever staged in St. Louis!

a phantasmagoria of scrumptious spring '61 fashions plus the year's most exciting ideas on the decorating scene—in sbf's collegienne

FASHION JAMBOREE!

FEATURING

Cool Refreshments and

HOT MUSIC
namely

SINGLETON
PALMER

SEVENTH FLOOR, DOWNTOWN

SATURDAY, MARCH 4

11 A.M. TO 4 P.M.
COME AT ANY TIME
RUNS CONTINUOUSLY

FASHION JAMBOREE!

AND ALL THAT JAZZ!

NOT 1 BUT 20 STAGES

48 LIVE MODELS 48

JAMBOREE
SODA SHOP
RIGHT ON OUR SEVENTH FLOOR

SEE THE LATEST FASHIONS POSED IN THE LATEST ROOMS!

52
GLORIOUS DECOR THEMES
DESIGNED BY OUR DEDICATED DECORATORS TO MAKE THE MOST OF YOU!

And

presented by Mr. Stanley Herbert and the St. Louis Civic Ballet

14 PRANCING DANCING GIRLS 14
PRANCING DANCING GIRLS

WOW
SATURDAY,
11 A.M. TO 4 P.M. SEVENTH FLOOR

Seventeen Magazine's new Book of Decorating inspired this fantastic festival of fashion. See it tomorrow!

FREE FREE FREE

WATCH
ONE STORE!
KEEP AN EYE ON
STIX FOR THE
FIRSTEST & THE MOST-
EST IN FASHION,
FURNITURE
AND FUN!

STIX BAER + FULLER

CHAPTER V

HOME

The changes taking place in home area marketing are important to chart before a study of its retail advertising is made. Observers point to the growth in bed and bath, upholstery fabrics, home-entertaining electrics and cookware and general remodeling and replacement items.

Bill Dunlap, president of Campbell Mithun Inc., the Minneapolis agency that handles Naugahyde brand fabric and 3M's Scotchgard says: "The growing importance of consumer advertising in the home furnishings and home-related products can certainly be attributed in part to the population bulk (76 million baby boomers who are setting up households) but we are also looking at the remodeling and replacement market, the entire population of homeowners who wish to build on or remodel instead of move or build".

Arlene Petroff, president of the New York chapter of the National Home Fashion League and home furnishings fashion coordinator for the J.C. Penney Co., affirms this trend: "Because of today's economy, people are staying home more, whether they want to or not. There's a great deal of remodeling and refurbishing going on. For greater personal pleasure at a lesser cost, this is especially true in the bed and bath area. We are also finding people are freshing up living areas by changing upholstery fabrics."

Jill Wiltberger, a spokesperson for Wearever, defines the kitchen as the new family room: "Home entertainment in a casual atmosphere will continue to grow in popularity as will men's interest in cooking". She also sees a desire for time-and-work-saving appliances and utensils built for quality, durability, versatility and compactness for diminished storage and counter space.

All in all, it's an exciting, challenging time for the home area retailer!

How do you make a TV dinner look special?

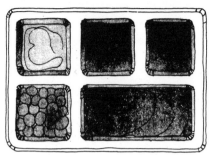

Set your table with good linen, company flatware, a big bouquet of fresh flowers and one of nine beautiful dinnerware patterns by Denby and Hornsea. Now at savings.

SHAMROCK
44.99

Denby cook 'n' serve dinnerware
The strongest, most chip resistant dinnerware made from clay. You can put it in the oven — handy for warm-ups. Put it in the freezer. And you don't have to worry about patterns fading because it's dishwasher safe and detergent proof. Family proof, too! Good looking dinnerware in six great patterns that are easily accesuorized for appealing dining. Well, are you convinced that this is a pretty fantastic line of dinnerware? We are.

Hornsea dinnerware
Three attractive patterns sure to make an eye-catching table! Saffron, Bronte or Heirloom Brown. Available in 20 and 45 piece sets; or you can try a coffee set, teapot, mugs or cereal bowls. (But we're convinced you'll like them so much, you'll want to have the whole set!) Dishwasher safe and detergent proof dinnerware to make your meals a pleasure — even TV dinners! From our China department, all 3 stores.

Hudson's Bay Company

| DENBY ROMANY **44.99** | DENBY POTPOURRI HONEY **39.99** | DENBY MAYFLOWER **42.99** | DENBY GYPSY **54.99** | DENBY CANTERBURY **39.99** | HORNSEA HEIRLOOM BROWN **24.99** |

Denby prices above are for a 16 piece starter set; Hornsea price (same for all patterns) is for a 20 piece set.

DOWNTOWN DAILY 9:30 - 6, THURS. AND FRI. 'TIL 9, SAT. 'TIL 5:30. SOUTHGATE DAILY 9:30 - 5:30, WED., THURS AND FRI. 'TIL 9. LONDONDERRY DAILY 9:30 - 9:30, SAT. 'TIL 6. 24 HR. TELE-BUY 424-0141.

One of the freshest item promotions we've seen in a long while. The Bay, Edmonton, knows that there are TV-dinner-days in everybody's life experience. And so to make things look brighter and more cheerful, the store suggests: "Set your table with good linen, company flatware, a big bouquet of fresh flowers and one of nine beautiful dinnerware patterns by Denby and Hornsea. Now at savings." We bet that the next time people in Edmonton have a TV dinner, they'll remember this promotion.

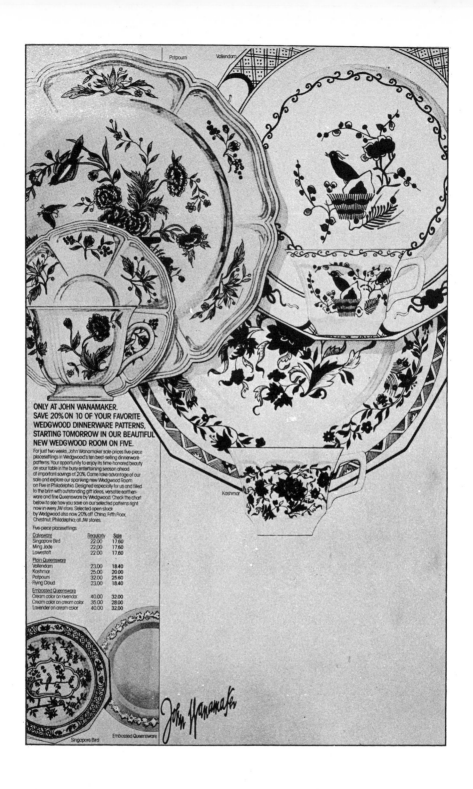

You are seeing a dinnerware sale page that means more and makes a greater impact than any ad anywhere. This year or any year. What you don't see is the superb color, a fantastic drawing reproduced beautifully by the Philadelphia Bulletin. John Wanamaker knows how to make advertising the customer sees, loves, and responds to.

Choose from the greatest collection of decorative arts in the world.
That's what we did.

TIFFANY & CO.

This page by Fortunoff came popping out of the paper with the force of an explosion. No copy. Only a headline, a bold brash statement. A gigantic poster, clean, organized, beautifully rendered, and making one point—one message—unforgettable. Powerhouse stuff.

Building confidence. Explaining merchandise. Going back in history and describing the quality standards of a fine manufacturer. A friendly, informative, brilliant job of research and copy. A total job selling an idea, selling a quality brand name and selling the store. This is what it took to make the grade in 1975 and Fortunoff did it well.

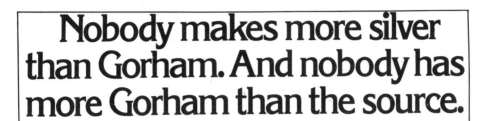

Nobody makes more silver than Gorham. And nobody has more Gorham than the source.

If you're looking for Gorham, the source is the place to look. We sell every pattern Gorham makes.

Every piece of every pattern. And Gorham makes more patterns than anyone else who makes silver. As a matter of fact, Gorham makes more silver than anyone else.

And we have it all. Simple Gorham, ornate Gorham, stainless Gorham, sterling Gorham, even pewter Gorham.

Gorham from 1831 to 1974.

In 1831, Jabez Gorham, in his little Providence, Rhode Island silver shop, began making forks, spoons, and knives. One at a time, carefully, slowly, and painstakingly. On a good day, he might make 20 spoons.

Today, at Fortunoff, we still have silver patterns Jabez Gorham designed. They're right here on our "wall of silver" along with Gorham silver designed this year, and all the years in between.

Forty-two people to make a spoon.

When you've been making silver as long as Gorham, you become pretty incredible craftsmen. You can learn a lot in 150 years. And when you see, hold, and eat with Gorham silver, you know they did.

Every piece of Gorham silver is worked on by at least 42 people. And Gorham is so particular about the quality of their silver, they're the only silver makers in the world who buy their own raw silver and melt it down and roll it out themselves.

They were even the first in America to develop a method for manufacturing pewter flatware.

Gorham from punch ladles to melon spoons.

When we say we have Gorham flatware, we really mean it. Not just your everyday forks, knives and spoons, but every unusual serving piece they make. In every pattern. Ice cream forks, jelly servers, bonbon spoons, cake breakers, baby sets, oyster forks, even salt spoons.

And we have just about all of it in stock, so you won't have to pick out your silver and then wait a month to get it. You can probably take it all home

when you buy it. And eat with it that night.

The bowls, pitchers and épergnes.

And we have still more Gorham. All their gorgeous holloware. From little things like decanter labels and wine goblets to gigantic things like épergnes, tremendous, swirling, curling, intricate centerpieces.

And we have Gorham serving dishes, baby bowls, gravy boats,

even sterling silver Christmas ornaments.

But Gorham's just the beginning.

In addition to Gorham, we have every famous brand name in sterling silver, silverplate and stainless you've ever heard of. And a lot of other names you haven't. Not to mention the 478 spectacular patterns we design, manufacture and import ourselves.

All in all, we have over 1,000 patterns for you to choose from.

And with a selection like that, your only problem will be narrowing it down to one.

So come to the source.

Now you know about our tremendous selection. And you've probably always known about our great prices.

But if it all sounds good, come and see it. It's even better in real life.

And after you've seen our thousands of forks, knives and spoons, maybe you'll want to see our thousands of rings, bracelets, watches, earrings, clocks and necklaces. Our antiques.

Because whatever you're looking for, we have it. And probably more of it than you've ever seen in your life.

And for better prices.

But what else would you expect, from the source?

Fortunoff, the source.

239

One winter, almost every retailer had the opportunity to promote Ice Sculptures by Ice Art. But it took the people at Dayton's to bring the concept to life, to melt hearts. Breathe there a human so cold that he/she could not respond to the question: "Pardon me, but isn't that a polar bear in your punch bowl?" We also love the easy way Dayton's explains just how they make the bear: three line sketches of the process. This is the way to sell concepts . . . and bears.

240

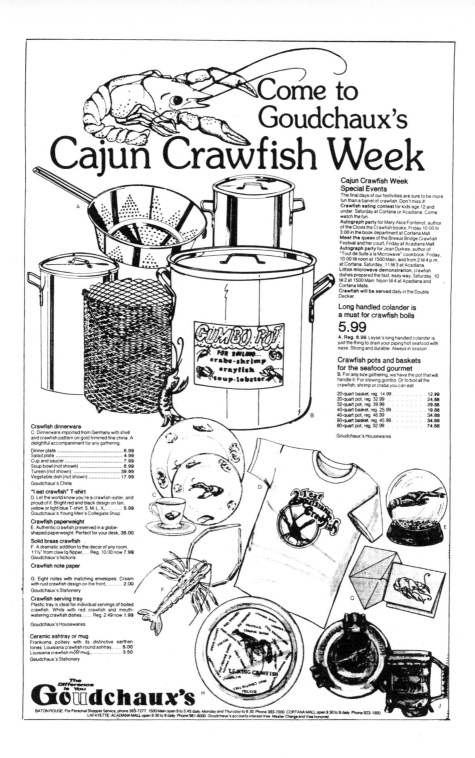

We've had many meaningless "weeks" lately but here is a week we can relish! Goudchaux's staged a Cajun Crawfish Week complete with crawfish eating contests, cooking demonstrations, cookbook autograph parties plus the Queen of the Crawfish Festival. Obviously everybody had a snappy time. Those yankees far to the north would never dream there would be so many special gadgets to honor this delectable crustacean.

This ad is an eye-opener.

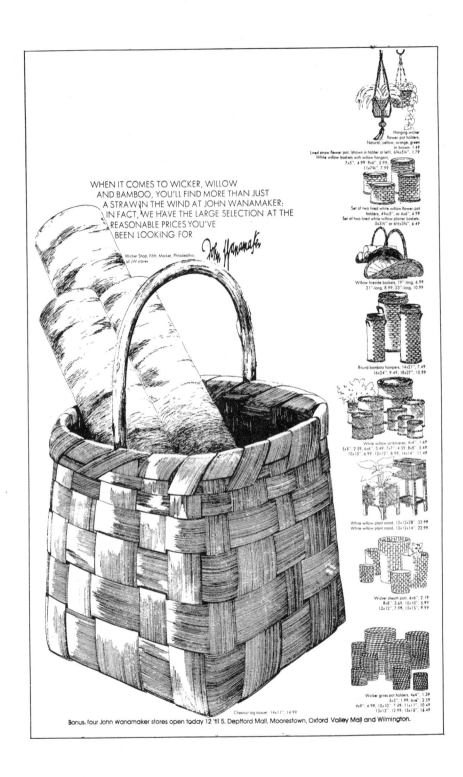

WHEN IT COMES TO WICKER, WILLOW
AND BAMBOO, YOU'LL FIND MORE THAN JUST
A STRAW IN THE WIND AT JOHN WANAMAKER:
IN FACT, WE HAVE THE LARGE SELECTION AT THE
REASONABLE PRICES YOU'VE
BEEN LOOKING FOR

Wicker shops have proliferated all over the country, in all sorts of stores, but leave it to Wanamakers to single it out and make impact on the customer. This is an example of what it takes to sell the store, taking one classification of exciting merchandise at a time, and presenting it to the people convincingly. It's an outstanding advertisement.

242

Macy's makes a parody on one of the popular TV coffee commercials and gives New York one of the great ads of the year. This one has everything—eye-stopping power, curiosity, creativity, and good copy.

Above:

Time changes are such a bother! But they are almost worth it when A&S is on hand with its brilliant "Hour loss is your gain" page. A page of clocks. But not ordinary clocks, these. A clock with its own sculpted hands, a crystal vase clock, plus the traditional Grandfather clock and striking clock. The selection of the theme at the moment of importance, the selection of the most interesting merchandise in its category, the clear presentation . . . all contribute to making this ad important.

Right:

The children do seem to enjoy the clock and we do, indeed, enjoy Wanamaker's advertising. The Charles Addams sketch contributes to the scene and it's all good.

The May Co's sentimental thoughts about telephones made a lot of impact on Cleveland. This is advertising that draws many eyes and creates conversation in the home. When advertising can do that it is serving its purpose well.

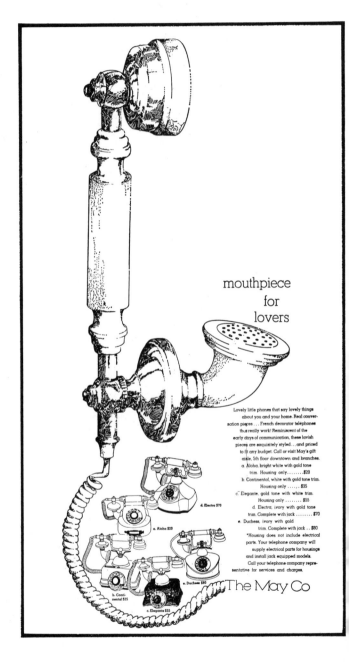

mouthpiece
for
lovers

Lovely little phones that say lovely things about you and your home. Real conversation pieces . . . French decorator telephones thus really work! Reminiscent of the early days of communication, these lavish pieces are exquisitely styled . . . and priced to fit any budget. Call or visit May's gift aisle, 5th floor downtown and branches.
a. Aloha, bright white with gold tone trim. Housing only $20
b. Continental, white with gold tone trim. Housing only $35
c. Elegante, gold tone with white trim. Housing only $55
d. Electra, ivory with gold tone trim. Complete with jack $70
e. Duchess, ivory with gold trim. Complete with jack . . $80
*Housing does not include electrical parts. Your telephone company will supply electrical parts for housings and install jack equipped models.
Call your telephone company representative for services and charges.

The May Co

But Sony's apartment stereo has a rich hi-fi sound even at low volume!

Sony's HP-180 lays down a full, dynamic sound at any volume level, low or high. You'll hear it all, from the thundering low bass notes of the pump organ to the sparkling high notes of the violins . . . without turning your neighbors into a committee of complainers! The cost? Only $319.95

Here's where all that fabulous sound comes from!

Before Sony, to get a great stereo sound in a small apartment, you had to turn the volume way up.

The speakers include two 6½-inch woofers and two 3-inch tweeters in the walnut-finish enclosures. Each speaker reproduces the entire range of sound with effortless clarity and no distortion—particularly the basses!

The tuner uses expensive FET transistors which are highly sensitive to distant stations. It performs beautifully on AM and stereo-FM programs, adding up to a lot of listening pleasure with 28 radio stations in the Dallas-Fort Worth area!

The turntable is German-made by Dual. It meets professional broadcast standards of accuracy, operates as a record changer or manual turntable. Complete with cueing device and single-play adapter.

The cartridge is Pickering's V-15 magnetic unit. The built-in dust brush sweeps the grooves while the record is playing. And the precision diamond stylus preserves the life of records for years!

Sanger-Harris

STEREOS, LOWER LEVEL DOWNTOWN, ALL SUBURANS EXCEPT HIGHLAND PARK

Here's an ad designed to reach a responsive cord in the heart of every apartment dweller! Sanger-Harris shows a doorway-full of neighbors ready to lynch a music lover. The three-column headline-and-copy story tells all about the new Sony apartment stereo with "rich hi-fi sound even at low volume!" The lesson here: Involve the reader and then tell him the whole story.

Macy's salutes Kohoutek's comet, shows an authentic sky map, and ties
in ten Tasco instruments. An exciting, informative advertisement.

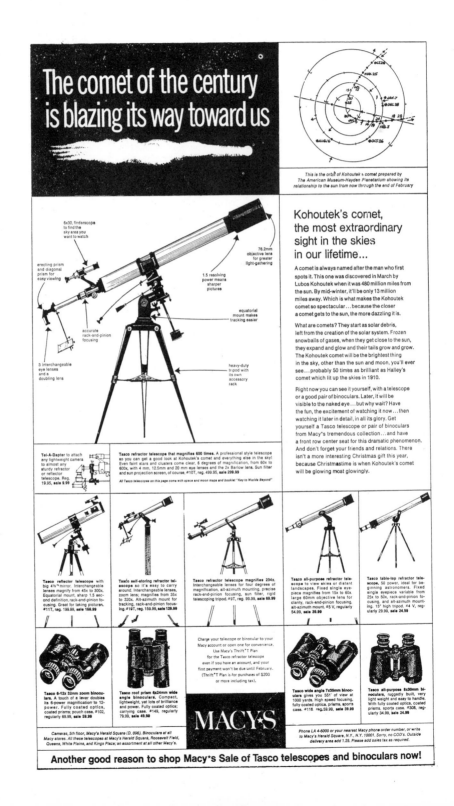

248

Call it obvious if you will. But people love the obvious, especially if the pun can be made so adorable. This bright-eyed quartet with the funny ears captured every New York Times reader that day. And they made a considerable statement for the merchandise, too. Dear Gimbels, can't we have this talented team make further appearances in support of your merchandise?

Left:

Ask almost every retail advertising person! "Mattresses are boring. They are big and dumb and, visually, the only difference we can show is whether their covering is striped or floral or striped and floral." The almost everys work at other stores.

The fews are from Wanamaker's where creativity is given the opportunity to flower. "A mattress ad! Let's try to top the last one. Let's make this the most memorable ad in the store's history." And so, the Wanamaker fews dump out the contents of a bottle of Snooze-x and stuff a mattress in that empty bottle.

Sizing up a good mattress can be a bit of a gamble so Eaton's, Toronto, does a careful copy job of it, explaining sizes, cushioning qualities, construction features, Eaton's Research Bureau, and giving to boost to the mattress salesman. It's a thorough job of selling a brand name done with full information and humorous sketches. A great combination.

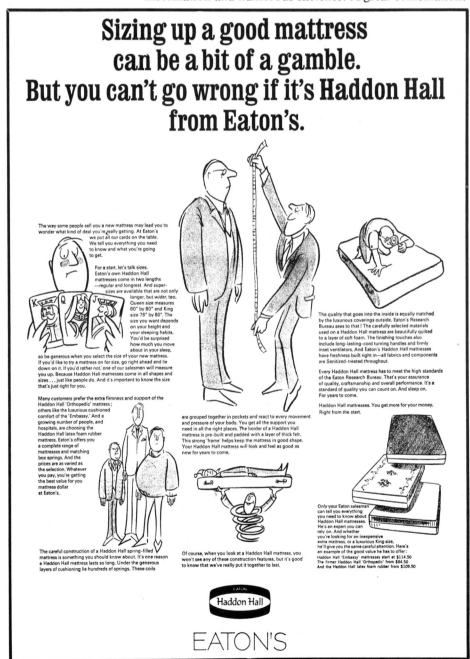

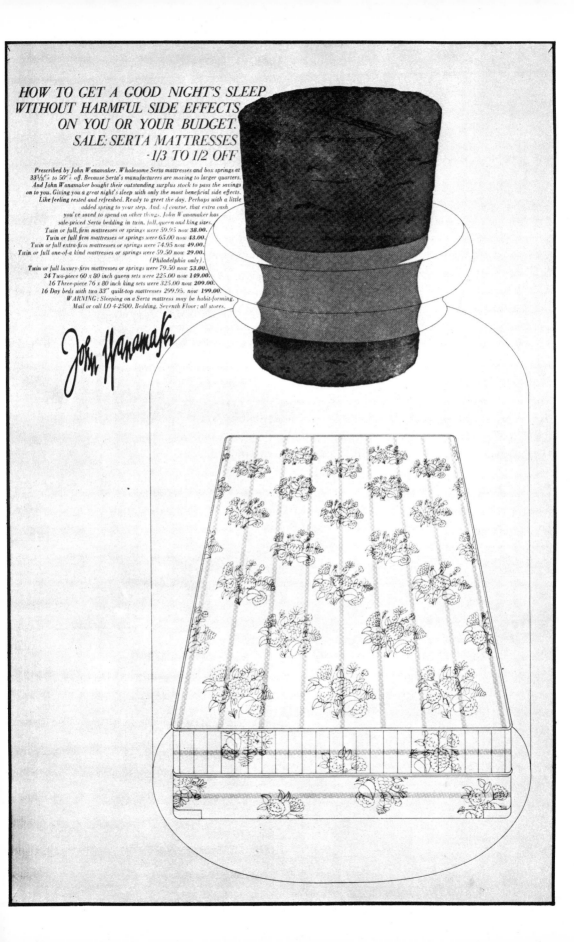

The talking pillow made impact all around the country and stores went all out to make the news visible and exciting. Some did the cartoon strip bit but May Co. in Los Angeles did it best. Not only the delightful sketches but the informative copy reach out irresistibly to the customer, Surely the best seen and best studied ad of the week.

It was inevitable for Kliban's precocious pussycats to appear one day on merchandise. Leave it to the May Company to develop a squeezable, teasable ad on the subject, pull together Kliban merchandise from several departments, and give the customers a cheerful, wonderful advertisement. You have to be a cat admirer to tolerate this ad . . . but then, who but cat admirers would tolerate this merchandise? Printing in two colors helps to reach out to the customers.

This has got to be a major breakthrough in newspaper advertising.
It illustrates a pillow case, in full color, and just about actual size.
The copy reads, "clip this from your newspaper and place it on your pillow
and discover what a great new look. . . ." Lowenstein's has given the
customer the next best thing to actual merchandise.
A convincing do-it-yourself bit of salesmanship.

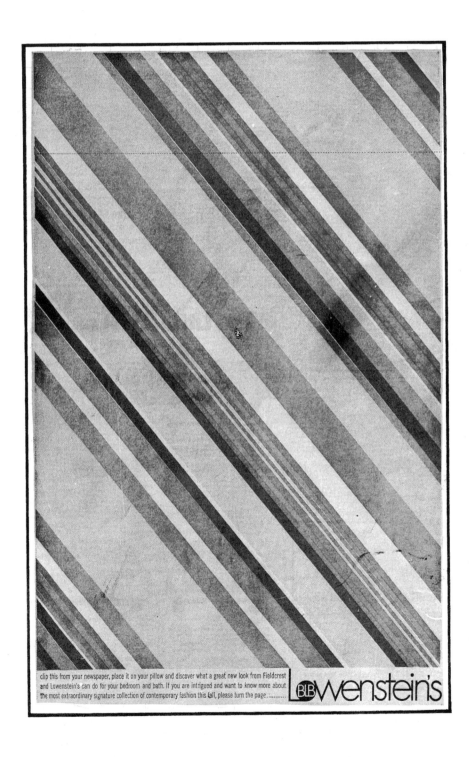

A lot of hard work and attention to detail went into this ad! Carson's promotes a "Village Bath Products Extravaganza" with a charming old-fashioned omnibus of spaces for vegetable beauty bath, mineral bath salts, hand-rolled soap balls, hand-cut slab soap and more. There's even an endorsement by "an American beauty: 'And I owe it all to Village Bath Products,'" signed Renee Malvoux.

Dayton's Consumer Service Memo Number 17

re: ENERGY CONSERVATION

115 things you can do in your home to be a power-pincher

It is estimated that Americans lose approximately two-thirds of the energy they consume and that half of the energy we use could be saved through conservation practices. The days of low-cost, unlimited energy are over while the need of it is ever increasing. Until the time when solar energy is both practical and economical, conservation of fossil fuels is important to all of us. Here's an idea list of some of the things you can do to save energy. . .and money!

IN HEATING

POWER POINTERS: Heating and cooling consume 11% of our total energy used in the United States and offer one of the most important areas in which savings can be made. Inefficiencies in your heating system alone can increase fuel consumption as much as 10%

1. Dial down. During the day preferably to 65°. At least to 68°. Wearing an extra sweater costs you nothing. Every degree above 68° adds 3% to your heat bill. At night, dial down to 60°. And during vacations, turn your thermostat to 55°.
2. Clean and change furnace filters frequently.
3. Clean thermostats yearly to assure proper readings.
4. Clean dust from registers, grills, air returns and baseboard heaters.
5. Have your entire heating plant cleaned and adjusted by a service person each year to make sure it is operating efficiently.
6. Understand your heating system. Hot water and steam radiators must be bled of air periodically. Some oil and gas plants have fans and motor bearings which require oiling.
7. Make sure heat registers and cold air returns are open and unobstructed by furniture or draperies.
8. Repair any leaks in ductwork with adhesive duct tape, especially at connection points.
9. Reflect heat from freestanding radiators on exterior walls by placing a large sheet of heavy-duty aluminum foil on the wall.

IN COOLING

10. Dial up. 75° or even 78° will feel cool inside when the temperature outside is 90° and you'll save up to 20% more energy than at 70°.
11. Use room fans or window fans instead of air conditioning units.
12. Use a kitchen exhaust fan to draw off cooking heat.
13. Use a bathroom exhaust fan to remove heat and moisture.
14. Shade whole-house and window units from direct sun with trees or awnings.
15. Close draperies to prevent direct sunlight from entering.
16. Clean grills and filters regularly.

POINTS OF PURCHASE: Buy right. An air conditioning unit that's too big wastes money. One to small will not cool adequately. Rule of thumb is 18 BTU's for every square foot to be cooled. Look for high "Energy Efficiency Ratios" which are listed on every unit and range from 4.7 to 12.2. 8.0 and above is considered to be a good rating.

IN FIREPLACES

POWER POINTERS: While efficiently heating the room they are in, those dancing, marshmallow toasting flames are pulling furnace-heated air from the rest of your house and causing your furnace to work harder.

17. Shut doors to other rooms while using your fireplace.
18. Lower your thermostat when you have a fire going.
19. Close damper when fireplace is not in use.
20. Install a fireplace chimney cap which minimizes loss of warm or cool air through your chimney.
21. Use glass fireplace doors which lessen heat loss and help to radiate warmth into the room.

POINTS OF PURCHASE: When building a new fireplace, have it designed so it uses outside air for combustion and has vents which return heated air into the room.

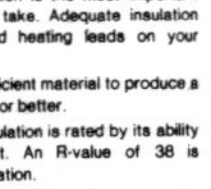

IN ATTICS, WALLS, BASEMENTS

POWER POINTERS: Insulation is the most important energy-saving step you can take. Adequate insulation can reduce the cooling and heating leads on your equipment by 15%.

22. Insulate attics with sufficient material to produce a heat loss value of R-38 or better.

POINT OF PURCHASE: Insulation is rated by its ability to resist the flow of heat. An R-value of 38 is recommended for ceiling insulation.

23. Wrap ductwork with 1½" of insulation, especially where it passes through unheated areas or outside.
24. Weatherstrip windows and doors.
25. Make your house ship-shape by caulking joints between window frames and siding, between window and door drip caps and siding, at joints between door frames and siding, at sill plate where wood siding meets the foundation, where masonary meets the siding, where porches join the house, around outside water faucets and basement windows, where pipes and wires penetrate exterior siding.
26. Install storm windows and doors. Generally they pay for themselves in approximately five years, then continue to help save money and energy.
27. Use batts of insulation inside of house between joists and studs at foundations.
28. Install ventilation louvers in eaves and roof gables to prevent moisture collecting on insulation in the winter and to let out warm air in the summer.
29. Humidify with a furnace unit, a portable unit, pans of water near heating outlets or by having lots of moisture-creating plants. Your house will be as comfortable at 68° as a dry one at 75°.

POWER POINTERS:

If outside temperature is:	Inside humidity should be:
20° or above	35%
20° to 10°	30%
10° to 0°	25%
0° to -10°	20%
-10° or below	15%

IN WATER HEATERS

POWER POINTERS: Hot water heaters are the second greatest users of energy in your home and an area in which energy-saving will cut costs.

30. Lower water heater temperatures. 140° is sufficient for homes with automatic dishwashers; 110° in homes without them. Add a 3% increase in your water heating costs for every 10° over 140°.
31. Wrap older water heaters with a blanket of fiberglass insulation. But only after calling your utility company to learn necessary precautions.
32. Insulate hot water pipes from source to point of use.
33. Turn hot water heaters down when on vacation.

POINTS OF PURCHASE: Select a unit with high efficiency rating and heavy insulation that is in proportion to family size. Rule of thumb is a 40-gallon oil or gas tank or 80-gallon electric tank for a family of four.

IN BATHROOMS

34. Turn off running water as often as possible when shaving or brushing teeth.
35. Replace worn out washers. It's drippy to let leaks waste water, energy and money.
36. Reduce the amount of water required by each flushing by setting a water-filled plastic bottle or a few bricks inside the tank of the toilet.
37. Take showers instead of baths.

TEST A THEORY: Stop the drain next time you shower and see how much water you use in comparison to the water level for a bath. Short showers generally use considerably less.

38. Install a shower head which restricts the flow of water to three gallons per minute. A normal shower head delivers about seven gallons per minute.

IN LAUNDRIES

39. Wash with warm water and rinse in cold.
40. Wash only full loads of various sized items. Water level and temperature selectors help reduce cost of small loads but full loads save more.
41. Don't overload or use too much detergent.
42. Hand set gentle or slow wash cycles to high speed spin to remove greater amounts of water and save drying time.
43. Pre-soak heavily soiled items to save second washings.
44. Use special features such as soak and short cycles, suds savers.
45. Remove clothes promptly from dryer. You'll prevent wrinkles and save ironing time.
46. Dry items of similar weight and texture together.
47. Dry consecutive loads to avoid dryer warmups.
48. Damp dry clothes which will need ironing. It saves sprinkling.
49. Vent electric dryers inside your home in winter to increase humidity.
50. Hang clothes to dry in the sun or on inside lines in winter to increase moisture in your home.
51. Operate and maintain washer and dryer according to manufacturer's recommendations.
52. Clean lint filter after each washing or drying load.

IN YOUR KITCHEN

53. Keep freezers and refrigerators filled to capacity for maximum efficiency.
54. Maintain and operate food storage units according to the manufacturer's directions.
55. Minimize length and number of refrigerator and freezer door openings by removing or replacing several items at once, by knowing what you want and by teaching children to do the same.
56. Cover all liquids to reduce moisture evaporation.
57. Set refrigerators at 37° to 40°; freezers at 0°.
58. Unplug a second refrigerator when not in use. Unplug all refrigerators when leaving for a long time. Clean, turn off and put in an open box of baking powder. Be sure to leave the door open.

TEST A THEORY: To check your refrigerator and freezer for cold retention, close doors on a piece of paper. If it pulls out easily, you'll need to adjust the latch or replace a gasket.

POINTS OF PURCHASE: Choose a refrigerator based on family needs, generally 14 cubic feet for a family of four with two additional cubic feet of space for each additional member. For freezers, you'll need two cubic feet per family member. Two-door refrigerator / freezers use less energy than one-door models. Frost-free models and side by side models use more energy than two-door uprights. Automatic ice makers and liquid dispensers also increase energy usage. Look for refrigerators without heater strips around doors or models with power switches that turn them off in less humid weather. Chest freezers use considerably less energy then uprights.

POWER POINTERS: Never use range surface units or ovens for anything but cooking.

59. Turn off surface and oven units before removing pans to utilize "hangover heat."
60. Use tight fitting covers on cookware to help foods cook faster.

61. Cook with flat-surfaced, straight-sided pots and pans that extend more than one inch over cooking unit.
62. Use hot tap water for boiling and use a tea kettle instead of an open pan.
63. Use only enough water in cooking to make steam and prevent sticking. You'll save energy and retain more flavor and nutrients in your food.
64. Keep reflector pans clean to reflect heat better.
65. Lower cooking heat with Teflon-coated utensils.
66. Cook full meals in oven when possible. It's more economical than using both oven and surface units.
67. Pre-heat oven only when necessary and then only for a short time . . . try it on your favorite recipe.
68. Don't peek. 25° of oven heat is lost when you open the door.
69. Use glass or ceramic bakeware and reduce heat 25°.
70. Schedule baking all at once and put as many things as possible in at one time.
71. Bake enough for two or three meals at once. Reheating takes less energy.
72. Defrost frozen foods to save time in the oven.
73. Rearrange shelves in oven before heating.
74. Warm foods in ovens at 200° or less.
75. Use "hangover heat" on burners for warming, plates, rolls, etc.
76. Use a timer and a thermometer to prevent over cooking.
77. Brown foods at high heats then reduce to medium or low. You'll save energy, reduce shrinkage and spattering.
78. Check gas range pilot light for clear blue color. If yellow, call a service person to adjust the combustion. If burner flame is yellow, clean with pipe cleaner.

POINTS OF PURCHASE: Carefully compare the advantages of both self-cleaning and continuous cleaning ovens and select the type that offers greater efficiency for your particular baking / broiling habits.

79. Run dishwasher only when full.
80. Remove large particles from dishes with a cold water rinse.
81. Load dishwasher properly and use recommended amount of detergent.
82. Turn off dishwasher after final rinse in cool months and allow dishes to air dry.
83. Run dishwasher in cooler hours during summer months to avoid extra heat and moisture. This also helps to keep operation away from peak power times.

POINTS OF PURCHASE: Dishwashers with partial load cycles, rinse only and mid-cycle turn-offs help to save energy as will models with power switches to turn off drying cycles automatically. Look for models with heavier insulation to reduce noise and retain heat.

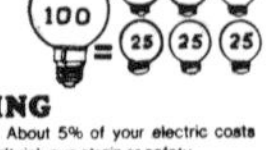

IN LIGHTING

POWER POINTERS: About 5% of your electric costs are from lighting so don't risk eye strain or safety

84. Use a single high-watt bulb instead of several smaller ones. It takes six 25-watt bulbs to give the light of one 100-watt size.
85. Turn off lights when leaving a room . . . even for a short time. Only fluorescent tubes can be left on for up to a half-hour without using more energy.
86. Use fluorescent lighting wherever possible. Fluorescent wattage gives five times more light and lasts ten times longer.
87. Light small areas rather than entire rooms.
88. Leave lights off whenever daylight is sufficient.
89. Use long-life bulbs only in hard-to-reach areas. They may last three times longer but they give off 20% less light.
90. Keep bulbs and lighting fixtures clean for maximum lighting. Dusty bulbs give one-third less light.

POINTS OF PURCHASE: Consider replacing incandescent lighting with fluorescent; light switches with solid-state dimmers that allow choice of light level. Choose 3-way lamps for the same reason. Select outdoor lighting that uses photo-electric cells for automatic operation.

IN GENERAL

POWER POINTERS: Appliances that heat use more energy. Use them sparingly and be sure to turn them off when through. Save money and energy by purchasing appliances according to life cycle operating costs rather than initial price tag. A more expensive model may cost a lot less in the long run.

91. Turn off television sets when no one is watching. Tube types use more power than solid state models and color sets more than black and white. Instant-on sets draw energy unless unplugged.
92. Sleep under an extra blanket when you turn the heat down.
93. Use a towel to dry hair instead of a blower.
94. Set hair in curlers or pins instead of electric rollers.
95. Use only cold water in garbage disposers.
96. Use trash compacters only when full.
97. Entertain by candlelight. It's more romantic.
98. Empty dust bags in vacuum cleaners frequently.
99. Cook small meals in counter-top appliances rather than ranges.
100. Use a timer to turn radios and lights on and off when you're on vacation.
101. Heat a ceramic tile for your bread basket when baking dinner instead of using an electric warmer.
102. Close draperies to keep out cold on winter evenings. Open them on sunny days for warmth and light. In summer, keep them closed to block heat and sun.
103. Cover large windows with clear vinyl or plastic sheets during winter months. It's one way for apartment dwellers to save energy.
104. Hang thermal draperies.
105. Carpet bare floors with carpeting having an R rating of 4 or more.
106. Close off heat and doors in bedrooms and congregate in one room. Family relations are sure to warm up while you save energy.

IN FASHION AND CLOTHES CARE

POWER POINTERS: It's fashionable to save energy. This year's layered look is just what's needed for cooler homes, offices and factories. Even famous designers are contributing with such things as fancy, warm underwear by Fernando Sanchez and long, over-the elbow arm stockings from Halston. Sweater up and be in style.

107. Dress with several light layers of clothing such as shirt, sweater and jacket or vested suit.
108. Wear ribbed or opaque pantyhose for greater warmth.
109. Choose natural fibers for extra warmth. They usually are produced with less energy, too.
110. Choose man-made fibers to save ironing.
111. Wear flannel pajamas to keep warmer at night.
112. Use a shawl, afghan, blanket or throw while watching TV or reading.
113. Iron at lowest possible temperature settings.
114. Do a week's ironing at one time to cut down on numerous heatings.
115. Turn iron off minutes before you're finished and if interrupted.

IN OUR STORES

We've taken steps to be power pinchers . . .

1. Lowered temperatures in stores to 64°; to 62° in our Distribution center for heating months. Set temperatures up to 78° for air conditioning.
2. Reduced hours of operation for escalators, elevators, air flow equipment, steam presses and steamers.
3. Upgraded maintenance schedules to improve efficiency of mechanical equipment.
4. Installed capacitors to correct power factors where ratings were under 95%.
5. Lowered temperatures of hot water used by customers and employees.
6. Added insulation to store roofs, entrances and loading doors on docks.
7. Turned off air doors in Minneapolis and St. Paul.
8. Installed timers on electrical circuits in many areas.
9. Reduced use of spotlights and show window lighting.
10. Recircuited lighting for better control of specific areas.
11. Reduced wattage, where possible, by using fewer fluorescent tubes in fixtures.
12. Installed demand limiting equipment in Minneapolis, Ridgedale, St. Cloud and the Distribution Center.
13. Turned off snow melting equipment for sidewalks.
14. Eliminated outdoor display lights on holidays.
15. Burning trash to create steam for heating in the Minneapolis store.
16. Working with newly hired, Dayton Hudson Corporation energy consultant to reduce power consumption in new and existing stores.
17. Encouraging employees to help with energy conservation methods.

FOR MORE INFORMATION . . .

Visit Dayton's Major Appliance Booth and Home Furnishings Booth at the Energy Savers Show in the Minneapolis Auditorium, September 8 through 11.

Visit the NSP Consumer Information Booth when it comes to the Dayton's store nearest you September 15 through 23 and talk to the representative who will have pamphlets on many energy saving methods and narrate a Residential Energy Conservation Slide Show, an informative 15 minute presentation followed by a question-and-answer session.

Ridgedale: 3 p.m., September 15, Major Appliances
Southdale: 7 p.m., September 15; Housewares
Minneapolis: Noon, September 16; Major Appliances
St. Paul: Noon, September 17; Major Appliances
Burnsville: 3 p.m.. September 17; Housewares
Rosedale: 3 p.m., September 19; Housewares
Brookdale: 7 p.m., September 19; Housewares
Fargo: Noon, September 21; Housewares
Rochester: Noon, September 22; Major Appliances
St. Cloud: Noon, September 23; Housewares

For reprints: write Dayton's Customer Service Memos
700 On the Mall, Minneapolis, Minnesota 55402

This page:
Smoke detectors are coming in strong and customers are in a quandary about what, why and how. Macy's in San Francisco does an in-depth study of the subject, reviewing the merits of the devices, giving good advice, and offering a price reduction. This is the kind of informative, person-to-person conversation this subject has been needing and here it is, done beautifully.

Page left:
Dayton's produced 17 full newspaper consumer memos on subjects that are important to its customers. Each ad invites customers to send in for complimentary reprints, and as continued proof of the readership and real interest, the store received 500 to 1500 requests per ad. These requests came from individuals as well as a large number of schools and clubs. Dayton's was right! As merchandise selection gets more complex and the conservation of natural resources gets more crucial, customers will read every word of real information presented to them ... particularly if it is presented by a store they trust. In the fall of 1977, Dayton's memo on energy conservation was presented in the Congress of the United States and reprinted, in its entirety, in the September 16, 1977 Congressional Record.

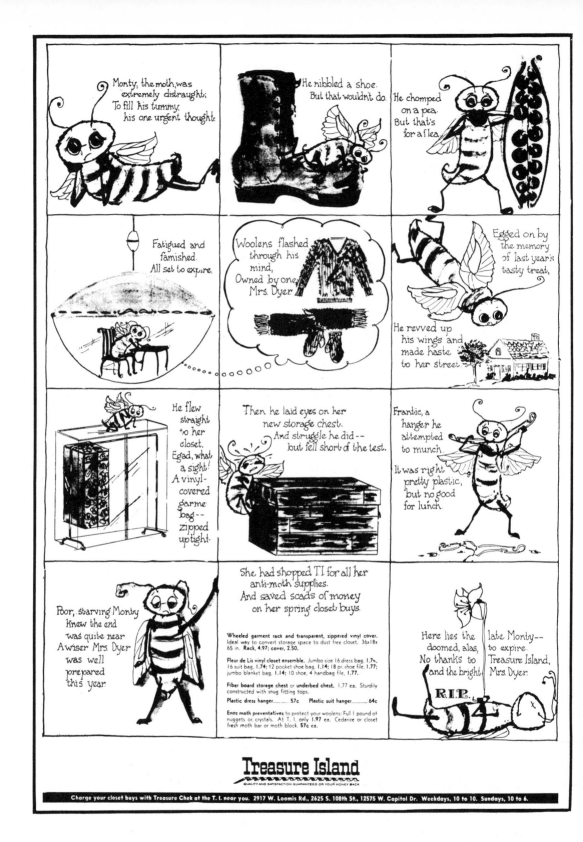

The life history of a moth who got tangled with modern anti-moth supplies,
as told in verse by Treasure Island. This ad gets a lot of attention.

258

There is growing evidence that customers are impressed with assortments and a wide range of merchandise to choose from. Gabberts shows a wide range in a particularly inviting manner, each chair in an attractive setting. No descriptive copy. Why write words when a picture does so much? Beautiful job.

You'll find your home in our range.

From our $650 Chair and Ottoman to our $480 Modern Swivel.

From our $400 French Provincials to our $275 Wingbacks.

From our $250 Modern Tub Chairs to our $200 Lounge Chairs.

From our $150 French Canebacks to our $70 Americana Rockers.

Gabberts

Across from Southdale on 69th Street, open weekdays noon to 9:30, Saturdays 10:00 to 6:00, Sundays 12:00 to 5:00, Phone: 927-7033

259

The apartment, the hi-rise, the condominium. Carson's is paying close attention to a life-style of smaller rooms, lower ceilings, and less space. This advertisement, one of a series, is timely, authoritive, and distinctive.

260

It is particularly refreshing at the start of a new year to find a retailer doing one sale a year. One. "If you miss it, you'll have to wait until 1983." Workbench, with retail outlets throughout the New York area, makes this once-a-year sale a month-long event and reduces the prices of "practically everything." The copy in this ad carefully explains what this means. Read it. This is a top-notch job of selling the sale, conversational, pleasant to read, convincing.

There is a fascination about this advertisement by The Broadway. It is hard to resist. The simplicity of language and the narrative style makes it extraordinarily readable and convincing. There are those who say, "people don't read long copy." This may be so in many cases but here is an ad that will be well read and understood. This is today's advertising; real, honest, informative, and a pleasant departure from the usual sale-on-sale of most retailers. The art is also an example of beautiful technique and an understanding of today's customer.

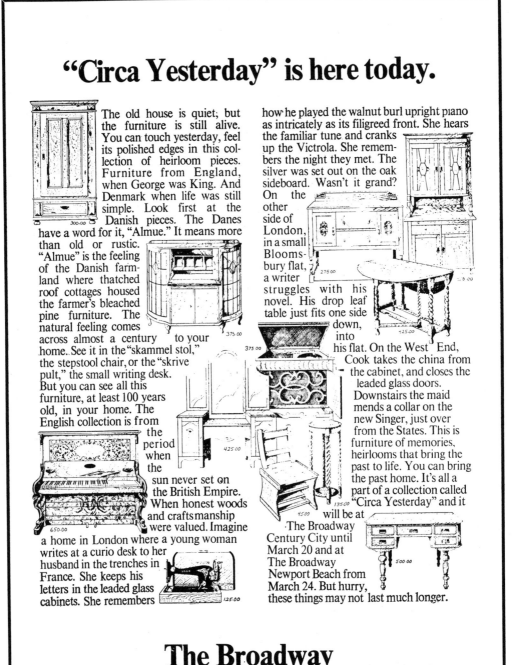

"Circa Yesterday" is here today.

The old house is quiet; but the furniture is still alive. You can touch yesterday, feel its polished edges in this collection of heirloom pieces. Furniture from England, when George was King. And Denmark when life was still simple. Look first at the Danish pieces. The Danes have a word for it, "Almue." It means more than old or rustic. "Almue" is the feeling of the Danish farm-land where thatched roof cottages housed the farmer's bleached pine furniture. The natural feeling comes across almost a century to your home. See it in the "skammel stol," the stepstool chair, or the "skrive pult," the small writing desk. But you can see all this furniture, at least 100 years old, in your home. The English collection is from the period when the sun never set on the British Empire. When honest woods and craftsmanship were valued. Imagine a home in London where a young woman writes at a curio desk to her husband in the trenches in France. She keeps his letters in the leaded glass cabinets. She remembers how he played the walnut burl upright piano as intricately as its filigreed front. She hears the familiar tune and cranks up the Victrola. She remembers the night they met. The silver was set out on the oak sideboard. Wasn't it grand? On the other side of London, in a small Blooms-bury flat, a writer struggles with his novel. His drop leaf table just fits one side down, into his flat. On the West End, Cook takes the china from the cabinet, and closes the leaded glass doors. Downstairs the maid mends a collar on the new Singer, just over from the States. This is furniture of memories, heirlooms that bring the past to life. You can bring the past home. It's all a part of a collection called "Circa Yesterday" and it will be at The Broadway Century City until March 20 and at The Broadway Newport Beach from March 24. But hurry, these things may not last much longer.

The Broadway

Shop weekdays and Saturday from 10 a.m. and all weekday evenings. All stores open Sundays. Order board open 24 hours a day. Dial 1-800-252-9174.

262

This has got to be, without any question, the most appealing advertisement of the week. Not only did every reader of the New York Times stop here but this is the kind of advertising that gets passed around in the home and gets talked about. When an ad succeeds in getting talked about its value per line increases ten times. Einstein Moomjy buys its linage very cheap.

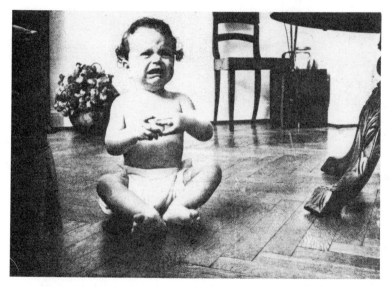

"I want my Moomjy."

From now through Sept. 29th, 570 bottom-warming, shiver-stopping, anti-freeze winter carpets will be on sale at Einstein Moomjy. Shags, shimmers, softs, for $5.99. (Were $7.99.) Plushes for $6.99. (Were $8.99.) Furries for $10.99. (Were $17.99.) Even our practically thermal Antron⁺ nylon for $11.99. (Was $15.99.) Give your bare little floor its big, warm Moomjy before, baby, it gets cold outside.

Einstein Moomjy
The Carpet Department Store

*DuPont registered trademark.

PARAMUS, 526 Route 17 (201) 262-4100   BLOOMFIELD, 326 Broad Street (201) 743-1900   N.Y.A. (201) 944 Route 22 (201) 233-9800   (N.J.) (201) 344 Route 10 (201) 887-1600
WAYNE, 1502 Willowbrook Mall (201) 785-1333 (just outside the Mall)   (Just our to Departs store 201-201 Route 1 (603) Sec. (1:00). Stores open daily to 9 pm, Saturday to 6 pm.
HOW TO GET FROM NEW YORK TO OUR PARAMUS STORE: Cross George Washington Bridge. Take Route 4 to Route 17 North. Follow Route 17 for 2.5 miles. Einstein Moomjy is on your right.

That's using your head!

We wouldn't say you have to go to the length our be-wigged Britisher has gone to. We merely suggest you put Lees 'Melody Mood' on your floors, not on your head. And why the be-wigged Britisher to make the point? That's just Higbee's sly way of breaking the most exciting decorating news in a generation: BRITISH is BIG! All things British, from practically every century. And when it comes to floor coverings, you're using your head when you carpet with Lees Melody Mood. It's plush. Just the ticket for any room, informal or not so, in English manner. The pile is Acrilan® acrylic, sturdy, mothproof, non-allergenic. Cortez red, avocado, Tucson gold, frosted honey, Burma gold, cloudy jade, vanilla bean, bronze, royal blue, Grecian olive, pearl beige, bottle green, fresco blue, ivory cream. Sq. yd. 8.95, on Higbee's Sixth Floor Downtown, Westgate, and Severance... a correct carpeting to underline

English...the well-bred look

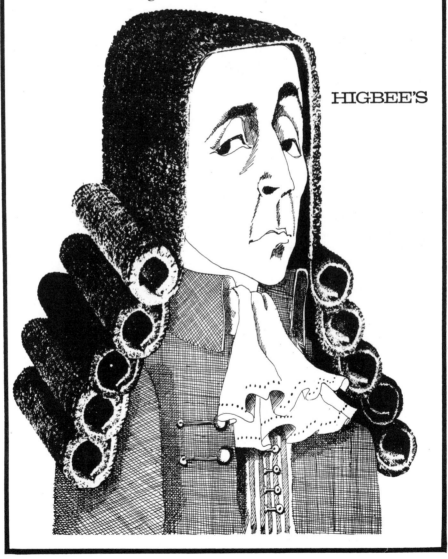

HIGBEE'S

Higbee's tells the story of the well-bred English look in carpets.
This is advertising that gets talked about.

May Co's guide for the successful carpet shopper

once upon a time carpet shopping was simple. First you decided on color, texture and pattern. Then you took your choice of wool, wool or wool. Times change. There's still wool. There's also acrylic, modacrylic, nylon, polyester and polypropylene. Bewildering? Yes . . . but starting today May Co is publishing a series of weekly ads that will clear the air

about carpeting. We'll discuss how » buy it. What to look for; What to expect in the way of personal service at May Co . . . important things such as our decorator service, installation and follow-up service. At the same time we'll show you just a few of the floor coverings available from our tremendous selection. Stick with us and in no time at all you'll be the most successful carpet shopper you know!

facts about fibers The fiber alone does not determine the quality of a carpet. The more fiber, the better the carpet. Here is a summary of carpet fibers and their particular advantages.

Acrylic fibers include Acrilan®, Creslan®, Orlon® and Zelkrome®. All have good resistance to abrasion, medium to high resiliency and good soil and stain resistance. They are non-allergenic, mildew and moth proof. Acrylic fiber is perfect for a bedroom or study where, with minimum care, it will stay fresh and lively for many years to come.

Nylon is rated as the longest wearing fiber. It is very durable and easy to clean. Great for heavy traffic areas such as hallways, stairways or living rooms. Most nylon carpet fiber is texturized to make it resistant to pilling and fuzzing. Nylon is non-allergenic and mildew and moth proof. It is also less expensive than other man-made fiber carpets.

Cotton rugs, introduced after World War II, are easily dyed to almost any color and are washable. The best are vat-dyed and pre-shrunk. Because they are economical they make good temporary coverings. But consider carefully where they will be used. Cotton has low crush resistance and tends to mat more than rugs of other fibers. Cotton is a thrifty covering for areas of minimum traffic.

Modacrylics (modified acrylic) such as Dynel® and Verel®

are used alone in bath or scatter rugs and have the hand and feel of wool. Perfect for taking the chill off cold bathroom and hallway floors. When used in carpeting they are almost always blended with an acrylic. They have the same characteristics as acrylic besides being fire resistant (self-extinguishing).

Polyester fibers are the newest man-made carpet fibers and go by such names as Dacron®, Fortrel®, Kodel® and Vycron®. They have a hand and appearance similar to wool. They have outstanding durability and crush resistance, and are stain and soil resistant. They also are non-allergenic and mildew and moth proof. Another good fiber for heavy traffic areas.

Polypropylene (olefin) is used for indoor-outdoor carpets. Because of its outstanding stain resistance and low absorption factor (water beads up on it), it is perfect for carpeting bathrooms, kitchens or patios. Vacuum it indoors, hose it down outdoors. Excellent colorfastness lets you select it in many lively colors. Polypropylene is comparatively inexpensive and has very good abrasion resistance. The backing for indoor-outdoor carpeting should also be man-made.

Wool is the traditional carpet fiber and its use is believed to go back as far as 2000 B.C. It is easily cleaned and has excellent resiliency. It also has good soil, stain and flame resistance and color versatility. All good wool carpets today come permanently mothproofed. A good choice for creating memorable rooms, that also can take years of wear. Wool holds its shape and luster the longest of all carpet fibers. When buying wool, don't skimp. A poorly made wool rug is worse than an inexpensive man-

made fiber carpet. Good wool costs a bit more, but there is incomparable personal satisfaction in the luxury of wool.

Carpetmobile service

We've put the store on wheels for those who prefer to see carpet samples at home. Our carpetmobile has a complete selection of all the carpeting we have on the floor. At no extra charge one of our carpet experts will help you select just the right color to go with your furnishings, take measurements prepare an estimate and even

handle credit. All in your home. Call MA 3-8211, ext. 2392, or one of the toll-free numbers listed below.

where to shop

If you've read this far, we assume you are interested in carpeting. We have men in 16 stores who will be happy to tell you more. You can start by asking them about the carpets described at the right,

Coronet's Imperial Luxuriously thick Kodel® polyester pile broadloom that retains its beauty, resiliency and liveliness for years. Easy to maintain, moth and mildew proof, with excellent wearing qualities. 15 exciting colors. Spanish gold, tropic fern, Wedgewood blue, claret red, burnt orange, lemon yellow, antique gold, cactus green, seamist, sapphire, ruby red, empire green, moss, bone beige, mellow gold.
sq. yd. installed, 12.99

Coronet's Iridescence An extra-heavy, hi-lo sheared nylon pile carpet, Nylon, the longest wearing carpet fiber known, resists dirt and stains. It's moth and mildew proof, non-allergenic, and extremely durable. Cationic-dyed in 10 multi-tone effects including peacock, copper, latin olive, bronze, red, dark gold.
sq. yd. installed, 10.99

Prices include complete installation over heavy rubberized padding and custom tackless installation by May Co carpet experts.
floor coverings 32—all 16 stores

MAY CO

May Co. L.A. cuts through the mysteries and misconceptions of carpet copy and tells it like it is. The grateful customer will long remember the store that knows what it is talking about. A first rate job.

AARGHH might well have been the sound of the seventies and Ayres offers an antidote. That's what this ad is all about. Ideas like this are what it takes to sell—ideas that stop the reader instantly, talk to her, sympathize with her problems and offer her solutions. Old-timers won't like this ad but we can't be too concerned as long as the young-in-heart get a stimulation out of it.

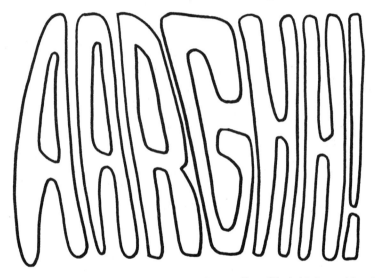

L.S.Ayres + co.

Until Now
There Was But One Word
To Describe Shopping
for Ready-Made Draperies

You've all uttered, moaned or screamed that word at least once in your life, right? It means you've been pushed beyond the limit of endurance; you just can't take any more! You found just the right texture of drapery for that big picture window but the store only stocks that particular drapery in single widths, right? So you good-naturedly proceed to pick out another texture and, lo and behold, they do have the right sizes! However, it comes only in the ever-popular shades of moon-over-Miami blue, crab-apple pink and startling scarlet! So again, in your mild-mannered way, you go on to find a color you like. You find the color, the right size! . . . and, with will-wonders-never-cease amazement, discover the fabric is the all-new, in-now, flame-proof, water-resistant, insect-repellent cheesecloth! By now, you've begun the city's first fight-against-windows movement.

You can think only of draping your windows with black mourning cloth. We can't blame you, but we can help you. It's not hopeless, so don't despair. There is a drapery to fit your window! Ayres' now has in stock a large selection of drapery sizes and colors. 14 Colors and 30 sizes in Croscill's Victorian Royal Antique Satin draperies, 4 colors and 23 sizes in Dacron® polyester Voile Sheer underdraperies, 4 styles of valances and an outstanding selection of tie-backs and other accessories. Almost any window can be fitted immediately; almost any color preference is available, like now. If you're shopping for draperies now, or perhaps you will be later, keep Ayres' in mind. We may not have just the thing you need for, say a ship's porthole, but we'll probably come closer than anyone else you may try! **Another AARGHH** antidote . . . bedspreads to match! Available: Draperies. Seventh Floor, Downtown; also Glendale, Greenwood, Lafayette and Fort Wayne.

This week, Ayres' salutes the Indianapolis Section of the National Council of Jewish Women for their humanitarian efforts in the fields of education, community service and social action

Right:
Horne's advertising for the Decorating Studios is beautiful beyond compare. The copy is written as a want-ad, easy to read and loaded with ideas. Actually a strong selling job! The art is in color and the total impression is unbelievably exciting.

Bloomingdale's takes a refreshing approach to "savings that turn the clock back." The copy is loaded with information, items and price-appeal. Phone numbers are listed and there is even an announcement of a new store coming up. News is the key and everything about this page suggests news including the nostalgic movie-set photo.

Right:
Abraham & Straus proves that form can follow function beautifully even though the basis of operation is a Brooklyn Brownstone dating from the ever-gay nineties. It's lovely.

HELLO, CENTRAL?
GIVE ME BLOOMINGDALE'S CUSTOM SLIPCOVER AND CASEMENT DRAPERY SALE

THIS IS NO LINE . . . USE OUR CONVENIENT SHOP-AT-HOME PHONE SERVICE . . . OR HURRY IN FOR SAVINGS THAT TURN THE CLOCK BACK

30% savings on Peter Kaufmann casement fabrics for draperies . . . Only a phone call away when you use our convenient Shop-At-Home service. Take time for that extra cup of coffee while our representative shows you our vast array of casement fabrics. Airy, open-weave designs that permit sunlight to stream through . . . yet create a mood of intimacy and privacy. All Imported weaves . . . in ecology-conscious hues. Earthy brown . . . sand . . . and palest oyster. Some fabrics woven in a single shade . . . others multi-toned. Cottons, linens, acrylics and blends now only 3.85 to 4.70 the yard (regularly 6.50 to 6.75 the yard). We'll transform the fabric of your choice into handsome pinch-pleated draperies right in our own workrooms. You'll discover our magnificent obsession for detail. Never satisfied: every mitered corner, every blind side

stitch has to be just so. All you do is call. We'll do the rest.

25% off on custom-made slipcovers for sofas, loveseats and chairs. Choose from four amazingly diverse collections. Our "Spectra V" group has a marvelous mix of printed florals, damasks and stripes woven of 100% cotton. One sofa and one chair, custom covered for only 149.00* (regularly 199.00). Sofa and two chairs, only 199.00* (regularly 269.00). But there's much more. Plump corduroys . . . opulent textures . . . country quilteds in prints and solids. All in three other collections at slightly higher prices. Just one phone call will bring fabric samples and expert advice to your home.

*Prices for tufted 84" sofa with up to three seat cushions; chair with one seat cushion.

Fabrics for the Home, New York and all stores.

STAY AT HOME AND PHONE US if you're too busy to come in. We'll bring samples (within 50 miles of our New York store) and help you make your selection. New York 832-2965; In New Jersey, call Short Hills at 379-1000, ext. 246 or Bergen County at DI 3-3200, ext. 332. In Connecticut, call the Stamford store at 348-6812, ext. 285. In New Rochelle, call NE 6-1234, ext. 249. In Manhasset, call 627-3840, ext. 217. Custom Fabrics for the Home, 4th Floor, New York and all branch stores.

AND THEN THERE WERE TWO
Once upon a time there was only one Bloomingdale store specializing in Home Furnishings . . . Manhasset. In this unique environment, our Long Island customers can find a dazzling array of home furnishings in every period and price.
Now, we are proud to announce that beginning in early November, Manhasset will be joined by a sister store . . . Scarsdale. Here you will find Living Room, Bed Room and Dining Room furniture, Bedspreads, Rugs, Draperies, our internationally acclaimed Designer Rooms, our Decorating service, and much, much more.

BLOOMINGDALE'S, LEX. AT 59TH, N.Y. 10022, PL 2-1212. BERGEN, FRESH MEADOWS, MANHASSET, NEW ROCHELLE, SHORT HILLS, STAMFORD. OPEN LATE MONDAY AND THURSDAY NIGHTS

Custom-made by A&S (THE SHADES, THAT IS)

No matter what your architectural taste may be, A&S will draw up the
perfect plan for custom-shading your windows. Come in and see our exciting collection of fabrics
and trims and you'll agree that form can follow function in a beautiful way!

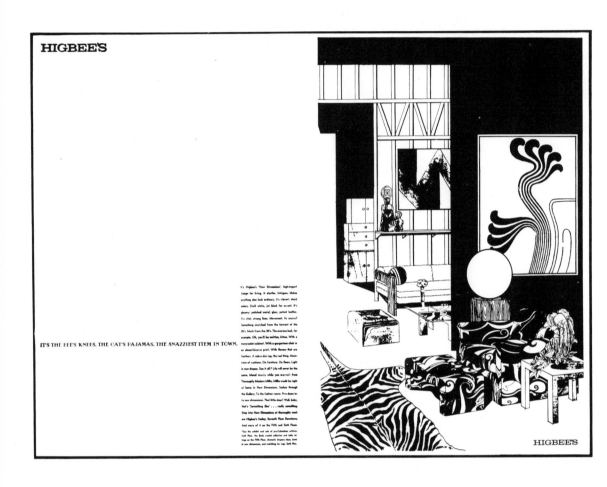

Higbee's takes a new look at design for living, calls it New Dimensions and does an opening series that startles calm old Cleveland. "Oh, you'll be smitten, kitten" the copy says. We are.

Right:
"A happening is finally happening in the world of home furnishings," says Macy's and they have Peter Max to demonstrate what it is. He has a lot to show, and so does this fascinating page.

Another victory for Vectra!

It withstood the onslaught of sun, stain 'n' rain in patio carpeting... now in upholstery, it weathers the assault of cowboys and indians, too!

This is the same invincible Vectra polypropylene fibre proven outdoors 'on the carpet', that Quaker Fabrics has woven into upholstery. Just as resistant to abrasion. Just as resistant to fading — the lively colours are locked right in. Just as stain-resistant — no costly added finishes needed, the resistance is built right in the fibre. Any spills can be simply washed off with household detergent. Happily however, Vectra upholstery only performs like outdoor carpeting... it looks and feels like softest wool in herringbone, checked and tweed patterns. Eaton's introduces Vectra upholstery fibre first in Canada on contemporary furniture designs by Sklar, Selig, Richardson-Nemschoff — on indoor-outdoor designs in Featherweight aluminum and redwood — on Colonial designs by Vilas — and on convertible sofa-beds by Simmons. All are sale-priced now at Eaton's College Street — a selection at our other Toronto Stores, Oshawa and Hamilton.

Eaton's Downtown Stores, Don Mills, Oshawa open 9:30 a.m. to 6 p.m. Yorkdale, Shoppers' World, Warehouse Store, open 9:30 a.m. to 9:30 p.m. Catalogue Sales Area, Warden Avenue, open 9:30 a.m. to 9:00 p.m. Phone 861-5111.

EATON'S

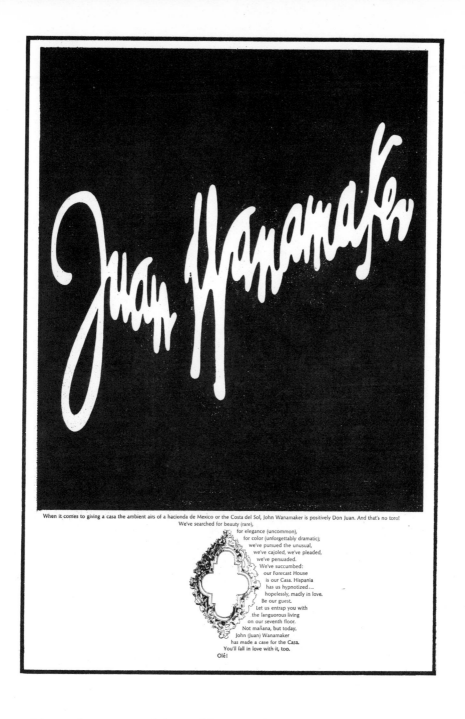

When it comes to giving a casa the ambient airs of a hacienda de Mexico or the Costa del Sol, John Wanamaker is positively Don Juan. And that's no toro!
We've searched for beauty (rare),
for elegance (uncommon),
for color (unforgettably dramatic);
we've pursued the unusual,
we've cajoled, we've pleaded,
we've persuaded.
We've succumbed:
our Forecast House
is our Casa. Hispania
has us hypnotized...
hopelessly, madly in love.
Be our guest.
Let us entrap you with
the languorous living
on our seventh floor.
Not mañana, but today.
John (Juan) Wanamaker
has made a case for the Casa.
You'll fall in love with it, too.
Olé!

It's good to see one of the world's most glamorous symbols made more
glamorous than ever. "Juan Wanamaker" has gone all out for Spanish
"and that's no toro." Read the copy. It's all joy.

Left:
Those Toronto Cowboys and Indians are getting wilder
but Eaton's shows how to cope with the situation.
A provocative approach high on human appeal.

273

Altman's keeps giving us lessons on how to write great copy. This one is on Karastan and how Altman's has featured the line for 46 years. Altman's makes it a Broadway show and ends with, "if they gave awards for a show like this, we'd be a cinch to win a 'Ruggy'." A carpet ad with no carpet illustration? This one is a great job.

See the floor show that's been a hit for 46 years

Five Homers, 3 by Ruth, Slug Yankees to Title; Cards Go Down, 7 to 3

It opened in '28. Roaringest year of the roaring '20s. Luxury liners sailed at midnight in a flurry of confetti. If you were really the cat's whiskers you knocked on a certain door and said: "Joe sent me." You watched the Yankees win the World Series, and dreamed of driving a Duesenberg.

That was the year **Karastan®** and Altman's teamed up. Our stellar cast of **rugs** had been getting rave reviews all over town for decades, and when Karastan brought us their first samples, we knew we had another hit on our hands. "This is real star quality," we said. "Class." That's why, 46 years later, Altman's and Karastan are still collaborating as successfully as Gilbert and Sullivan.

One applause getter, Beautiful Broadloom. It gives you long-running performance because Karastan looms with a unique patented process, **Kara-Loc®** Every individual tuft of fiber is woven right into the backing **permanently.** Clean your carpet, wash it, vacuum it; the pile won't shuffle off to Buffalo.

And it's **pure wool pile.** It's got life. It's got pure, living color. Because wool is protein, dyes soak in deeper. Mother Nature built a unique, coilspring construction into the fiber to keep wool looking and wearing better over the long run. A tough, natural outer casing keeps clinging dirt on the surface, so you can vacuum it off as quickly as you can say Flo Ziegfeld. Wool is safer, too. If your Dapper Dan drops a lighted panetela on it, wool won't support combustion.

PURE WOOL PILE
The Woolmark is your assurance of quality tested carpets made of Pure Wool Pile

See that **Woolmark** label? Guarantees you a quality-tested broadloom that's passed more tests than a kid trying to make it big on Broadway.

Come see why our show has 'em standing in the aisles. See 116 exciting colors 116. Feel the socko textures. Creamy velvets. Plushy plushes. Loopy piles. A show-stopping chevron pattern. A cut-and-looped pile with checkerboard squares of color. Every one a smash hit. Square yard 24.00 to 28.00 (carpet only).

No cover, no minimum charge if you'd like an Altman decorator to help you plan your own stage setting.

If they gave awards for a show like this, we'd be a cinch to win a "Ruggy." Fifth floor, Fifth Avenue, with road companies at White Plains, Manhasset, N.Y., Short Hills, Ridgewood/ Paramus, N.J., St. Davids, Pa.

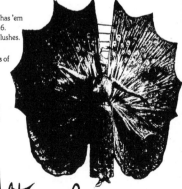

B Altman & Co

274

The striking feature of Einstein Moomjy advertising is the consistency.
Year after year this technique of reaching out to the customer is continued.
This retailer has found an advertising formula that gets action.
The formula is basic: brilliant copy, a subtle sense of humor, and a page
set in type that is superbly inviting and easy to read. A dozen items are
described and priced, plus an institutional message that gets seen and
remembered. Advertising could do no more.

Einstein's theory of relativity:
Give strangers the same price you give your relatives.

From now through Saturday, July 24, blood won't be thicker than broadloom at Einstein Moomjy's Carpet Department Stores.

We're giving you family prices. The prices we give our own family.

Example: The trace of grace. It's our popular tracery carpet. Recommended by our Aunt Fanny's fanny.

She paid $4.99 a sq. yd. She saved plenty.

You'll pay $4.99 a sq. yd. You'll save plenty.

We can give you our Saxony shag for $5.99. We can give you our softies (with soft little bursts of color) for $6.99 and $8.99.

A satiny is $8.99. An earthy is $10.99. A sumptuous Saxony is $11.99.

A heavier plush than heavy plush is just $12.99. A silky, just $13.99.

Even our $35.99 wool Berber has been sheared to just $23.99.

Rya rugs as big as a room are down to $119. Couristan Oriental designs as big as a room are up for sale at $199. Art Decos, Art Nouveaus and all sorts of area rugs for all sorts of areas are now reduced by the dozens to the same low prices we give our cousins.

Ditto our Orientals, hand woven in India. We're handing them over for $$$$$ less.

Mr. Moomjy charged his mama only $5.99 for this gorgeous carpet. And that's all he's charging you.

And all of our Back Yd. prices are in permanent rollback, of course, which even our grandma admits is pretty grand!

You may say to Einstein Moomjy: "You're giving me the same prices you give to your relatives.

Okay, terrific.

But how do I know I'll love your carpets? How do I know I'll find what I want?

Your papa's posh plush could very well be my poison. It's all relative."

Ladies, you're right.

Maybe our warm bedroom carpet (it's down to only $7.99) will leave you cold.

Maybe you'll think our feathery finish (it's down to only $10.99) is for the birds.

Think nothing of it. We've got hundreds more carpets in hundreds more colors.

We've got hundreds more styles and piles and prices to show you.

We're The Carpet Department Store. We've got more of more for your floor.

Please drive us crazy until you find the carpet you want at the price you want.

After all, our relatives have been driving us crazy for years at

Einstein Moomjy
The Carpet Department Store

Bon Marche quotes facts and figures to prove their underselling policy. Another in a dramatic series that made Seattle sit up and take notice.

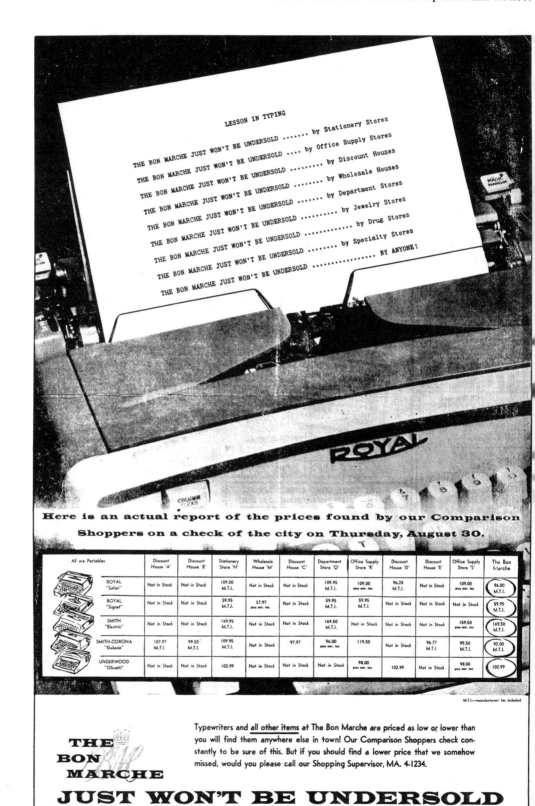

In January, finding more for your money at Gabberts is a cup of tea.

Lots of stores get all steamed up about their January Sales. But not Gabbert's. You see, offering more for your money is a year-round thing for us.

Still, we've got some pleasant surprises brewing for you this month. And while they're raising a tempest in a teapot about sales — we're serving 24 varieties of imported tea, free, in our coffee shop.

So come savor some tea. And sample our every day low prices. You'll find them both mighty easy to swallow.

Traditional 90″ tuxedo sofa of untraditional multi-colored Matelasse. $549.

Rich exotic tapestry weave tuxedo sofa, 90″, $399. The 60″ loveseat may be just your size at $309.

Traditional roll arm lounge chair of cushy brown velvet. Roll it away for $199.

Perk up your room with a contemporary 90″ sofa or 60″ loveseat of blue/brown cut velvet. Go for the sofa at $229. You'll love the loveseat at $199.

A contemporary stripe 83″ sofa hides a queen size sleeper. Very smart. Very economical at $499.

Grace any room with a graceful Queen Anne wing chair of fresh multi-color floral print for $145.

Quietly elegant traditional lounge chair of quiet moss green velvet, $209. Shhh…

There's plenty of comfort hidden in a traditional low back recliner of doe-soft beige velvet, $299.

Gather the whole family on a big 95″ traditional roll arm sofa of snappy yellow printed chintz, $299. Pretty as a picture.

Dynamic 82″ contemporary sofa, geometric multi-color print. Live like a jet-setter for $479.

Traditional wood frame occasional chair cuddles warm gold velvet upholstery. Wrap your arms around it for $95.

Classic Henredon officer's chest commands a formation of 5 coordinated occasional tables. March one home for $145 to $255.

Henredon Circa 76 occasional table group. Take home a piece of American history from $185 to $319.

Down-home country pine table group in friendly brown. Priced individually from $99 to $189.

Straight forward country English 5-piece oak table group. Priced individually from only $95 to $199. Blimey!

Bamboo to you too. 5-piece occasional table group combines refreshing bamboo style and Old English finish. A treat at $159 to $309.

Have a ball choosing from the Conant Ball Sierra 5-piece table group. Soft light oak finish. $99 to $309.

The original ginger jar lamp. White pleated shade. Yellow, green, brown, black, white, red, orange, blue ceramic base feels at home in any decor. $29.50.

Fresh as a breeze crisp dotted Swiss bedspread trimmed with lace. Machine washable. Pink, blue, yellow, white. Twin size $26.00. Full size $32.00.

Bright country garden pucker print bedspread hemmed with ribbons and ruffles. Springtime colors on white. Machine washable. Twin size $26.00. Full size $32.00.

Stately grandfather clock, 72¼″ tall. Timeless mahogany finish. Weight driven Westminster rod chime movement. You'll get a big bong out of it for $349.

No-frills contemporary 5-piece bedroom of sun-washed driftwood finish. Triple dresser, pair of mirrors, full/queen size bed, night stand, $719.

Hibriten country French 4-piece bedroom. Fine Pecan finish. Big triple dresser, mirror, full/queen bed, night stand, $1,182.

Antique white Mediterranean 5-piece set makes any color scheme a delight. Triple dresser, pair of mirrors, full/queen bed, night stand. $742.

A fine Thomasville Mediterranean 4-piece bedroom. Satiny pecan finish. Triple dresser, mirror, full/queen bed, night stand, $764.

Swahili contemporary area rugs, textured shag. 4′ x 6′, $129.00. 6′ x 9′, $279.00. 9′ x 12′, $539.00.

Dark oak Mediterranean 4-piece bedroom lends an air of mystery. Triple dresser, mirror, full size bed, night stand, $688.

Youth 4-piece bedroom. Oak finish with kid-proof simulated slate top. Dresser, mirror, bunk bed, night stand will take 'em right through college, $538.

Live in your own little bit of Italy with Thomasville's Villa Romano 4-piece bedroom. Dusky Florentine finish. Dresser, mirror, king/queen bed, night stand, $567.

Serene Oriental 4-piece bedroom. Light oak finish. Triple dresser, mirror, king size bed, night stand, $330.

Versatile apartment 5-piece dining set. Natural finish wood grain. 40″ extension table with heat resistant top. 3 side chairs and 1 hostess chair. $419.

Give your kitchen a face lift: casual butcher block top table with chrome base, 4 Bentwood side chairs, $299.

Set a great table — Thomasville's country 5-piece dining set. Paint and oak finish. Inviting 44″ pedestal extension table, 3 mate's, 1 captain chair, $769.

Thomasville Fountain Head pine 5-piece dining set. Velvety Honey finish oval extension table, 4 side chairs, $895.

Contemporary sculptured high-low nylon shag. Immediately available in 8 colors. $8.95 square yard.

Rich, heavy, textured nylon plush. Immediately available in 8 colors. $10.95 square yard.

Caucasia imported wool area rugs, 3 handsome multi-colored designs. 4′ x 6′8″, $36.50. 5′6″ x 9′2″, $69.95. 8′3″ x 12′2″, $135.00.

Kasal imported wool area rugs, 3 delightful designs, 3 colors. 4′ x 6′, $169.00. 5′6″ x 8′, $269.00. 8′3″ x 11′6″, $539.00.

13342 Midway Road. Just North of L.B.J. (635)/Open weekdays noon to 9:30/Saturday 10:30 to 6 Phone 233-3232 Ft. Worth phone 263-4551.

A free cup of tea is one reward for shopping at Gabberts in January. Other rewards are listed—38 exciting items. "Offering more for your money is a year-round thing for us," the copy says, in contrast to bombastic price reductions by competition. This is a daring and unusual approach which should have an effect long after January.

A fantastic ad. Serious but exciting copy, handsome drawing, breathtaking layout. And a compelling twist—the cast shadow of a chair! This is the detail that makes the difference and John Wanamaker is expert at doing such details.

278

World's best tranquilizer.

[At a rocking good sale price.]

Nobody should ever grow up in a house without a rocking chair.

Nothing else ever invented seems to offer quite as many soothing and beneficial effects to both mother and child.

Nothing quiets the crying quite as fast, or brings up the bubbles quite as decisively, or hurries the sandman quite as surely. Or brings the mother such private moments for hope, plans, and peace.

Since we know about these things, in our own way, some time ago we purchased a nice stock of traditional solid hardwood rockers, now arrived.

They were made to sell for $39.95.

But Mother's Day is coming. So starting tomorrow, for as long as they last, and one to a customer, we've priced these wonderful chairs at just **$18.00** each.

If you wish, you can take yours with you for only $2 down, and pay us the rest later.

Like we say, nobody should grow up in a house without a rocking chair.

Especially a new mother.

Even if the diamond earrings have to wait.

Henry M. Goodman makes you comfortable

Even on Sunday

A smashing example of the new approach to advertising. Copy and art as simple and as direct as human minds can create it. A great message selling an $18 item. This is advertising at a level few stores achieve.

Dayton's makes sure that every reader of the Minneapolis Tribune knows the Garden Shop is open for business. At the same time the Marine Shop opens and the two announcements make a team that will not go by unnoticed.

Dayton's big Southdale Marine Shop opens Monday

Ahoy there matey, here's what you'll find in our very complete boating section:

- 8 popular Scott motors
- Arkansas Traveler aluminum and fiberglas boats
- Sailboats, 12' and 14' fishing boats
- Holsclaw trailers
- Swim masks, water skis, fins
- Motor parts, spray paint, oil, extra props, gas tanks, engine cleaners
- Control boxes, cables, other rigging supplies

Marine Shop — Dayton's 66th and France Avenue South, Southdale

Dayton's

SHOP MONDAY TILL 9:00

Sssssst! Dayton's Southdale Garden Shop opens Monday

Don't let summer sneak up on you . . . start planning now for those fun-filled days out-of-doors! Our Southdale Garden Shop has everything you need for garden, barbecue and patio . . . all gathered together for quick, convenient shopping!

Dayton's

SPRINKLERS . . .
POWER MOWERS . .
BARBECUES . . .
RAKES . . .
WHEELBARROWS . . .
GLIDERS . . .
TRIMMING SHEARS . . .
. . . FLOWER SEEDS . . .
PLANT FOOD . . . GRASS
SEED . . . ALUMINUM
LAWN FURNITURE . .
BUG CONTROL . . .
GARDEN GLOVES . . .
CRAB GRASS KILLER
. . . PATIO FURNITURE
. . . CHARCOAL . . .
HOSES . . . SPADES . . .
SWING SETS . . .
PICNIC TABLES . . .
HOES . . .
. . . AND MORE!

A separate building at 66th and France, Southdale, is devoted to your garden and marine needs. Open 9:30 to 9 Monday, Thursday, Friday; Tuesday, Wednesday, Saturday till 6. Plenty of parking space, too.

IN THE TWIN CITIES AND SUBURBS, PHONE DAYTON'S, FEDERAL 2-6123

Left:

A great store must carry great assortments, but does the customer know? How often is the story of assortments told? Hudson's is giving Detroit a demonstration of what it means to be a great store—and the customers love it. These assortment advertisements are the talk of the town.

When living plants begin talking to the customer something wonderful happens. This page by The Bay had to be the best seen and most talked-about advertisement in Montreal. The copy is first person, me to you, and great. Why can't all advertising have this wonderful rapport with the customer? (Love the sign-off, too.)

CHAPTER VI

ANNIVERSARIES

The yearly celebration of a store's founding is not only an occasion to run one of the best accepted sales of the year but also an opportunity to renew all the aspects that make up that organization.

Is your store known for its community involvement and for its in-store services? Is it respected for its outstanding merchandise assortments and its high standards of merchandise? Is it known for its day-to-day value prices? This is the time to reaffirm what all of this means to the customer.

Unfortunately, what the retailer and the customer perceive about the same store can sometimes be two different things. We recently heard of a department store president who was exceptionally proud of his return policy. He was shocked--actually angry and disbelieving--when he was presented with a consumer study done by a local media supplier. The study placed him sixth in his market in terms of return policies. Obviously, he had the message, and maybe he stopped voicing it years ago because he thought that everyone in town knew all about it. But babies have a habit of growing into adult customers, people have a habit of moving from city to city. And so, after five years of not restating his policy, it was forgotten. What better time than at the store's anniversary to tell of his liberal policy on merchandise returns!

The most recent Celanese study indicates that the lack of retail selling service is a major complaint of the female customer. Approximately 44 percent of the women interviewed agreed that they were willing to spend a little more money to get better and more individualized service. If you pride yourself on your friendly, knowledgeable sales-people, we can't think of a more important message to give your customers at anniversary time.

Study the ads in this section. Perhaps the yearly restatement of the services you offer your customer will become a pleasant tradition.

To Simpsons from Eaton's

Heartiest congratulations on your 100th Anniversary year. No doubt about it, you're a very sprightly 100. For 103 we're pretty spry ourselves. Could it be all that healthy competition that's kept us both so young? It's been a grand hundred years. Happy New Year and thanks for being such a good neighbour.

EATON'S

Eaton's, Toronto, gets the cake ready, lights the candles and sends the chef over to Simpsons with its 100th Anniversary wishes: "Heartiest congratulations on your 100th Anniversary year. No doubt about it, you're a very sprightly 100. For 103 we're pretty spry ourselves. Could it be all that healthy competiton that's kept us both so young? It's been a grand hundred years. Happy New Year and thanks for being such a good neighbor."

Congratulations also are in order to Eaton's for its public recognition that healthy competition keeps retailers young and alive, for a "good neighbour" policy that contributes to the total climate of the city's business community.

You are all invited to Eaton's College Street tomorrow to help us celebrate our 37th. Anniversary Party. It's going to be bright lights all the way with pink carnations, gala decorations and, most important, big birthday savings for you. You'll find hundreds of low special prices and hundreds of special things on every floor of the store. The festivities start at 9:30 in the morning and go until 6:00 at night. So put on your best birthday smile and come on down. After all, it just wouldn't be a party without you.

(Watch tonight's evening papers for special College Street Birthday Bargains)

EATON'S

An outstanding approach to an Anniversary Party. One paragraph of good copy presented as a page of pictorial impact. The best things in advertising are usually the simplest and the most direct.

How do you say Confidence? J.P. Allen says it by going back in history and looking at the beautiful women of Atlanta who helped make this store what it is today. This is a terrific editorial, simple in phrase, written with charm and sincerity. And the photograph of 70 odd years ago makes a great attraction. 1975 was the year to re-state the case for the store and here's a fine example.

"Since 1908 I've been making the women of Atlanta my business."

In 1908 J. P. Allen said "The women of the South should have a store as beautiful as they are" and in the heart of Atlanta he opened a fashion emporium of such taste and elegance that Mrs. Cornelius Vanderbilt journeyed from New York City to shop there.

J. P. Allen was from Atlanta. He had a deep appreciation of Atlanta women and the Atlanta way of life. He knew how they liked to dress up, and how

they liked to dress down. He knew just what clothes were required for living the Atlanta life to the hilt.

J. P. Allen has spread from the first downtown store to five stores in the Atlanta area. Each of them is so geared to how Atlanta likes to look and live, that they'll have exactly the dress, just the sportswear, precisely the accessory you're seeking.

J. P. Allen looks at hundreds of fashions so you

don't have to. You'll peruse carefully edited collections of things all so right and so beautiful, the only problem is choosing.

J. P. Allen is making Atlanta history again, right now. Their stores have never been prettier, their clothes have never been more geared to helping make Atlanta famous for its fashionable women.

Come in, we'll look wonderful on you. *J.P. Allen*

J.P. Allen

NEW DOWNTOWN • LENOX SQUARE • GREENBRIAR • NORTHLAKE • CUMBERLAND MALL

286

A second century dawns at Forbes Wallace and here is the ad to prove it. A fabulous layout, and the second line of copy would turn anybody on. Happy second hundred years, dear F & W. With a start like this you're going to make it great.

Here it comes.

Our second hundred years dawned this morning at 7:19 a.m.
You were so nice about the first hundred, we thought we should do it again.

FORBES & WALLACE

Here's to 100 years of hill-climbing...

Thirteen years after Roos and Atkins opened their first store Andrew Hallidie started his cable cars climbing the hills. Since Roos/Atkins has also become something of a San Francisco tradition, we're especially proud to join the cable car centennial festivities.

View photos of the people who help to make the cable cars run today in the windows of our Market Street store. **Ride** a cable car and win a prize. For the next ten days we'll be taking daily pictures of people on the cable cars and display the photos in our Market Street windows with the faces of ten people circled. If you can pick yourself out we'll give you a genuine piece of cable handsomely encased in clear lucite. **See** R/A's own decorated car in the parade tomorrow and throughout the celebration.

Roos Atkins

Dressing Active Westerners Since 1860

Those who know San Francisco know that this is the 100th anniversary of those hill-climbing cable cars (now a landmark—never to be eliminated). Roos-Atkins salutes the occasion with a world of special events, give-aways, and a fun ad. Love it all.

Right:
Time marches on in Atlanta and for Rich's it's "114 years of pure polish." A superpowerful eye-compelling page that gently pats the store on the back and winds up with, "We hope you'll join the celebration of our Anniversary Sale, this week only." Serene copy, proving again that less is more.

114 years of pure polish...that's Rich's

It's our birthday and we're wearing a hand-rubbed shine that
we're proud of. For over a hundred and fourteen years we've been
ahead of the times. And our famous traditions are still our
foundation. We hope you'll join the celebration of our Anniversary Sale,
this week only. At Rich's...the time is always now.

It's good to know there is a Timothy Eaton Rose . . . "most beautiful of all our special 100th Anniversary projects." It's good to know a great company, in the midst of conducting a vigorous anniversary campaign, can identify with a rose (2.39), and what it will do to "beautify the street where you live." A great idea, a fine ad.

How do you greet your great great grandfather on his birthday?
Eaton's, a mere Century 2, extends a friendly salute to The Bay as that
company enters its 4th century. It's a beautiful tribute and a distinguished
drawing by Eaton's of Winnipeg.

This tribute to a great pioneer of retailing makes a beautiful statement for the store. The history of J.C. Penney deserves to be reviewed and the customers, too, will be interested. In this age of restlessness and change it is good to know that "what's important!" has not changed at Penney's. It is a beautifully written editorial, giving out facts lightly and entertainingly. We like the last line, too: "Thank you for reading all these words. We promise not to write another ad like this till April 14, 2002." Why wait so long?

75 years ago this month James Cash Penney opened his first store in Kemmerer, Wyoming.

Today everything has changed except what's important.

On April 14, 1902, James Cash Penney unlocked the door of his new store and started the business. He was 27. He'd been in dry goods since he was nineteen.

"I went to work in Hale's store (J.M. Hale & Brother, Hamilton, Missouri) at the age of nineteen. The sum of $2.27 a month was certainly modest pay. But I felt strangely contented. I knew if I could get into something connected with dry goods, I could sell. At least I'd found my work in life."

Penney had to leave Hale's store and Hamilton because of his health. A doctor sent him off to Colorado (which must have been good advice; he lived to be 95).

He got a job in Longmont, near Denver, with a retail chain of several stores.

"I wasn't interested so much in the wages I would get or bothered by long hours. I was looking for opportunity."

He found it. The firm sent him to work in their Evanston, Wyoming store, then gave him a shot at his own store, in Kemmerer. Opening day was April 14, 1902. At dawn.

"When we locked the store at midnight and went upstairs to our attic room after the first day's business to figure out

how we stood, there was an astonishing—to us—wealth in pennies, nickels, dimes, quarters, and half dollars. Our first day's sales amounted to $466.59."

The "we" and "our" in Mr. Penney's quotes refer to Mrs. Penney.

Second Kemmerer store. In 1904, Penney moved his store to a "better location" but he took the mud puddle with him.

The "Mother Store." This pretty storybook store is an artist's conception, drawn from the only existing, very fuzzy photograph of Penney's first store. In the real world of 1902 Kemmerer, nothing was very "pretty." Penney describes a permanent mud puddle in front of the store.

Part of the James Cash Penney legend. Testing samples of fabric with soap and water in his hotel.

Painting of Mr. Penney against backdrop of Kemmerer, Wyoming.

"My wife worked in the store side by side with me as much of the time as she could, wrapping the baby in a blanket and putting him down for naps under the counter while she waited on customers."

Opening day was no fluke. The store continued to do well.

"We were soon so busy that we had to hire help. Whereas the company stores of the mining company treated their customers rather callously, in our store the people were quick to notice a different atmosphere, which made them feel welcome and appreciated. They realized that we sold goods at just one price and gave good values.

"These were people who took the saving of so much as a penny seriously. To save pennies for them we had to save them for ourselves. We threw away no wrapping paper, no short ends of string, no empty boxes, no nails, even though they were bent, because we could straighten them out and use them over again."

Fashion. From an early Penney newspaper ad.

Fashion. From a current Penney ad.

At the end of the first year, the store had done $29,000 worth of business. By 1907, Mr. Penney had saved enough to buy out his partners and the company took off. In 1913, 36 Golden Rule stores were incorporated as the J.C. Penney Company. This was the year "The Penney Idea" (at right) was adopted.

In 1924 the company acquired its 500th store, J.M. Hale & Brother in Hamilton, Missouri. Remember? In 1941, the company opened store number 1600.

The number of stores was no longer a meaningful measure of company growth. Bigger stores replaced smaller stores. The company moved into more types of merchandise, went into the catalog business, acquired other businesses.

In 1971, James Cash Penney died. The only ambition he had that he didn't achieve was to live to be a hundred. He only missed by 5 years. The company he founded is 75 years old today.

Generally we look ahead and focus on the changes in the Penney Company. There've been plenty of them. But on a birthday—and a 75th birthday to boot—it seems appropriate to talk about the things that never change, because they're grounded in the basic needs and wants and expectations of human beings.

There are things you expect from your Penney store that haven't changed at all—like getting good value for your money, like being treated as the welcome guest you are, like getting complete satisfaction if ever anything goes wrong. All these things are as impor-

tant to us and to you today as they were to James Cash Penney and his customers on the famous opening day of April 14, 1902.

Thank you for reading all these words. We promise not to write another ad like this till April 14, 2002.

Adopted 1913

◄1►
To serve the public, as nearly as we can, to its complete satisfaction.

◄2►
To expect for the service we render a fair remuneration and not all the profit the traffic will bear.

◄3►
To do all in our power to pack the customer's dollar full of value, quality and satisfaction.

◄4►
To continue to train ourselves and our associates so that the service we give will be more and more intelligently performed.

◄5►
To improve constantly the human factor in our business.

◄6►
To reward men and women in our organization through participation in what the business produces.

◄7►
To test our every policy, method and act in this wise: "Does it square with what is right and just?"

In the year 1913 the Penney partners approved this code of principles to guide them. "The Penney Idea" became, and is today, a moral as well as business basis for decision-making.

JCPenney. Everything has changed except what's important.

• Cinderella City • Northglenn • Boulder • University Hills • Villa Italia • Westminster • Aurora Mall • Downtown Aurora • Downtown • JCRS

292

CHAPTER VII

STORE-WIDE PROMOTIONS

Ads that proclaim that the whole store has magically turned itself into a giant map of the United States, or into Britian or Mexico or the Pacific Islands or Ireland, take the customers' minds off specific shopping chores and put them in the mood to be entertained. There is special merchandise to see. There are events to enjoy, foods to try. A visit to the store has been turned into a free trip through the amusement park.

Lois Patrich, divisional vice president of advertising and sales promotion for Carson Pirie Scott, Chicago, explains: ''Store-wide promotions are the way of the 80's, establishing a differential in the market''. She points out that Carson's has done an event every spring and fall since 1958, only missing one year, and that was for a special 125th anniversary celebration.

''Back in the 60's,'' she recalls, ''they were called import fairs, but now we all are much more sophisticated. Customers have traveled more. They're not as interested in that little mosiac pin as they once were. Today, they are looking for things they had wished they had brought back with them, merchandise of quality, items that can't be duplicated here. For instance, a wonderful mohair lap throw from Scotland''.

She also explains that stores need not search for a new store-wide event every year. In the mid-60's, where Carson's first presented its Scandinavian promotion, it was found that Scandinavian home products were so new to the mid-west that the promotion was repeated in the home area for several years after that.

The ads in this section are invitations to all the excitement of store-wide promotions. See if they would persuade you to spend a fall Saturday touring the store!

293

In 1967, Carson's was a vision of the Pacific and this page captures the spirit.
It is printed in yellow and shocking pink and it is as hot as blazes.
Which is what it should be.

Carson's eighth floor auditorium was converted into a typical Ulster town square in 1966.
It makes sense because, in 1842, young Pirie and young Carson met there.
This interesting editorial makes sense, too.

Philadelphia was the scene of another British invasion and it looked like it would be the biggest in 200 years. "The British Lion is rampant" this advertisement announces, and the variety of special events and British merchandise boggles the mind. Who can miss stopping here and reading every bouncing, exciting word of this copy. What a beautiful, colorful, innovative job!

Hello, Mother.
Surprise! How are you?
Stick out your mother
tongue. Oh, don't be so British.
We're all family. English is spoken here.
English classes, English majors, English lit.
English ivy, English bulldogs, English horns,
English setters, English walnuts, English sparrows.
We even put English on our billiard balls.
Forgive and forget. That was 200 years ago we threw
you out! You know we still love our mother country. Why,
look at all the trouble we've gone to, bringing back the
British, capturing England, dragooning everything that's
truly, purely British right into Wanamaker's
for the whole month of October—
British woolens, tweeds, twills, teas,
cheese, chocolates, sterling,
crystal, houndstooth checks,
pleats, vests, cravats,
hats, hacking jackets,
blankets, boots,
bumbershoots,
and all the best.
A real British fair:
Britannia '76!
Philadelphia '76!
Think of it!
For a whole
month, the
British Lion
rampant! The
sun never
sets, right?
Aren't you
proud of
your son,
the Eagle?

THROUGHOUT OCTOBER: BRITANNIA '76/PHILADELPHIA '76. A BICENTENNIAL SALUTE TO THINGS BRITISH. TRANSPORTATION ARRANGED THROUGH **British airways**

296

"Can't escape the winter? Let California come to you . . . at Eaton's." This is pure drama, staged in February, to give the good people of Winnipeg a lift in spirit just when they need it most. This cover of an eight page pre-print section is a drooling scene of California's famous Farmers Market. Eight pages of gorgeous sketches and photographs, plus a full scale campaign of follow-up ads, in-store events, the works. A first rate job.

Right:
Carson's was wild with Mexican excitement in 1968, a riot of color, music and happy people. Merchandise, too, which makes it all worthwhile, and good advertising like this.

Below:
"The Great American Shape-Up" was a 1975 flight, a complete special-events plus advertising program. Diamond's does it with flair and great attention to detail. This page describes the seminars, demonstrations, and in-store activities that have been scheduled. A smash ad and a smash idea.

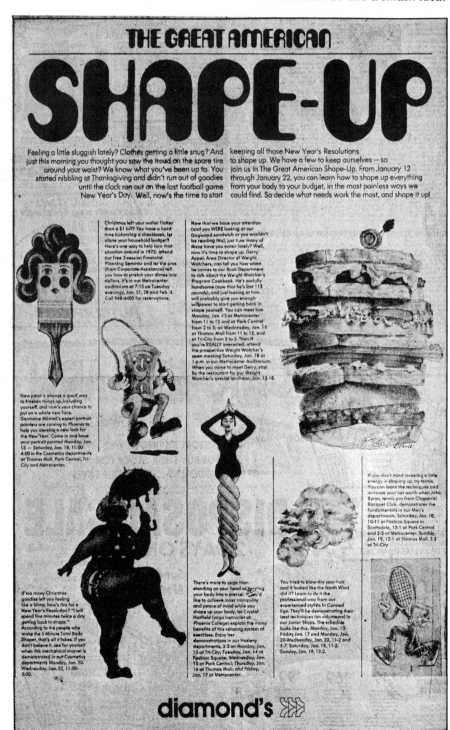

COME TO THE ZOCALO!

IT'S CARSONS AUDITORIUM-TURNED-MARKETPLACE, RIMMED BY A MEXICAN RESTAURANT, WROUGHT IRON BALCONY WORK & HAND-CARVED DOORS, WITH A MEXICAN SKYLINE OF ROOFTOPS & TREES. IT'S THE HEART OF OUR ¡SALUD, MEXICO! EVENT, DESIGNED & BUILT FOR CARSONS BY THE CONSEJO NACIONAL DE TURISMO OF MEXICO. WITHIN THE ZOCALO SEE MEXICAN CRAFTSMEN AT WORK, MEXICAN SHOPS BURGEONING WITH GIFTS, GLASSWARE, & MORE. IT'S GREAT! ON EIGHT. ON STATE. TODAY. OLE!

WATCH SOME BARK PAINTING

Painting upon bark, that is, by Pauline Martinez of Taxco. See how he paints charming bright-colored primitive designs on sheets of bark. Demonstrations daily 10 to 5; Monday and Thursday also 'til 7. The paintings will be available for purchase.

HI, AMIGO! I'M AN ARMADILLO WITHOUT A PECCADILLO

But I'm surrounded by squirrels, rabbits, and more friends, all hand-carved by Indians in the mountains of Mexico. Come see us, take one (or several) of us home with you.

EVERYTHING UNDER THE AZTEC SUN comes to Carsons via Mexicana Airlines. Want to put yourself under the Aztec sun? Shop all Carsons for resort wear, then ask the Mexicana representative in our marketplace about the delights of Mexico and the delights of getting there via Mexicana Airlines, the airline that knows Mexico best.

A TIN I-TINERARY

Check your list, we've cockatoos to chandeliers, all exclusively Carsons and excitingly colored in the flamboyance of Mexican folk art.

SI. SI. A CERAMIC SNAKE

And turtles, ducks, and geese made in miniature by Jorge Wilmot of Tonala. More: pottery from Oaxaca. All typically Mexican in craftsmanship and designs ours alone.

JUST ASK IT! WE'VE A BASKET

Any shape, any size, any use. Reed baskets to totes by the trio for taking along on a trip through our Marketplace or toting along to Mexico.

Carson Pirie Scott &co

¡SALUD, MEXICO!
NOW THROUGH JANUARY 27TH
ZOCALO, 8TH FLOOR, STATE STREET

FLORES, SENORES!

Watch those proud paper flowers being made by a charming Senorita. Demonstrations daily 10 to 5; Monday and Thursday also 'til 7.

designer/
craftsman

TWO WEEKS OF PROOF THAT PEOPLE STILL HAVE MORE TALENT THAN COMPUTERS

Like Ron Thomas, one of the few people around spinning pewter by hand. Or Candace Laird, who still weaves her lovely baskets from split oak logs. Our Arcade runneth over with inspiring people like these, from studios and workrooms hidden away under our very noses in nearby West Virginia. Their work, much of it for sale, bears the designer/craftsman's unmistakable stamp of ingenuity and creativity. Two beautiful qualities to be found in extra measure throughout Pogue's during the next two weeks.

Pogue's

Design America is indeed a beautiful idea and Franklin Simon is
making the most of it. The list of designers is something to behold and
the same goes for each advertisement.

Left:
Pogue's has a smashing idea: "People still have more talent than
computers" is a refreshing and reassuring note in this age of
mechanized monstrosities. A beautiful series, done in 1968.

One of the most beautiful invitations of the season! Neiman-Marcus invites all of Dallas downtown for its Ireland Fortnight with this misty, romantic photo. The Irish gentleman and his lady, dressed for Fall '76 in their country wools, lead their horses in from the fields. Suddenly the mood is established. A simple copy statement further defines it for the reader: "Next Monday, meet us in Ireland! Discover its romance, legend, beauty, goods, fashion, art, crafts, food, wit, music, laughter and people . . ."

NEXT MONDAY, MEET US IN IRELAND!

Discover its romance, legend, beauty, goods, fashion, art, crafts, food, wit, music, laughter and people

as we celebrate IRELAND FORTNIGHT, OCTOBER 18–30 at Neiman-Marcus, Downtown.

At Dayton's you are the star. The ''Go Hollywood'' event was a store-wide production reflecting the nostalgia of yesterday and the spirit of tomorrow, a gigantic extravaganza, beautifully staged and directed. It came in three acts, as you see here, the total store gone Hollywood with fashions, shows, star appearances, movies, contests, sneak previews, palm trees, lights, cameras. When the winds blew cold in March Dayton's was warm and happy, as only Hollywood can do it. What a fantastic show!

THE DAYTON'S PRODUCTION OF

Starring Dayton's and You

[Join us March 4 through April 14]

ACT I: THE FASHION

SCENE: *Somewhere inside Dayton's. The store has gone Hollywood. Posters. Palm trees. Photos of your favorite stars. We're showing YOU around.*

YOU: *[Impressed]* Oh, this is wonderful. The lights, the action. But what about the cameras? I don't see any...

US: Never mind about cameras. Just look at these clothes. All these things for spring. Do they remind you of anything?

YOU: Why, yes, they do. They remind me of everything I've ever seen up on the silver screen. *[Runs over to suit rack.]* Crawford would have worn this one in Grand Hotel. *[Draping US from department to department.]* And the shorts, and the slides and the strapless dresses. *[Dreamily]* Boy, you sure could catch a California tan in these.

US: That's just the beginning. Even the sunglasses kind of take you back, don't they? Those were the days, the golden days. *[Lovingly]* Stars were stars. And bit players.

YOU: What's that over there? *[Points.]*

US: Our Home Furnishings area. Like it?

YOU: Love it. Looks like a Hollywood set with all that glamorous Art Deco stuff. Fred would feel right at home here.

US: Your husband?

YOU: *[Sitting at table]* Astaire, silly. He was one of the greats.

US: *[Sitting opposite]* You're not so bad yourself, kid. In fact, you're on your way.

YOU: Oh, but I don't want to leave yet. The fun's just beginning.

US: No, no, no. We mean you're on your way to the top. Go Hollywood is your first starring role.

YOU: *[Tearfully]* Well, I couldn't have done it without all the little people who...

ACT II: THE OVAL ROOM*/VOGUE SPRING FASHION SHOW

SCENE: *Wednesday, March 7 at 12 noon. Downtown Minneapolis 8th floor Auditorium.*

Our premiere event, featuring Vogue Editor Liz Groves in a cameo role. Your 3.00 ticket includes a tote lunch (Hollywood Mix, Fresh Fruit Salad with citrus dressing, Egg Twist Roll, Pecan Pie Square and Beverage), and the chance to view some of the best performances by designers this season. You'll see Calvin Kleins, Anne Kleins, Ralph Laurens, Yves St. Laurents, dresses, eveningwear, outerwear. Plus movie costumes on live mannequins. Call 375-3018 for reservations tomorrow, March 5.

US: *[Glancing at our watch]* Hurry, the show's about to start.

YOU: They can't do that, dahling. I'm the star.

US: *[Shouting above the crowd]* Oh, Say, can we have your autograph?

YOU: Delighted.

US: And that's not all.

YOU: So tell me more. I'm not due on the set for an hour.

ACT III: THE EVENTS

SCENE: *Inside Dayton's, everywhere you look.*

Movie Costume Display, today through Saturday, April 14, Downtown Minneapolis. See actual costumes from the films "My Fair Lady," "Mame" and "Funny Lady."

Win a Hollywood Trip, one week for two, in Hollywood, California. Includes flight via Western Airlines, hotel accommodations at the Hotel Concorda, rental car, and VIP tour of Universal Studios. Travel arrangements courtesy of Dayton's Travel Service. Here's how to enter: pick up an entry blank at any Dayton's store. Drop your entry into our store drop boxes between March 4 and April 14, 1979; one entry will qualify you for all 3 drawings. One trip winner will be selected by random drawing every two weeks. 3 winners in all. Complete details available at Dayton's.

Hollywood Tabletop Contest, Downtown Minneapolis only, March 5 through March 10. We've set 10 tables (5 on our 5th floor, 5 on our 6th) with close to movie titles. Guess all 10 correctly and you'll have a chance to win a complete 8-piece setting of dinnerware. How to enter: pick up an entry blank, fill it out and turn in to entry boxes on 5th or 6th floor at our downtown Minneapolis store by March 10, 1979. Winner must answer all questions correctly—in case of a tie, a random drawing will be conducted. Complete details available at Dayton's.

Universal Studio's Roadshow, "Catch Hollywood in The Act," Monday, March 5 at 2:30 pm, 4:30 pm and 7:30 pm in Downtown Minneapolis 8th Floor Auditorium. Tuesday, March 6, same times, in the Ridgedale Mall Lower Level Central Court. A 30-minute show featuring animal acts (Baretta's bird), live-action scenes by stuntmen, and a monster make-up session.

Be A Star at Dayton's—Kids Style. Saturday, March 10, 2:00 pm at Burnsville. Sunday, March 11, 2:00 pm at Rosedale. Saturday, March 17, 2:00 pm at Ridgedale. Sunday, March 18, 2:00 pm at Brookdale. Thursday, March 22, 4:30 pm at Southdale. Saturday, March 31, 1:00 pm at Minneapolis. Children's fashion show using local children. Shirley Temple look-alikes tap dancing and singing at each show. Western Flight Wings giveaways to kids at the show while they last.

A Salute to the Stars by Clarke University's "13x13" Women's Musical Troupe, Saturday, March 10 at 4 pm in the Sky Room, 12th floor, Downtown Minneapolis. Admission free. Seating reserved. Call 375-3018.

Mademoiselle's "Management Style." Thursday, March 15, 5:00 pm at St Paul Exhibition Hall. Friday, March 16, 12 noon at Minneapolis Junior Dept. Saturday, March 17, 1:00 pm at Southdale Indeed Sportswear. Mademoiselle Fashion Editor Sandy Hill-Solomon and Career Editor Jennifer Kintzing will conduct a panel discussion with 4 local career women. The subject, women at work.

The Sneak Preview of "Ken Murray Shooting Stars" will take place in Dayton's Skyroom, 12th floor, Downtown Minneapolis. Monday, March 19 at 8:30 pm. Be on hand for champagne (compliments of Western Airlines), and an hour of home movies Hollywood-style, featuring all-time great movie stars. No admission charge. For reservations, call 375-3018.

Roller Disco, Downtown Minneapolis Junior area. Saturday, March 24 at 2:00 pm. See top local disco skaters from the St. Louis Park Roller Gardens in a demonstration of disco dancing on skates. Plus a fashion show for Juniors. Doorprizes, too: 100 complimentary tickets to the Roller Gardens will be given away, plus "Go Hollywood" T-shirts and disco records.

Elizabeth Stewart Swimwear Show. Downtown Minneapolis, Thursday, March 29 at 12 noon. Ridgedale, Friday, March 30 at 12:30 pm. Southdale, Saturday, March 31 at 3:00 pm. See all the season's sleekest styles, formally modeled.

CONTEST RULES

1. All winners will be notified by mail, by April 1, 1979, for Tabletop Contest, by May 1, 1979, for Hollywood Trip.
2. Hollywood Trips must be taken between May 1, 1979, and May 1, 1980, or forfeited.
3. For a complete list of winners, send a self-addressed, stamped envelope to: Special Events, Dayton's, 700 on the Mall, Minneapolis, Mn. 55402
4. Entrant must be at least 18 years of age.
5. Contest is not open to employees (and their immediate families) of Dayton-Hudson Corporation or Western Airlines.
6. No purchase is necessary to enter or win.
7. You need not be present to win.
8. Prizes are not transferable or refundable. No cash equivalent or substitute prizes are offered.
9. Winners are responsible for all local, state and federal taxes.
10. Contest open only to residents in geographic areas in which it is displayed or advertised and where legal. Offer void wherever prohibited or restricted by law. Offer void outside U.S.A., all federal, state and local laws and regulations apply.

DAYTON'S

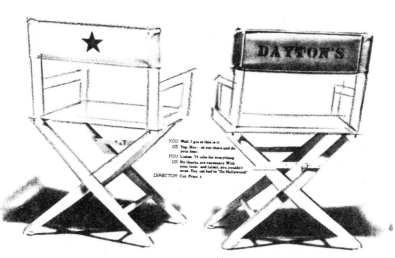

YOU: Well, I gue ss this is it.

US: Yep. Now ... out there and do your best.

YOU: Listen. Th anks for everything.

US: No thanks are necessary. With your look and talent, you couldn't miss. You ...ust had to "Go Hollywood."

DIRECTOR: Cut. Print t.

CHAPTER VIII

INSTITUTIONALS

What does the future hold for the traditional retailer? Nothing but challenge! There are discounters, direct mail companies and electronic shopping services with at-home videotex and cable television systems ready to woo away the already disenchanted customer.

The 1982 Celanese study we have referred to throughout this volume says: ''The most important finding uncovered by the study is the fact that many women do not like to shop''. For Celanese, this means a full 40 percent of women polled. And this phenomenon transcends age, market size, income, employment status and degree of interest in fashion.

For those retailers who have dedicated themselves to offering what today's customer wants (that is, selection, service and value for her money), the problem is how to convey the message. Particularly in these hard economic times, immediate-results oriented retail managements may balk at the expense of newspaper ads that don't seem to return a dime to the register. But, in the long run, how wrong they are. A retailer is in business not only for tomorrow's sales figures -- but for five years of tomorrows, ten years of tomorrows.

We invite you to study the ads in this institutional section. Look with the eyes of a customer who has experienced lack of service and find institutionals that announce friendly salespeople, a direct-line phone number for every department, late night hours, free parking. There's even an ad that shows a man who bears the store's name at the head of that institution, taking full responsibility for it! Look with the eyes of a customer who is concerned about value for her money when you read ads about merchandise quality and the meaning of a sale. And look with the eyes of a customer suspicious of establishments when you go over ads that showcase the store as a long-established and very important member of the community.

Are these ads worth the money? The hard answer is: only if the product you're selling, YOUR STORE, is worth the investment!

This is a singularly timely and worthy idea. Thalhimers lines up a vast array of experts on a variety of subjects and invites customers to phone for information. Moreover, if you're downtown, you can step into the corner window and meet the expert in person. It's a beautiful community service idea presented in a handsome advertisement.

Right:

Brandeis is promoting telephone orders and writes a great editorial about the Brandeis Personal Shopper, telling in detail what she will do for the customer. "She does get a bit weary around 5:30...", proving she is human too, a girl we'd like to know. The ad is made up of testimonials from customers who have had good experiences ordering by phone from Brandeis. Altogether a happy, enthusiastic advertisement, beautifully executed.

Below:

Hutzler's makes a bold statement few stores today can make. To the customer it means "the Hutzler family is still minding the shop." This is Hutzler's opening shot in their 115th Anniversary year. It's a good beginning. It means that, after 115 years, Hutzler's is still putting the store owner's neck out a mile. That's the way to run a store. Dear Mr. Hutzler: We wish you a good year.

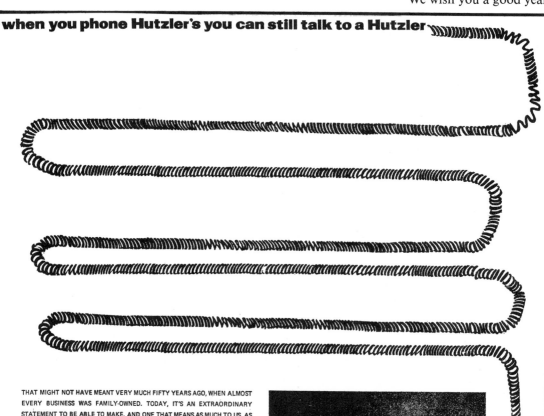

when you phone Hutzler's you can still talk to a Hutzler

THAT MIGHT NOT HAVE MEANT VERY MUCH FIFTY YEARS AGO, WHEN ALMOST EVERY BUSINESS WAS FAMILY-OWNED. TODAY, IT'S AN EXTRAORDINARY STATEMENT TO BE ABLE TO MAKE. AND ONE THAT MEANS AS MUCH TO US, AS IT DOES TO YOU. IT MEANS WE BELIEVE IN BALTIMORE AS DEEPLY TODAY AS MOSES HUTZLER DID WHEN HE MOVED HIS FAMILY AND BUSINESS HERE FROM FREDERICK IN 1840. IT MEANS THE HUTZLER FAMILY TAKES AS ACTIVE A ROLE IN THE COMMUNITY TODAY AS DAVID HUTZLER IN 1909, WHEN HE SERVED ON THE CITY'S CHARTER COMMISSION. IT MEANS THE HUTZLER FAMILY IS STILL MINDING THE SHOP, JUST AS THE FOUNDERS INTENDED WHEN THEY OPENED THE BUSINESS BACK IN 1858 AT 71 NORTH HOWARD STREET. IT MEANS WE DEDICATE OUR 115TH ANNIVERSARY YEAR TO THE CONTINUATION OF OUR TRADITIONAL STANDARD OF SERVICE TO OUR CUSTOMERS. A TRADITION ESTABLISHED OVER FIVE GENERATIONS. A TRADITION SYNONYMOUS WITH THE NAME HUTZLER'S. MOSES HUTZLER WOULD BE PLEASED TO SEE THE WAY HUTZLER'S HAS THRIVED AS BALTIMORE'S FINEST STORE. WE THINK HE WOULD BE EQUALLY PLEASED TO KNOW THAT FOR EVERY YEAR THERE'S BEEN A STORE NAMED HUTZLER'S, THERE'S BEEN A HUTZLER IN THE STORE.

HUTZLER'S
1858 - 1973 OUR 115th ANNIVERSARY YEAR

Quotable quotes from friends who use our Personal Shopping Service.

"Thank you so much for your prompt handling of this small order. Such interest in small details mean so much."

"Sincere thanks to you for your time and effort to locate a pair of stocking slippers for me."

"Sorry I'm so late in dropping you a line. The navy and red pant suit you chose for me was perfect."

Put our personal shopper to work for you. She loves her job!

"Just a line to tell whoever took my long distance call last week is a most thoughtful and courteous young lady. And so helpful."

"Hi. I feel you are a personal friend only from our telephone conversation."

"I received my rush order before Christmas and found everything perfect and wrapped beautiful."

"Thank you for your courtesy, specially the way your personal shopper handled all requests."

"thank you for calling Brandeis"

342-8482

Amazing what dialing 342-8482 can do for you! A complete department store is at the end of the dial-tone and Brandeis Personal Shopper is waiting to take your order, anything from baby booties to a roomful of furniture. She'll check every item on your list, the correct size, the right color, going from department to department to find what you want, even have it gift-wrapped and mailed for you. There's no one like her in town! She does get a bit weary around 5:30, so she turns on a tape-recorder for "after-hours" calls, and by 9 the next morning she's processing your order. Fantastic? We think she is. It's so easy, so simple and so convenient for you. Use your credit? Of course.

BRANDEIS...**BETTER** for service

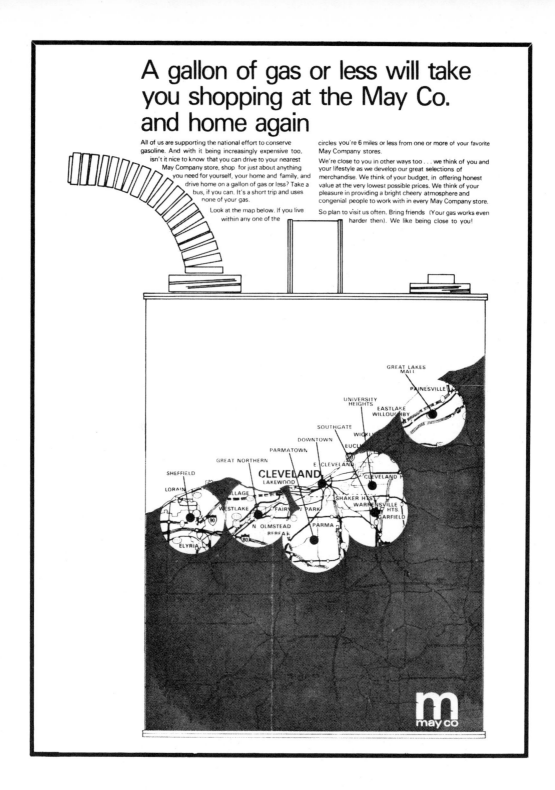

A gallon of gas or less will take you shopping at the May Co. and home again

All of us are supporting the national effort to conserve gasoline. And with it being increasingly expensive too, isn't it nice to know that you can drive to your nearest May Company store, shop for just about anything you need for yourself, your home and family, and drive home on a gallon of gas or less? Take a bus, if you can. It's a short trip and uses none of your gas.

Look at the map below. If you live within any one of the circles you're 6 miles or less from one or more of your favorite May Company stores.

We're close to you in other ways too . . . we think of you and your lifestyle as we develop our great selections of merchandise. We think of your budget, in offering honest value at the very lowest possible prices. We think of your pleasure in providing a bright cheery atmosphere and congenial people to work with in every May Company store.

So plan to visit us often. Bring friends. (Your gas works even harder then). We like being close to you!

In Cleveland there is a May Co. within six miles of most customers. That became the subject of the most informative and exciting program we've seen on the subject of gasoline conservation. Here is advertising everybody talks about.

Right:
Buffums' Italian Import is a distinguished human interest story. This is the kind of advertising that builds confidence and wins new friends.

Italian import.

He's Nicholas Defiore, and he came all the way from Rome, Italy.

Mr. D, as he's known around here, is a master tailor. He was an apprentice at the age of eleven. He then became a journeyman, and finally after twelve very busy years of tailoring, he earned the title of master.

He is truly a tailoring specialist. That's why we hired him at Buffums'. (Everyone at Buffums' is a specialist at one thing or another.) In Mr. D's case, it's tailoring

Because of expert tailors like Mr. D, and because we don't charge for alterations, whether you buy a fine suit or just a sport jacket at Buffums', you can be sure you won't get stuck.

There are Buffums' in Long Beach, Marina, Palos Verdes, Pomona, Lakewood and Santa Ana. Mr. D works in Santa Ana. It was the one closest to Rome.

Visit the Buffums' closest to you, and you, too, may never want to roam again.

Every department's a specialty shop at
Buffums'.

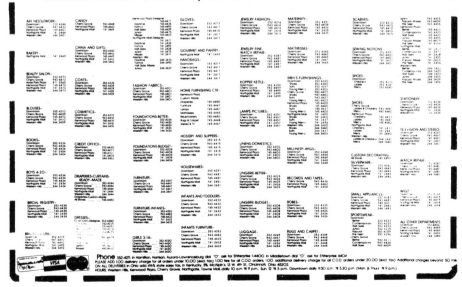

We are seeing many practical solutions to gasoline shortage situations and some stores are featuring telephone ordering as one way to go. McAlpin's goes a giant step further and advertises every telephone number in every department in every store location. What a colossal job of coordination! There is nothing spectacular about the ad but it is the sort of page that gets saved out of the newspaper for future reference. A practical, sensible job.

Every store in the world has a gift wrap program but very few do a free wrap with every purchase. Ivers has wraps to sell, too, but that free wrap is outstanding and surely a pulling factor with the customers. The ad is outstanding too, the wraps are shown in crisp black-and-white, flat-on, and big enough to mean something to the customer. An example of taking an obscure service and making it a smash hit.

Some call them
our finest hours.

Barney's, New York

Open every night till 9:30,
including Saturday.

Barney's man-in-the-moon tells a simple story of service: "Some call
them our finest hours". The lower-Manhattan retailer is, of course,
open until 9:30 p.m. including Saturday. This gem runs often as a
small-space ad.

Barney's, New York. The service remains gracious. The parking remains free.

Barney's, New York

Seventh Avenue and Seventeenth Street. Open 9:30 to 9:30. Free parking.

Again, a Barney's institutional that gets right to the point. And here, the point is free parking, a great inducement for a retailer out of the mainstream. We also like the general reference to the service remaining gracious.

It's friendly time at Dayton's with gold butterflies stuck to the fronts of employees, gold butterflies and smiling employees stuck in a full-page ad. It's Dayton's way of communicating to the customer that everyone in their store is out to be extra helpful and courteous, and it's not because their employees might win a million-dollar bonus. Dayton's says: "We feel you (the customer) deserve it. And it's time we let you know..." A great idea!

Don't ask why this page by Rich's deserved to be the bell ringer of the week.
How could it fail! It is audacious, brazen, flamboyant, flashy. It doesn't
even do a selling job, in the usual sense, on the subject involved. It's just
there, one big blast. And who can miss it! Without doubt the best seen and
most talked-about ad of the week. The store card, issued to ''Ms. Loise
Laine'', is sheer inspiration. We love it all.

WE SAID IT FIRST AND WE'LL SAY IT AGAIN

Quality for quality

Rich's will not be undersold

We don't really mind if others **hop on the Rich's bandwagon...imitation is** often the most sincere form of **flattery!** Our customers know that it has **always been Rich's policy** to meet the **fair market price** on merchandise of the same quality. This was **established** by Rich's founder, Morris Rich, **over 115 years ago. It's no news** then that our **prices of identical merchandise remain as low,** or lower, **than any place in town.** It's only what our customers expect at Rich's! So, if you find **an item locally at a lower price,** we want to know about it. If it is currently advertised, **bring the ad** when you come to make your purchase and we will make the **adjustment on the spot.** If it is **not advertised,** but you see it locally at a lower price, **we'll** go so far as to **check it out** on the day of your purchase at Rich's and **send you the difference.** And, we do it all **with a great big smile!** Others may think that this is a unique concept, a news-making event, an unexpected service...but, **Rich's customers know it's** just **our established policy! SO what's new?**

RICH'S

ALL YOU EXPECT, A LOT YOU DON'T

In recent years, inflation has made fearful editorial headlines. But in comes John Wanamaker with this institutional advertisement. It is a simple, truthful, brief statement. But what punch! What a triumph over inflation! One hundred and nine years of sound merchandising policies are rolled out for inspection. A sale is only as credible as its store. Please read the copy.

14.95

7.99

3.50

Slashing prices is a little like slashing tires. It's a curious way to fight inflation. If the prices are fair to begin with, they can be reduced a fair amount for a special occasion, or to close out a season or a line of merchandise. Ordinarily, prices can't be drastically reduced unless they were drastic in the first place.

After 109 years of careful study, John Wanamaker has two suggestions.

First, shop where *good* merchandise is fairly priced, consistently, without wild fluctuations. Where if you buy something this week for $14, you know it's worth $14 and you won't find other people buying it on sale next week for $3.99.

The only real way to fight inflation is to insist on value.

Second, next time you see someone slashing prices, listen. There may be a loud hissing sound as the air goes out.

John Wanamaker

Left:

We like the emphasis on "quality for quality" in Rich's price policy institutional. There's even a big "Q" to make the point.

And we like the way Rich's makes sure readers know that the policy was established by the store's founder, Morris Rich, over 115 years ago. This Monday editorial does more than explain a policy, it showcases Rich's as a store where high standards never change, a store that fulfills its promise.

318

2/29¢

Buy one get one free!
All prices slashed! Fantastic discounts! Bargains you won't believe!
Won't believe is right. If it's 2.99 today, why was it
12.99 yesterday? The ads may cluck and crow
but inflation keeps Plucking and plucking and
pecking away. What can you do? Insist on solid value.
Deal with stores who trim prices all they can *before*
the prices are marked. Who have realistic sales
for realistic reasons. Not the ones who promise
pie in the sky one day, then go running around
next day like Henny Penny yelling you-know-what.
Stick with the stores (Cox's is
seven of them) who stock first
rate goods at good, honest
prices, have good sales
when they can and who
don't go in for dizzy cut-price
claims. One store and
it's customers can't
beat inflation, but they
can sure help, and that's
where it has to start.
There's nobody here
but us chickens.

OCTOBER IS NINETY-EIGHTH ANNIVERSARY MONTH AT COX'S MONROEVILLE MALL,
EAST HILLS, NORWIN, WASHINGTON, CHARLEROI, McKEESPORT, BEAVER VALLEY.

Is everybody getting chicken? Is everyone offering "buy one get one
free?" Cox's discourages the Henny-Penny attitude by advising
customers to. . . "stick with the stores (Cox's has seven of them) who
stock first rate goods at good, honest prices, have good sales when
they can and who don't go in for dizzy cut-prices claims."
And to strengthen its message Cox's uses a beautiful four-color
sketch of two chickens in the pot. . . by Arnold Varga.

Left:
Sears has re-issued the editorial page that has been running for
several years. The new layout is distinguished for its simplicity,
clarity, and typographic handling.

319

For New Yorkers strolling or riding down Fifth Avenue, the eye always seems to group two monuments together. First, St. Patrick's, then Saks Fifth Avenue. Both gray stone, both elegant. It is truly fitting that Saks should take a full page to commemorate its neighbor's 100th anniversary. The face-on portrait of the cathedral with just a hint of Atlas from across the street at Rockefeller Center is perfect.

One hundred years ago, Saint Patrick's Cathedral opened its doors to the people of New York City. And, as the City rose about her, she was there...providing sanctuary, offering peace, and instilling inspiration and strength not just to those of us who live and work near her, but to peoples of all nationalities, all cultures, all religions. With respect and affection, we commemorate the celebration of the spirit of Saint Patrick's.

Saks Fifth Avenue

Saks Fifth Avenue at Rockefeller Center will be closed tomorrow in observance of Memorial Day.

"What this world needs now—is all the love you can spare." This is more than a message for the start of a new year. This is for now and forever. It would be hard to estimate the impact for Eaton's this advertisement created. Yet, somehow, we believe Eaton's would do an ad like this without considering the commercial side benefits. It's no wonder Montreal loves Eaton's.

What the world needs now.

Is all the love you can spare. It's needed all around you. and it's needed most where you see it least. Maybe that's why there is a new year. It halts our headlong rush just long enough to make us realize that we each hold the greatest gift of all. If we can just learn to give it away.

EATON'S

Suppose you are a visitor in Winnipeg

And want to:

Buy exquisite English China.
 Stock up on woollen blankets.
Treat yourself to French perfume.
 Get wool sweaters for the children.
 Buy a piece of Eskimo sculpture.
Enjoy a snack, or full-course meal.
Get tickets for Rainbow Stage.
Start a souvenir spoon collection.
 Buy a maple leaf sterling pin.
Get some fine English cutlery.
 Where do you go?

To Eaton's, of course.

EATON'S

Eaton's, Winnipeg, takes a good look at the wants and needs of
Summer visitors and socks it to them. Where should they go for English
china, a piece of Eskimo sculpture, a snack or a full-course meal?
"To Eaton's, of course." It's a great ad.

Kodak—you are our sunshine... with a 100 year start on tomorrow

There is a brilliant sunny sky over Rochester. It's been that way for a hundred years because Kodak ordered it so—how else does one make brilliant sunny photographs? Sibley's pays tribute to one of the giants of American industry with an ad printed in brilliant yellow. It's a smash hit.

*Higbee's is happening in Cleveland *

Once upon a time there was a housewife who had a very demanding husband.

1

He demanded she serve breakfast on time, and he demanded that she be loving, giving, and get his approval on all purchases.

2

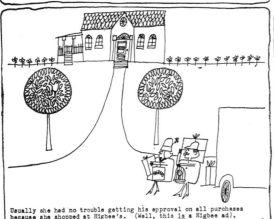

Usually she had no trouble getting his approval on all purchases because she shopped at Higbee's. (Well, this is a Higbee ad).

3

But one day she came home on the Rapid and showed her husband a lamp she had bought at Higbee's, and

he laughed, "Ho ho ha ha," and said, "Take it back."

4

So she took it back, and the salesgirl smiled and said, "Well, husbands are like that, and Higbee's understands and tut tut, you poor thing."

5

On the way out of Higbee's our housewife found something else she liked. So, if on the way home tonight, you find a perky housewife carrying a duck, remember she exchanged a very sensible lamp for it. Isn't that ducky? To have a store like Higbee's that not only exchanges things.. but is very understanding about demanding husbands?

6

Higbee's, the oldest store in Cleveland, thinks younger every year.

It is entirely fitting and proper that a message to Canada should be in the two languages of the realm. The message, of course, is one that every citizen south of the border feels intensely. There are beautiful people in the world and the Canadians proved it. And Hudson's said it well.

Thank you, Canada
Merci au Canada

To have harbored our people
D'avoir hébergé les nôtres

and brought them safely home
et de les avoir ramenés saufs et sains;

was an act of love
ce fût un acte de bonté

beyond the limits of
qui dépasse les limites normales

ordinary diplomacy.
de la diplomacie.

hudson's

Left:
Higbee's makes a penetrating study of Demanding Husbands and other factors that keep customers happy. This is advertising nobody will miss.

The impact is enormous. To see the President of the United States standing out of the newspaper, big as life, is breathtaking. What is even more breathtaking is Dayton's total approach to "We the People." Once again we see a great store assuming a responsibility and a privilege. We serve the people, we belong to the people. When business can say that, and live it, the wheels of this country roll ahead.

Generation Bridge

Books are a bridge between generations. Between cultures. Between countries. And in no place is the bridge firmer than at The New York Public Library. Specifically, the Central Research Library on Fifth Avenue. Used by more college students and their teachers than any other library in the world. Plus millions of other people. From novelists tracking down facts to art dealers tracking down paintings. From amateur genealogists to serious social historians. For inspiration for new fashions or new kitchens.

If you went to school in or around New York (or came home here on holidays with papers to write), you probably spent much of your time at the Library. Now a new generation is sitting in your chair. They may wear beards or minis, but they're here for the same reason you were. To learn.

The Central Research Library is unique in many ways. Its size: the 2-acre main reading room, the 80 miles of books. Its 21 special divisions. From material in 300 Indian languages in the American History Division to a million volumes in Economics and Sociology, bigger than most libraries in itself. From the playbills going back to 1750 and the 750,000 movie stills in the Research Library & Museum of Performing Arts at Lincoln Center to the 30,000 current magazines that arrive every week or month. Its matchless collection of Slavonic, Oriental, and Jewish literature. And so much more. Including 10 million catalogue cards, literally the key to anything anybody wants to know.

The Library is also unique in the way it's supported. If you want to know who feeds the Library lions ... well, you do. Or should. Because the Central Research Library, created at the turn of the century from the Astor, Lenox, and Tilden Foundations, is privately financed. It's a public library, but it lives mostly on income from endowments and contributions. And it's struggling. With rising costs. With the need to keep bridging generation gaps in knowledge. For example. The surge of books from young countries in Asia and Africa. The surge of new sciences that become whole disciplines overnight. What can you do? You can support the Library in every way you can. So it will continue to be open every day of the year. So it will continue to be the most used library in the free world. So it will continue to bridge the generations.

Why is Macy's telling you about the Library? Partly because it is New York's pride ... and New York's pride is ours as well. And partly because we, too, understand the need to bridge the generations. Which is why we're a very different store than we're a generation ago. Which is why, generation after generation, young people have been happily shopping at Macy's. Knowing that they'll find their things here. Which, of course, is why we became the world's largest store. And we still are.

Macy's
THE WORLD'S LARGEST STORE

Macy's says, "books are a bridge between generations, between cultures, between countries" and proceeds to give a great tribute to the work of the New York Public Library. Macy's explains that what belongs to New York belongs to Macy's, and advertising like this has its place in Macy's program.

What makes New York a great city is its fabulous people living elbow to elbow. For ten days in October the Parks Recreation and Cultural Affairs Administration sponsored a party which brought together the talents, cultures and traditions of 40 ethnic groups. Macy's, always true to the people that make the New York scene, took a page in the Times to let everybody know about it. This is one way a store can participate in matters that can mean so much to a community. To Macy's, bravo.

hoo·ray

(hŏŏ rā') interji., v.i., n. Chiefly Baton Rouge. Especially used to cheer for the champs in Goudchaux's First Annual East Baton Rouge Parish Spelling Bee. We, at Goudchaux's have always valued excellence in all things. That's why it's our special pleasure to honor these outstanding young Spelling Bee finalists. They're a credit to themselves as well as to all 365,000 of us in East Baton Rouge Parish. Join us for a well-deserved hooray. They have performed in the highest tradition of excellence as a personal hallmark.

Hans Sternberg, Chairman of the Board of Goudchaux's, congratulates the winners of Goudchaux's First Annual East Baton Rouge Parish Spelling Bee. The winners (left to right): Mike Sebastian, Episcopal High School; Laurie Couvillion, St. George Catholic School; Shane Johnson, St. Isidore Catholic School.

CONGRATULATIONS TO THE FINALISTS

**FIRST CATEGORY
GRADES 1-6**
Jenny Antoon, Villa Del Rey Elementary School
David Assaf, St. Thomas More Catholic School
Melissa Cannella, St. Pius X Catholic School
Wendy Cobb, Park Forest Elementary School
William Collins, University Laboratory School
Robert Craig, Bakerfield Elementary School
April Duhon, St. George Catholic School
Sheila Maria Earls, North Scotlandville Elementary
Brian Fenn, Westminster Elementary School
Jeannie Giroir, Delmont Elementary School
Rachel Haas, Southdowns Elementary School
Roy James, Eden Park Elementary School
Joseph Johnson, Nicholson Elementary School
Shane Johnson, St. Isidore Catholic School
James Key, Wildwood Elementary School
Sara LeBleu, St. Thomas More Catholic School
Cherie Rene Many, Mayfair Elementary School
Scott Marshall, Bernard Terrace Elementary
Danielle McMillon, LaBelle Aire Elementary School
Darren Robertson, St. Gerard Majella Catholic
Paul Sharon, Cedarcrest Southmoor Elementary
Coretta Smith, Glasgow Middle School
Jennifer Smith, Episcopal High School
Genell Thompson, White Hills Elementary School

Eric Toaston, Westdale Elementary School
Stephen B. Turner, Sherwood Forest Elementary
Chris Williams, Audubon Elementary School

**SECOND CATEGORY
GRADES 7-9**
Allison Adams, Broadmoor Junior High School
Angela Anderson, Broadmoor Junior High School
Carla Caston, St. Thomas More Catholic School
Laurie Couvillion, St. George Catholic School
Mary Alice Driggers, Episcopal High School
Kevin Gibson, Our Lady of Mercy Catholic School
Terri Renee Henderson, Glasgow Middle School
Duane Labbe, Prescott Middle School

**THIRD CATEGORY
GRADES 10-12**
Paul Bergeron, Catholic High School
Cristine Diane Crisler, Baton Rouge High School
Stephanie Gremillion, Broadmoor High School
Jan Jacob, Redemptorist High School
Susan Pearson, St. Joseph Academy
Mike Sebastian, Episcopal High School
Melissa Wells, Istrouma High School

Goudchaux's
The Difference Is You

BATON ROUGE: For Personal Shopper Service, phone 383-7277. 1500 MAIN open 9 to 5:45 daily; Monday and Thursday to 8:30. Phone 383-7000 CORTANA MALL open 9:30 to 9 daily. Phone 923-1000. LAFAYETTE: ACADIANA MALL open 9:30 to 9 daily. Phone 981-8000. Goudchaux's accounts interest-free. Master Charge and Visa honored.

Hoo-ray for Goudchaux's First Annual East Baton Rouge Parish Spelling Bee. An outstanding example of participation in civic affairs, with particular interest in the younger generations. The impact of an event like this, the parental approbation, and the favorable fall-out for the store cannot be measured. This is priceless and Goudchaux's will long be rewarded.

There was a lot of talk in Indianapolis when Ayres ran this page. The traffic-safety idea written into the last sentence of the copy makes this a serious public service advertisement. A tremendous job.

YIPPIE! school's out! And I betcha I'll climb the pare tree and lick lots of cake icing pans and look for a 4 leaf clover in the Grass and find a nickle Instead and make some mud pies in the vacent lot and visit Grammas House and find 3 new kittens under the bushes and go barefoot most all the time and ketch me some lighting bugs and stuff and and an Gee whiz MoM what'll I do the second day? ok I'll watch out crossing the street Mom but tell everybody else to watch out for me to cuz somtimes I forget.

L.S. Ayres + co.

Again, Fort Wayne keeps school playgrounds open all summer and assigns trained leaders to supervise them. Again, Wolf & Dessauer tells it to the people, giving school addresses and playground hours. Again, this is the way a great store proves it is the heartbeat of the community.

Published as a public service by

W&D

Pre-school children must be accompanied by an adult or older responsible child.

Hurrah! City Playgrounds open Tuesday morning at 9 a.m.

Playground locations:

ABBETT SCHOOL, 4341 Smith Street
BASS, at Bass and Hoagland
BLOOMINGDALE SCHOOL, 1300 Orchard Street
BOWSER, at Milan and Winter
BRENTWOOD SCHOOL, 3710 Stafford Drive
CAMP ALLEN, Camp Allen Drive at Huron
FRANKE PARK SCHOOL, 828 Mildred
GLENWOOD PARK SCHOOL, 4501 Vance Avenue
HAMILTON, at Spring and Jessie
HANNA PLACE, 1000 East Lewis
HARRISON HILL SCHOOL, Cornell Circle
HOLLAND SCHOOL, 7000 Red Haw Drive
KETTLER, Belmont Drive and Hoagland
KLUG, at LeRoy and Lawndale Drive
LAFAYETTE, Glencoe and Wilmette
LAKESIDE, Lake and California
LAWTON, at Clinton and Fourth
LIONS, North Carew Street
MAPLEWOOD SCHOOL, 2200 Maplewood Road
McCORMICK, at Raymond and Holly
McCULLOCH, at McCulloch at Eliza
McMILLEN, Hessen Cassel Road & Oxford
MEMORIAL, at Maumee and Glasgow
MINER, Miner and DeWald Streets
NORTHCREST SCHOOL, 5301 Archwood
PACKARD, at Packard and Fairfield
PRICE SCHOOL, State and Tyler
PSI OTE, Wenonah and Wendigo Lanes
RESERVOIR, Clinton and Creighton
RIVERSIDE SCHOOL, at Vance and Kentucky
ROCKHILL, Catalpa and Jefferson Blvd.
SHERMAN, Sherman and Pape
SOUTHERN HEIGHTS SCHOOL, Fairfax Drive at Gaywood
STUDY, at 2414 Brooklyn
WAYNEDALE, at Koons and Elzey
WEISSER, Hanna and Eckart

Again . . . it's time for summer fun at the playgrounds . . . athletics crafts, story telling, and many other activities for boys and girls of all ages. Under the supervision of trained leaders, all playgrounds are open daily Tuesday through Friday 9:00 a.m. till noon (with the exception of Bloomingdale School, which is open Monday thru Friday 1:00 to 4:30 p.m.) . . . And afternoons Monday through Friday 1:00 till 4:30; Evenings, Tuesday and Thursday, 6:00 to 8:00 (no later than 9:45 in case of a special event) at Bowser, Hamilton Lakeside, Lions, McCulloch, Packard, Waynedale, and Weisser Call 742-5341 for additional information if desired

Keeping up with the customer means stores have to turn on a dime these days. The bicycle wave is mounting high in New York and Bonwit Teller responds with a neat bike rack smack in front of the men's shop entrance. Many shopping centers now provide bike racks but big downtown stores are slow to move. Our thanks to Bonwit's for showing the way. It's a splendid ad, too, the spirit, the happy sketch, the copy, the flag— all of it is just right.

Bonwit's loves to make people happy. That's why we're not such big wheels that we forget you need a place to park your wheels

Next time you're pedaling by 57th and Fifth, be our guest and lock your wheels in the Bonwit Bike Rack. It's there for you. And it's there because we care about certain things. Like letting New Yorkers breathe a little easier thanks to more bikes, less monoxide. And getting a little healthy exercise while they're at it.

Bonwit's doesn't sell bikes, but we like the idea of seeing people wheeling around the city— somehow they seem more involved with each other than when they're encased in their separate glass and metal worlds.

Bonwit's racks up hours and hours of travel time searching the globe for the newest and most with-it clothes the world has to offer. But unless we try in different ways to give the city and our store a happier, friendlier atmosphere, we feel we're just coasting. And our Bike Rack is just the first stop. When it comes to making people happy, you can be sure we'll continue to keep the wheels in our heads turning.

This was the third time Abraham & Straus, Brooklyn, had promoted the Mayor's Office for Volunteers, a center which matches up citizen volunteers with organizations needing manpower. Checking the Mayor's Office the day after the ad ran, it was reported that hundreds of phone calls had already been received and that interviews of prospective volunteers had been booked. The Mayor's Office for Volunteers, a leading member of the Voluntary Action Center in Washington D.C., often receives requests for information from public and private offices around the country. During the time the ad ran, a copy of "Want to feel loved and needed?" went with the package.

An audience-participation concept that has far-reaching possibilities. Hochschild-Kohn is asking the children to submit their own ideas about "alive and aware." This is part of the store's back-to-school promotion and it's terrific.

Right:
Hudson's long sharp 500 mile needle pricked St. Louis where it hurt. The newspapers down there showed Hudson's ad, too! In 1968, it was malediction, mayhem, and murder.

BYE
BYE
BIRDIE

HUDSON'S Detroit's world-famous department store

you can use
your new voting privilege
only if you register by September 22

We believe in you young people of today . . . in your intelligence, your awareness, your sincerity, and your concern . . . and we believe in the kind of government which has granted you a voice in the shaping of your world. We urge you to register now to vote. Use your privilege wisely and well, carefully and conscientiously, and be among the first at the polls on November 2. After all, it's your city, your state, your country . . . and your privilege.

Register now thru September 22 at the Board of Elections, 410 South High Street, in the County Courthouse Annex. (Call 462-3100 for specific times daily). On Saturday, September 18, you can register at any public high school in Franklin County from 8:30 a.m. to 4:30 p.m. Public high schools will also be open for voter registration on Tuesday, September 21, and Wednesday, September 22, from 10 a.m. to 2 p.m. and 4 p.m. to 9 p.m.

LAZARUS THE PEOPLE PLACE

Lazarus performs a public service of great importance. This message to new voters needs to be given all over America and who should be doing it? Lazarus says we are "the people place", and thoughtful advertising like this proves the point. A beautiful job, a powerful impression. What more can advertising do?

336

Clean your closets!

Wednesday to Saturday you can clean up on castoffs

Eaton's and the Salvation Army's New-for-Old Trade-in Event

"You get a good deal and do a good deed—bring your castoffs to a trade-in depot at Eaton's". A neat plan for the benefit of Toronto's Salvation Army and Eaton's customers. In the late 70's we saw so many "coupon deals" but this one beats all. Everybody wins and most of all the Army and the destitute of the city. A thoughtful approach.

The Leaders
are the Readers.

RIGHT: Interior of the Hattiesburg Public Library as it appeared in 1930 soon after completion. The idea of a public library was conceived in 1927 and the project spearheaded by S.B. Berry, attorney and legionnaire, along with members of the American Legion's Allen Carter Post. Berry's son, Lieutenant General Sidney B. Berry (U.S. Army, Ret.) previously Commandant of West Point and now Mississippi's Commissioner of Public Safety, will speak during an April 20 reception commemorating the Library's 50th anniversary.

BELOW: A more recent view of the Library's downtown facility, much as it appeared originally. The land was purchased, the building constructed and an initial supply of books acquired for a total cost of $100,000 in 1930. Today the Hattiesburg Municipal Library System includes the Petal Branch, City Bookmobile, County Bookmobile and the 5th St. Community Center Reading Room.

The strength of a nation is measured by
it's literacy, for with literacy comes
Knowledge, and with Knowledge comes strength.

The world of the eighties will demand
much from all of us. We will need
all the personal and national strength
we can muster . . . if we are to
have any hope of coping with and solving
the problems of energy, disease, hunger
and peace. We must be informed.
We must learn. We must read.

IT'S NATIONAL LIBRARY WEEK,
APRIL 13-20

WALDOFF'S

It's National Library Week and Waldoff's takes notice in a way few citizens of Hattiesburg will miss. Or soon forget. A store belongs to the people and what is important to people becomes important to the store.

Right:
What is good for the community is good for the store. The Brooklyn Museum is sponsoring an open air "fence art show". It is a serious affair, representing serious painters, and it draws a great deal of public attention. In the middle of it all is Abraham & Straus. Naturally.

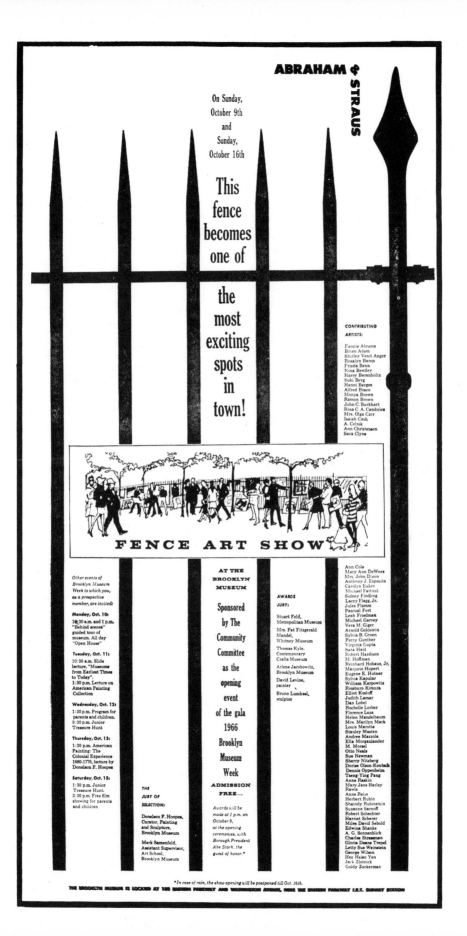

ABRAHAM & STRAUS

On Sunday, October 9th and Sunday, October 16th

This fence becomes one of the most exciting spots in town!

FENCE ART SHOW

CONTRIBUTING ARTISTS:

Fannie Abrams
Brian Adam
Shirley Venit Anger
Rosalyn Baron
Frieda Benn
Nina Bentley
Harry Berenholtz
Suki Berg
Hanni Berges
Alfred Bosco
Monya Brown
Ramon Brown
John C. Burkhart
Rosa C. A. Cambries
Mrs. Olga Carr
Isaiah Cash
A. Celnik
Ann Christenson
Sara Clyne

Ann Cole
Mary Ann DeWees
Mrs. John Dixon
Anthony J. Esposito
Carolyn Euker
Michael Fatizzi
Sidney Findling
Lacey Flagg, Jr.
Jules Flamm
Pascual Fort
Leah Friedman
Michael Garvey
Vera M. Giger
Arnold Goldstein
Sylvia B. Groten
Perry Gunther
Virginia Gupta
Sara Haid
Robert Hardison
M. Hoffman
Reinhard Hohaus, Jr.
Marjorie Hupert
Eugene E. Hutner
Sylvia Kapular
William Karpowitz
Risaburo Kimura
Elliot Kosloff
Judith Lamar
Dan Lobel
Rochelle Lorber
Florence Loza
Helen Mandelbaum
Mrs. Marilyn Mark
Louis Marotta
Stanley Masten
Andree Mazzola
Ella Morganlander
M. Morsel
Otto Neals
Sue Newman
Sherry Nitzberg
Dorise Olson-Koutach
Dennis Oppenheim
Tseng-Ying Pang
Anne Raskin
Mary Jane Harley Rawls
Anne Reiss
Herbert Rubin
Shaindy Rubinstein
Suzanne Sarnoff
Robert Schechter
Harriet Scherer
Miles David Sebold
Edwina Shanks
A. G. Sonnenblick
Charles Strassman
Gloria Deane Trepel
Letty Sue Weinstein
George Wilson
Hsu Hsiao Yen
Jack Zlotnick
Goldy Zuckerman

Other events of Brooklyn Museum Week to which you, as a prospective member, are invited:

Monday, Oct. 10:
10:30 a.m. and 1 p.m.
"Behind scenes" guided tour of museum. All day "Open House"

Tuesday, Oct. 11:
10:30 a.m. Slide lecture, "Museums from Earliest Times to Today".
1:30 p.m. Lecture on American Painting Collection

Wednesday, Oct. 12:
1:30 p.m. Program for parents and children.
3:30 p.m. Junior Treasure Hunt

Thursday, Oct. 13:
1:30 p.m. American Painting: The Colonial Experience 1680-1776, lecture by Donelson F. Hoopes

Saturday, Oct. 15:
1:30 p.m. Junior Treasure Hunt.
3:00 p.m. Free film showing for parents and children

THE JURY OF SELECTION:
Donelson F. Hoopes, Curator, Painting and Sculpture, Brooklyn Museum

Mark Samenfeld, Assistant Supervisor, Art School, Brooklyn Museum

AT THE BROOKLYN MUSEUM

Sponsored by The Community Committee as the opening event of the gala 1966 Brooklyn Museum Week

ADMISSION FREE...

Awards will be made at 1 p.m. on October 9, at the opening ceremonies, with Borough President Abe Stark, the guest of honor.

AWARDS JURY:

Stuart Feld, Metropolitan Museum

Mrs. Pat Fitzgerald Mandel, Whitney Museum

Thomas Kyle, Contemporary Crafts Museum

Arlene Jacobowitz, Brooklyn Museum

David Levine, painter

Bruno Lucchesi, sculptor

In case of rain, the show opening will be postponed till Oct. 16th.

THE BROOKLYN MUSEUM IS LOCATED AT 188 EASTERN PARKWAY AND WASHINGTON AVENUE, NEAR THE EASTERN PARKWAY I.R.T. SUBWAY STATION

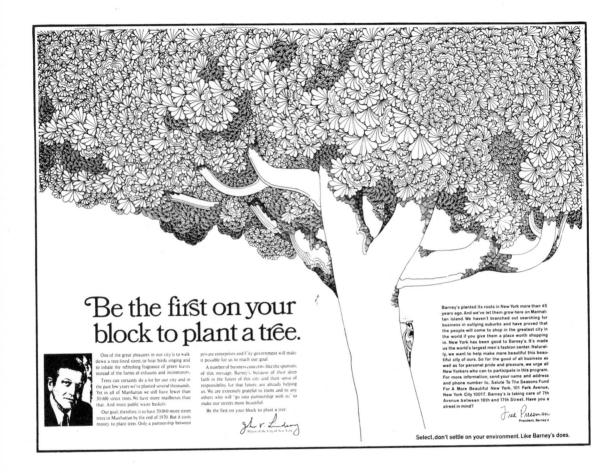

Be the first on your block to plant a tree.

One of the great pleasures in our city is to walk down a tree-lined street, to hear birds singing and to inhale the refreshing fragrance of green leaves instead of the fumes of exhausts and incinerators.

Trees can certainly do a lot for our city and in the past few years we've planted several thousands. Yet in all of Manhattan we still have fewer than 30,000 street trees. We have more mailboxes than that. And more public waste baskets.

Our goal, therefore, is to have 20,000 more street trees in Manhattan by the end of 1970. But it costs money to plant trees. Only a partnership between private enterprises and City government will make it possible for us to reach our goal.

A number of business concerns, like the sponsors of this message, Barney's, because of their deep faith in the future of this city and their sense of responsibility for that future, are already helping us. We are extremely grateful to them and to any others who will "go into partnership with us" to make our streets more beautiful.

Be the first on your block to plant a tree.

John V. Lindsay
Mayor of the City of New York

Barney's planted its roots in New York more than 45 years ago. And we've let them grow here on Manhattan Island. We haven't branched out searching for business in outlying suburbs and have proved that the people will come to shop in the greatest city in the world if you give them a place worth shopping in. New York has been good to Barney's. It's made us the world's largest men's fashion center. Naturally, we want to help make more beautiful this beautiful city of ours. So for the good of all business as well as for personal pride and pleasure, we urge all New Yorkers who can to participate in this program. For more information, send your name and address and phone number to, Salute To The Seasons Fund For A More Beautiful New York, 101 Park Avenue, New York City 10017. Barney's is taking care of 7th Avenue between 16th and 17th Street. Have you a street in mind?

Fred Pressman
President, Barney's

Select, don't settle on your environment. Like Barney's does.

Barney's, besides selling men's clothing, is selling the idea of planting trees in New York City. This doubletruck is a salute to The Seasons Fund For A More Beautiful New York. It's a beautiful cause, a beautiful advertisement, and the mayor of New York adds a tribute for which Barney's should be proud.

Right:
One way to make a community your own is to keep its history alive. For Calgary's centennial year, the Bay presented one ad a month (from March to June) commemorating 25 years of its community's history. The series was researched and produced by the store's art director and copy chief. In this page, art and copy tell of Sam Livingston who owned the two wild cows that gave the town its milk supply, the 1881 Mounted Police Barracks, the 1891 Bay store, the Chief of the Blackfoot who died in 1890. Handsome art and handwritten copy were printed in black and covered with a soft tan. A beautiful way to celebrate the centennial of a city!

300 Mounties started it all back in 1874 when they rode west from Manitoba, gunning for whisky traders. In 1881 Calgary consists of the Hudson's Bay Co., I.G. Baker's Store, the Mounted Police Barracks and the House of the Commanding Officer. Three years later, the C.P.R. locates their station on the west side of the Elbow, and the town moves! Permanent buildings replace tents and shacks, the population soars to 1,200, and buffalo bones sell for $7 a ton.

In 1884, the town's milk comes from two wild cows owned by Sam Livingston, who followed the California Gold Rush when a lad of 15. His farm is now the Glenmore Reservoir.

1890—the tall, lean and dignified Chief of the Blackfoot, Crowfoot, dies. Recognized as the Keeper of the peace, he led the Indians to a new life on the reserves. 1891— The Hudson's Bay Company buys out I.G. Baker and occupies a sandstone building on the northwest corner of 8th Ave. and Centre St. 1894— the town is incorporated into the City of Calgary, General Hospital is erected beside the Elbow River, the Alberta Hotel is the classiest place in town and the Bay was the place to go for boots, blankets and Perry Davis's Pain Killer. We've upheld our reputation over the years for service, selection and satisfaction, proud of our part in framing Calgary's colorful past. The Bay going and glowing with Calgary.

the **Bay**

a proud past... an exciting future

341

THE TALENT SEARCH IS ENDED

NOW

it can be told: Since October, 1963, the Elsie Talent Search sponsored by The Borden Company, with the help of the American Jersey Cattle Club, the 4-H Club, and Future Farmers of America has gone on...and on...and on. Across the nation, dairymen [and dairymaids] in

FIFTY

states have been looking at the lovelies in their herds...gazing into their eyes...glorying in their grace. The

CREAM

of the crop made the finals...a winner chosen! The judges have found their girl! Beautiful brown eyes, upswept nose, dainty walk, the right background...purebred.

HISTORY

is being made. Your first chance to see the "new" Elsie before she goes to the World's Fair in April.

Can a simple country girl find fame at the World's Largest Store and the World's Greatest Fair?

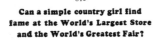

THE "NEW" ELSIE MAKES HER DEBUT AT

MACY'S
HERALD SQUARE
Thurs., Fri. and Sat., March

19, 20, 21

5th Floor Exhibit Centre. See the world's largest walk-around model of the World's Fair, the United Airlines display, Sinclair Dinosaur-land, super-duper souvenirs...and much more!

See the pride of the pastures. See the belle of the barns. See the brown-eyed beauty who's making red-hot news.

E L S I E

Elegant • Lovely • Scintillating • Intelligent • Enchanting

WHAT

were they looking for?
- Poise • Charm • Grace • Femininity
- Soft fawn tone
- Delicate face • Showmanship
- Purebred registered Jersey

AT LAST

"The new 'Elsie' is a 'natural'," say the famous judges including theater personalities, columnists and cattle pro's who chose this charmer from 10,000 herds of Jersey lovelies. Across the

NATION

in 50 states, the massive search has been underway since last October. In cloistered New England pastures, on palm-laden Hawaiian hills, across Midwestern plains.

HISTORY

is being repeated. The first Elsie made her debut at the 1939 World's Fair [but not under her real name of "You'll Do Lobelia"].

Come early... Elsie gets up with the cows.

Come one, come all to Macy's...where history is always being made and where you know we'll never steer you wrong

What can a store do to support the theatrical arts in its community? Ask Sanger-Harris. First, this delightful newspaper page acquaints the reader with TACA, the cultural benefit organization for Dallas. Second, it offers a week of "show" events at the downtown store: appearances by the Dallas Ballet Company, the Symphony Orchestra Brass Quintet, fashions from famous operas.

Left:
Many will remember that Borden's famous "Elsie" made her debut to the world on Macy's fourth floor. That was 25 years ago. Now the talent search is ended and there is a new Elsie.

People-minded A&S never slows down. Here is a store that believes people-to-people relationships must take precedence over all else. That's how a store survives and grows. This time it's the little league with a great big plus! No doubt the most seen and best remembered ad of the day. Or week. Or month. Or . . .

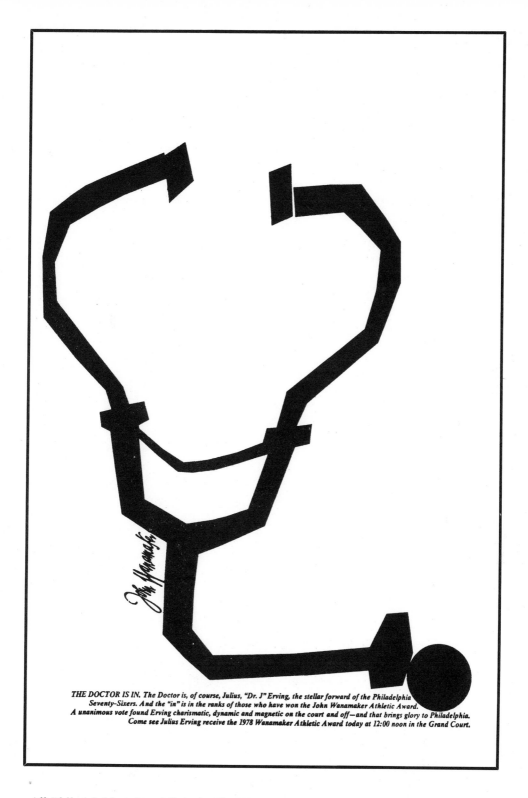

THE DOCTOR IS IN. The Doctor is, of course, Julius, "Dr. J" Erving, the stellar forward of the Philadelphia Seventy-Sixers. And the "in" is in the ranks of those who have won the John Wanamaker Athletic Award. A unanimous vote found Erving charismatic, dynamic and magnetic on the court and off—and that brings glory to Philadelphia. Come see Julius Erving receive the 1978 Wanamaker Athletic Award today at 12:00 noon in the Grand Court.

All Philadelphia takes delight in The Wanamaker Athletic Award, an annual affair that singles out the individual who makes a significant contribution in the realm of sports. This year it's Dr. Julius Erving of the Philadelphia Seventy-Sixers and this powerhouse advertisement makes the announcement to the people. Wanamaker's advertising has a way of overwhelming the eye, the emotions, the intellect. Plus sheer joy. What more can advertising do?

The great Higbee bicycle race includes all kinds of trikes and bikes and anybody, with wheels, big wheels or little, can participate. From tot class riding 50 yards to ABLA members riding 30 miles. It's fun and games sponsored by Higbee's. With loads of prizes donated by notable resources. This is one more way Higbee's says, ''more than a store.''

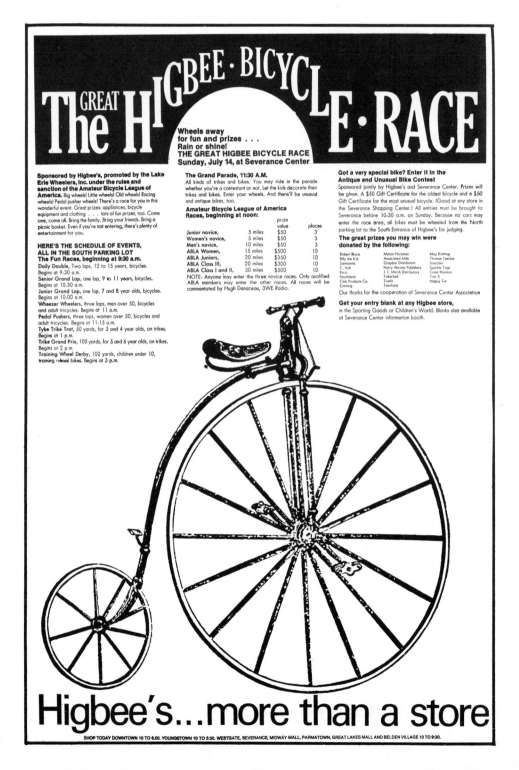

The store belongs to the people. Any store anywhere needs to associate itself with the things that people associate with. In Philadelphia the Orchestra is very much a people-thing, the pride and joy of young and old, rich and poor. John Wanamaker knows this, and has taken careful steps to tie in with the life of the Orchestra. This page of advertising, listing all concerts of the season, was tacked up in many homes, you can be sure of that. And that one line of small type at the bottom, announcing a fashion show at the Academy of Music, meant a sold-out house.

Came January 1970...a new decade...and Joseph Magnin puts
together the most significant advertisement in ten years...a review
of the sixties "drawn from JM fashion archives." Each fashion idea
is shown as it was advertised in the newspapers at the time.
A beautiful job.

It isn't often that a store stands up before the people and makes an honest-to-goodness resolution. Lazarus not only does it but you may be sure the store will live up to its promises. It's an inspiring advertisement featuring a great photograph.

349

"Hope...what a wonderful name for a brand, spanking new year—and for the nation embarking on its third century..." John Wanamaker pays this salute to hope, the new year, the new century, the new administration, in a beautifully organized piece of copy that sells Wanamaker in all its glory. All done up in a great layout. This is an exciting and thoughtful start into the new year.

What a wonderful name for a brand, spanking new year—and for the nation, embarking on its third century and a new administration. For the individual, hope is the optimism between desire and realization. This year, as always, our hope is that your John Wanamaker store, wherever it is, will continue to be important to your lifestyle. And that you will come soon and often to Philadelphia, Wynnewood, Wilmington, Springfield Mall, King of Prussia, Deptford Mall, Moorestown Mall, Northeast, Oxford Valley Mall, Jenkintown, Harrisburg, Reading, and Westchester—and before long to Montgomery Mall and Allentown. (Sometimes hope has very large dimensions!) Happy New Year. John Wanamaker

We must not let the new year get a day older without showing you the fabulous Neiman-Marcus 1969 calendar. Back then readers could write to N-M's advertising department for a full-size copy of this calendar printed in color. The demand for calendars exceeded expectations.

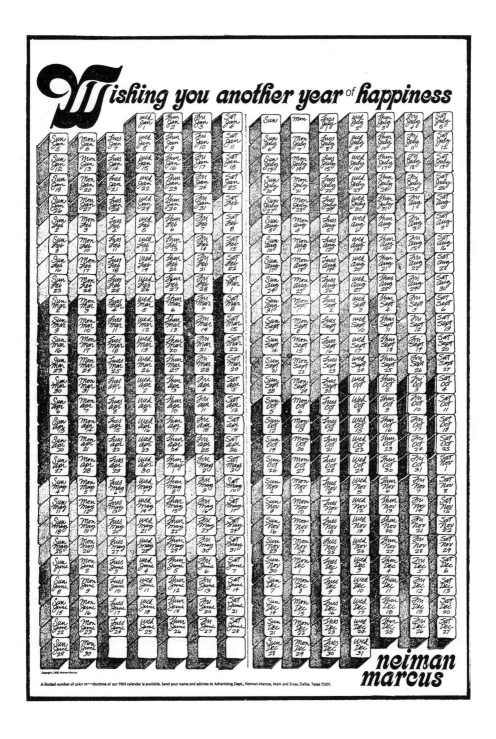

351

On Monday, February 1, "helpful Horne's" ran this full-page to help its Pittsburgh readers through the pitfalls of the month. Besides the usual ice and snow, there was the change in George Washington's Birthday, which had been on the 11th, then the 22nd, and this year was on the 15th. A Horne's writer researched other important February dates, as well, to prepare everyone for Groundhog's Day, Candlemas, The Abe-Val-George holiday weekend, Ash Wednesday...and for the possibilities of 2/27/72 and a February 29 and 30. The ad not only brought smiles to its readers...it is said to have caused Horne's calendar business to skyrocket.

After you've chosen a gift at Rich's for your Valentine (or Valentines...we'll never tell), use this page for gift wrap. Waste not, want not...even in love!

RICH'S

There are 110 hearts here, beautifully sketched and printed in brilliant red. It is Rich's loving love letter to everybody. But it is more. Down below we read, "after you've chosen a gift at Rich's for your Valentine (or Valentines...we'll never tell) use this page for gift wrap. Waste not, want not...even in love." What a beautiful idea! What a beautiful ad.

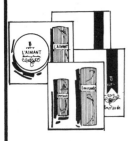

Where does it say "Just give her candy"?

You've gotta have a card,
maybe a serious one to tell her how you really feel . . .
but, don't you love the way she laughs? . . .
maybe a funny one . . . but, sometimes she
takes the funny ones seriously. Okay, the funny one first,
then the serious one! Candy and a card,
maybe some boxed silk roses? (4.00-5.00)
Now, for something nice. How
about a fragrance . . . What's her favorite?
Nina Ricci? Shalimar? Chanel? Can't remember, right?
Well, get her something new . . . She'll love it.
Well, how about something really sexy
and feminine . . . you know, a
nightgown or something. No, not flannel pajamas . . .
I know, you said she liked them . . . but, you
need to give her something frilly . . . extra special.
Like a Lucy Ann gown and robe set in fluffy nylon . . .
you know the type that makes her look beautiful.
Lots of white lace (145.00) or maybe the orchid print (178.00)
If you get her that, there's going to be no doubt
how much you love her. What? I know they're
not red, but, who cares, they're gorgeous! Hey, that's a lot.
maybe we should put back the candy?
No, you're right, she's worth it . . . any way, we're
going to eat most of the candy
ourselves, right?

Hemphill-Wells

You don't buy a man heart shaped candy for Valentine's Day.

Remember his macho image . . .
he'll never be able to tell the guys at work what
you got him! Then, again, if you
don't, he'll eat all the nut chewies out of yours . . . okay,
candy, but not heart shaped . . . not pink anyway!
(Russell Stovers Heart Boxed Candies 2.25-42.50)
Well, if you're giving him the pink heart-shaped candy,
you've got to give him something macho . . .
What? . . . no, not a sledgehammer, real funny!
Have you seen those jockey shorts with hearts
all over them? (7.50) . . . Can you
imagine him showing up in the locker room in those?
What a hoot! . . . Mr. Macho! Get 'em.
Wait . . . we've got to get serious . . . I mean pink
candy and dumb shorts are okay . . . but he's
going to think you don't love him. How
about the new knit shirts by Chaps? (Chaps by Ralph
Lauren 22.50-23.50) They're in red 'n white stripes and
solid red . . . real valentiny! Have you ever seen
a picture of Ralph Lauren? He's gorgeous . . . grey hair . . .
mmmmm. What? Oh, yes, well we could get some John
Weitz casual slacks to go with them (25.00).
They're in red or white too. Now that's taken care of . . .
we got everything at Hemphills . . . now what do you
want to do? Wait, before we leave, I want to show
you the cutest dress I saw yesterday in juniors . . .

Hemphill-Wells

Valentine's Day may be long gone but this kind of thing should not go unnoticed. Hemphill-Wells divides the space equally, one half for men only, one half for women only. Each half is a friendly, chatty, whimsical conversation with a man, with a woman (Purring—like telephone conversations. "Have you seen a picture of Ralph Lauren? He's gorgeous . . . gray hair . . . mmmmm . . .") and each is a sales pitch offering ideas and items. Dear Hemphill-Wells, you've made the world a little happier.

Left:
How do you make cosmetics exciting? February 14 is a good excuse for May Co.! The copy is a joy to read and the provocative gal wears a red heart on her shoulder. It's an ad to enjoy.

355

Left:
Without doubt this was the best seen, most talked about, and best remembered ad to appear in Atlanta that week. And real red lips...wow... those pretty Georgia girls! Take note of the thoughtful bottom line: "Newspaper gift wrap is all the rage...be a love and recycle this page!" Dear Rich's: you've made Valentine's Day a happy time to remember.

Below:
Bonwit Teller was a standout in the New York Times with a Valentine's series that showcased gift merchandise worn by nostalgic sketches of movie stars from other decades. We love the sentimental feeling of it all!

*Somewhere
deep under that bristling, spiny
exterior there's got to be a big-hearted
softie! We know this to be true of artichokes
and institutions and individuals.
In our era of chaos and confusing facts,
we sometimes forget that patience and
persistence usually manage to get to the
heart of matters. For our part,
more than ever before, John Wanamaker
is prepared to show you the
beauty and tenderness inside
its stone walls, and we
want to help you express your
Valentine's Day sentiment in the ways
you know best. John Wanamaker.
Ten stores that love you.*

A very realistic Valentine, this! JW compares itself to an artichoke with
a bristling, spiny exterior and a soft heart underneath. The ad was in
beautiful four-color art with green artichoke and red heart.

Peace

hope

brotherhood

joy.

Celebrate

them all today

in love.

Lord & Taylor, April 1979

Somebody at Lord & Taylor has an enormous grasp of human understanding and the power of words to express it. Retailers are often accused of commercialism and disregard for people. It is good to know that some in this business can and do transcend, can and do relate, can and do declare themselves. This advertisement, with emphasis on love, joy, and brotherhood, is universal.

Easter's Child is a Princess
From Polly Flinders

You call her Princess. And she's
clever enough to find a pea under
a pile of mattresses; caring
enough to rescue sparrows who
can't fly, puppies who need
a home and turtles she
builds castles for on her
window sill because she
says "He looked lonesome."
She's a Princess all right
and Dayton's knows how
beautiful little Princesses
should look. Polly Flinders does
too, so she designed these hand-smocked
dresses in Dacron® polyester that's easy to care
for and nary shows a wrinkle. They are for
all the little Princesses all over the world,
like yours.

Sheer mint hand-smocked dresses with
lantern sleeves, lace trim, fully lined skirt.
Toddlers' 2-4, $13. 4-6X, $15.

Sheer pink with angel sleeves and eyelet
"mock" apron. Hand-smocked bodice and
fully lined skirt. 4-6X, $15.

Sheer sleeveless lavender hand-smocked
dress, fully lined skirt, lace trim on
neck and armholes. Toddlers' 2-4, $13;
4-6X, $15.

Other styles $9-$16. Toddlers' and Girls' 4-6X
Departments. Call 339-0112.

Dayton's

®Registered, E.I. DuPont de Nemours Co.

Dayton's has brought joy to many this Easter with a children's wear series of extraordinary charm. Both art and copy radiate a warmth that's all too rare in advertising these days.

"Muffin, the cow, is going to have a calf" becomes a name-it contest in Higbee's Easter Barnyard. In Cleveland Easter wouldn't be Easter without Higbee's Barnyard. Staged every year, with a new twist, this becomes an important link between the store and the citizens. With all its headaches and problems events like this set a great store apart in the hearts and minds of the people who count most—the customers.
It's a super ad.

Let it not be said that we failed to note the nicest Mother's Day idea,
and the nicest advertisement on the subject. Dear Higbee's—you've
won all our hearts. And your readers, too.

the winners of the mother's day coloring contest

Thank you all for your enthusiastic response to our special contest. With so many colorful and imaginative pictures entered it was very difficult to choose. But to us you're all winners with first prize monis! We are showing portions of the winning drawings.

Maryann Merlo, age 8
Colonia (Woodbridge Center)

Jennifer Mish, age 9
Basking Ridge (Westfield)

Gregory Carter, age 5
Verona (Montclair)

Amy Leban, age 8
South Orange (Livingston Mall)

Mark Perrin, age 6
Montclair (Newark)

Garrett A. Dicks, age 6
Denville (Rockaway)

Many stores do a "make-a-drawing-of-Mother" contest for Mother's Day, and hundreds of entries come pouring in. But, after it's all over, who sees them? They may be displayed in the store somewhere but we never publish the winners. Hahne's customers were given a special treat with this ad. Six of their fascinating prize winners were published.

Children's art is true art. It has no precedent, no boundary. Always wonderful to see. The store that encourages it wins mucho brownie-points with parents. And what a joy to see the results in the paper!

Hahne's contest turned up wonderous stuff. Our favorite: Amy Leban's masterpiece—darling mother, all smiles, with two charming cats. And Gregory Carter's impish mother's earrings.

Our $20 dresses will take
Mom a lot more places
than a $20 tank of gas

Think about it. For $20, Mom will get a lot more
mileage out of one of these terrific little T-shirt knits
than she'll ever get from her car. Styled with enough
pep to race through the busiest days. And with a few
added options, even take her out to dinner. Here, in
super-charged colors: the V-neck classic with tie belt;
the deep V neck wrap with swingy side slit skirt and
the short sleeved V-neck. S-M-L. All of cool cotton/
polyester. Each a mere $20. In Miss Detroiter Dresses.

hudson's

Open Monday through Saturday: Northland, Eastland, Pontiac, Westland, Oakland, Southland and Twelve Oaks 9:30 till 9;
Lakeside, Fairlane and Ann Arbor 9:30 till 9:30; Flint 10 till 9:30; Downtown open 9:30 till 5:45

Hudson's says, "think about it." Yes, we all should. This headline is for today,
makes news, and gives the reader quite a jolt. Think how much more "hard sell"
is wrapped up in this ad than in any of the sales, off-price, and big bargain
headlines you've seen lately. Merchandise selling at regular price is the key to
profit. When you can make copy prove value you've got it. And Hudson's does!

364

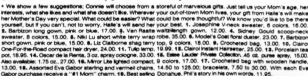

Halle's does indeed go the distance with this ad, provides service beyond the usual call of duty and even sends Mom a letter. It's a great idea. We see Connie Farkas here, doing her thing on the telephone. We also see a conglomeration of merchandise that staggers the mind. Fortunately an outline drawing of the 19 items helps a little to make ordering-by-phone a possibility. But the idea is good, the copy is good, and maybe—hidden in here—is a thought for shopping in this don't-let's-drive era.

365

The Monday before Mother's Day, Rich's ran this delightful red-spot color institutional with line after line of the same message: "Our heart belongs to Mom". The handwritten copy with its wavy lines, the "Mom" symbol with a red heart for each "O", it all makes a memorable statement. And Rich's didn't leave a thing to chance. The May 10th date is set in type at the bottom of the page.

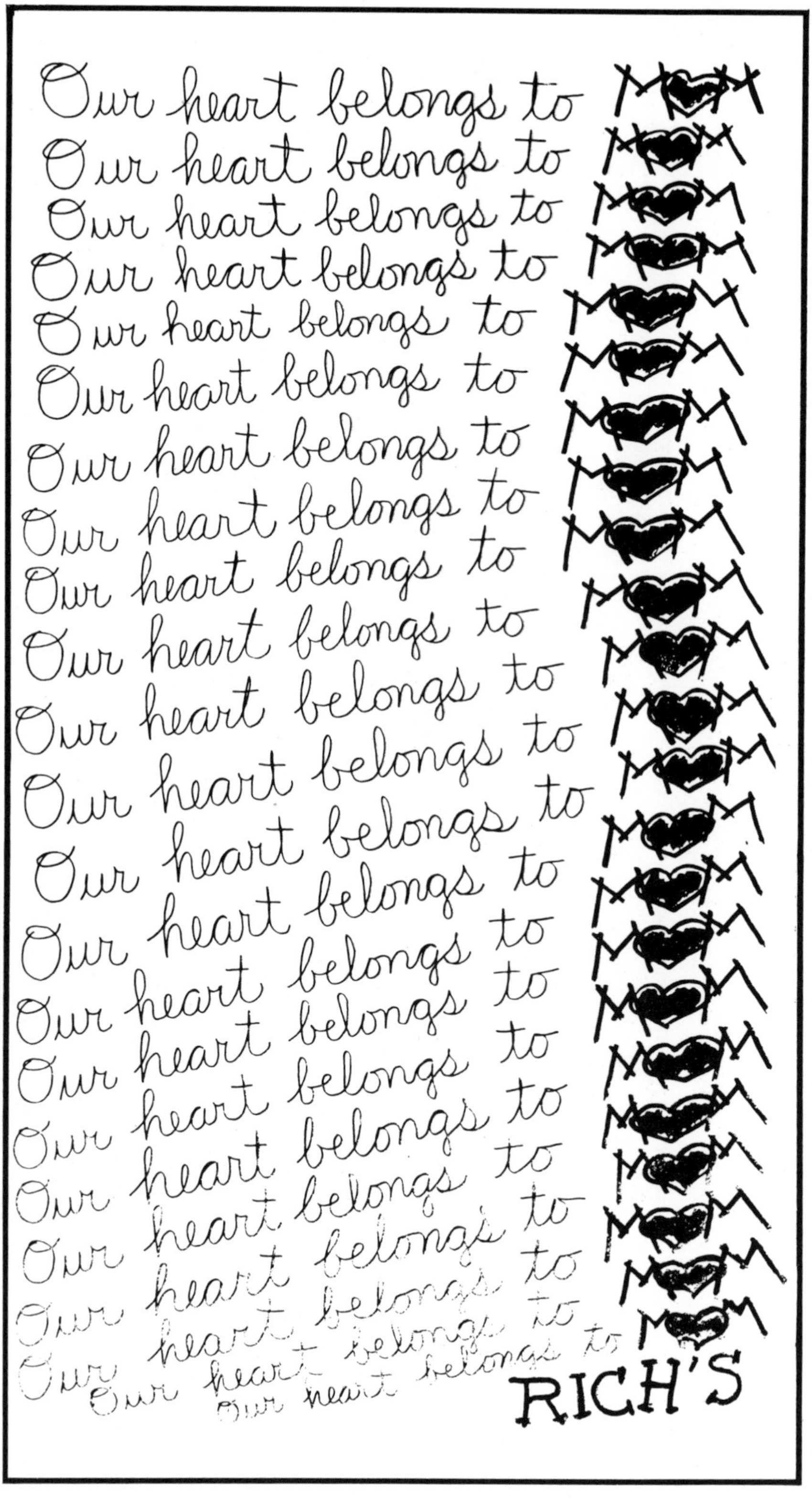

Our heart belongs to
Our heart belongs to
Our heart belongs to
Our heart belongs to
Our heart belongs to
Our heart belongs to
Our heart belongs to
Our heart belongs to
Our heart belongs to
Our heart belongs to
Our heart belongs to
Our heart belongs to
Our heart belongs to
Our heart belongs to
Our heart belongs to
Our heart belongs to
Our heart belongs to
Our heart belongs to
Our heart belongs to
Our heart belongs to
Our heart belongs to
Our heart belongs to

RICH'S

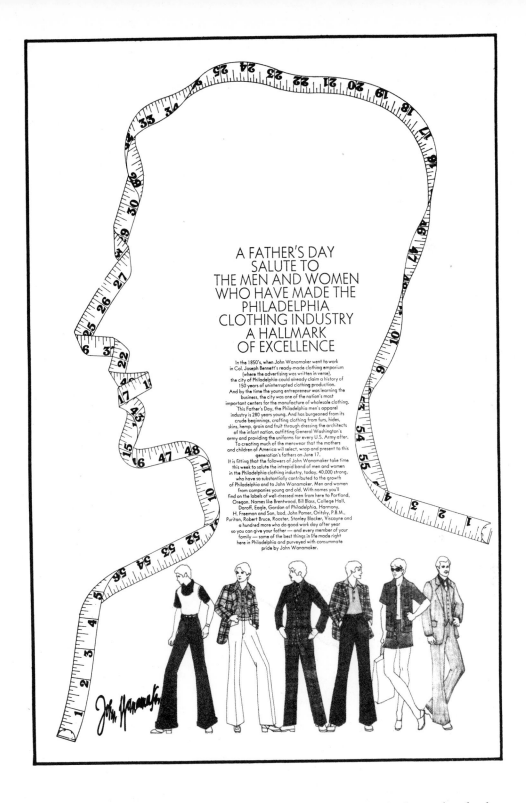

John Wanamaker salutes the men and women (40,000 strong) who are involved with Philadelphia's own menswear industry that is "280 years young." This is one of several striking layouts on this provocative theme. To complete the picture Wanamaker's windows this week tied in with the same salute.

How do you measure the value of an advertisement? How do you measure return on investment? If dozens of customers call in and request proofs, to frame, to tack up in homes, you know that ad is of priceless value. Such a reaction is indicative of another factor—the people's attitude toward their country. What a privilege it is to arouse that feeling! What an honor! The Denver deserves special commendation for this great July 4th advertisement.

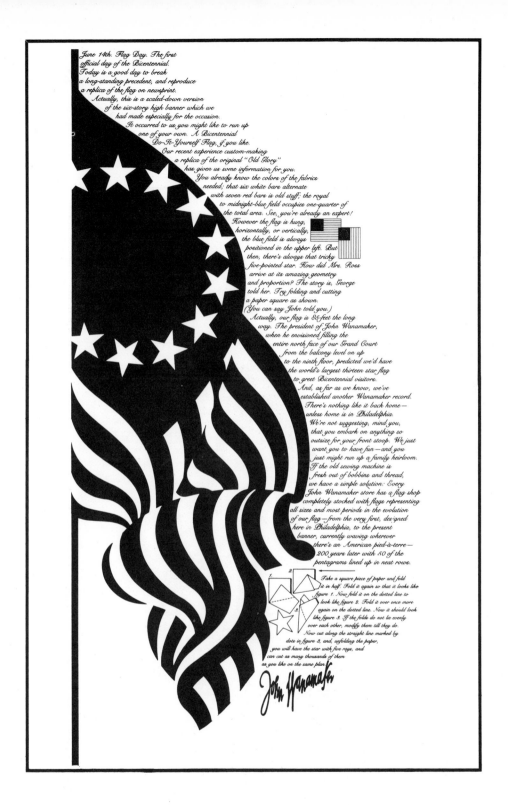

For Flag Day, the first official day of the bicentennial, Wanamaker's unfurls its red-white-and-blue art of the 13 star flag. Copy has a lot to tell the reader: how George gave Betsy the pattern for the star, how perhaps the largest 13-star flag in the world hangs in the Grand Court, how the flag shop is stocked with all sizes and most periods of our flag.

Lansons, Fort Lauderdale, gets women to trade up to major Christmas purchases with this page. And it does it with the promise of service. ''While your husband is at work, bring us his measurements—neck, sleeve length, waist and pants length. Then, we'll pick him out some Christmas goodies that'll knock his eyes out....'' The humor in the copy and art encourage us to read every word.

Does your husband deserve a belt?

Take it from us, ladies.

A belt under the Christmas tree isn't going to get you any whoopies. Same thing for pajamas, robes and after shave lotion. Not to mention flashlights, shotgun shells and fishing line.

You want whoopies, you got to do a sneaky thing.

While your husband is at work, bring us his measurements—neck, sleeve length, waist and pants length. Then, we'll pick him out some Christmas goodies that'll knock his eyes out.

Maybe a double-knit suit. Or a sport jacket. Or a pair of slacks. And maybe a few shirts and ties thrown in to spice things up. You want whoopies this Christmas? Trust us.

Lansons

Christmas is just around the corner, and so is Lansons.

What you see here is the start of Hudson's Christmas package...a quilt, especially commissioned and on view at the store, and duplicated not only for this introductory ad but for the store's Christmas shopping bags, place mats, catalogue covers, and store decor. A complete, fabulous package.

HUDSON'S IS
THE CHRISTMAS STORE

Quilting, the art of the ancestral home, had its birth in America with the early settlers. Long winter's nights were spent by the fire, where pioneer women pieced together quilts you see in museums today. Now, during our Bicentennial celebration, Hudson's revives the charm of the Christmas quilt and sets the stage for an early-American Christmas with all the trimmings.

The quilt was commissioned especially for Hudson's holiday season, 1975. See it in our central Woodward Avenue window, Downtown. The quilt motif is available as wrapping in Gift Wrap Service, place mats in the Table Top Shop and matching ornaments in our Trim-A-Tree Shop. Christmas. A good, old-fashioned feeling...starting today at Hudson's.

There's a store in Pittsburgh that pleases even Scrooge-like Christmas shoppers. JOSEPH HORNE CO.

Even Scrooge! With this fabulous portrait, Horne's says they have everything for Christmas.

We greet a friend a second year—the old boy (bloke!) himself and this time he's
making pointed remarks about Pittsburgh's "light-up", the traditional
Christmas event that won't take place this year because of the energy shortage.
Bringing Dickens up to date as only Horne's can do it.

Robert Merrill and six famous choral groups joined in an evening of song at Herald Square. The very idea gives a lift to the spirit. Let's hope this sense of joy somehow extends into the new year. Macy's has taken leadership in these affairs in New York. The opportunities for involvement are everywhere and for all seasons of the year. What can happen in your community in the months ahead?

tonight, join Robert Merrill, and go out to meet Christmas with a song

Robert Merrill, opera and TV star; Elly Stone, and a cast of thousands will meet you for Macy's Christmas Carol Sing-Along. At Herald Square, 8 p.m., Sunday.

You'll be there, red-cheeked and merry, part of an immense New York family, lifting your voice in the joy of the season. You'll be there with love and warmth filling your heart. You'll be caught by the sweeping spotlights that will turn the night bright as noon in Herald Square, one of the most history-packed sites in New York. Where the sense of New York Christmas, past and present, is almost tangible. You'll be part of a simply sensational evening that will lead you on straight to Christmas.

Star quality! Join your voices with all these famous choral groups. On three giant stages that will turn Herald Square into a pine tree-forested arena:

St. Patrick's Cathedral Choir
The Voices of St. Matthew's Baptist Church
The Boys' Choir of Harlem
V.I.P. Chorale
The Interfaith Neighbors Singers of Yorkville
The New Amsterdam Singers

We'll have song sheets for you—handed out by the Girl Scouts of Greater New York and all these volunteer Macy employee organizations: Our Lady of Fatima Club, St. George Association, Star of David Club, Retirees Tuesday Club.

Come sing "Jingle Bells" with us. And "Rudolph" and "Deck the Halls," and "Star of Wonder" and "Silent Night" and all the beautiful tunes that make the holiday what it is. Be part of it all: Herald Square—New York—Christmas—Macy's, a continuing romance. Tonight!

macy's
has so much to give

A tip of the hat to the Cleveland Newspaper Publishers' Association for recognizing a serious retail problem and doing something about it. This is an outstanding advertisement in concept, copy, layout, art, typography, and printing in two colors.

Why do Horne ads have so much gingerbread?

Because Horne's is full of ginger. All the holiday delights, gifts, ornaments, wrappings, confections, finery, frippery, bijouterie. Even gingerbread.

Left:

This is a fabulous happening. Who can resist stopping here, looking at every inch of it, and smiling over the headline? A reminder to us all that a great store must always be the talked-about store, must have the guts to do the unusual.

Below:

Higbee's "Christmas in the Country" warms the hearts of readers, recalling "simpler days bright with small pleasures." The four-color primitive announces the enchanted Grandma Moses Land with its mechanized scenes in the downtown store's tenth floor auditorium. Santa was there, too. And a special puppet show, starring Mervin the Mouse.

come with us to
Grandma Moses Land
for a wonderful
old fashioned
Christmas
in the
Country

Wander down Yesteryear Lane through simpler days bright with small pleasures . . . here in enchanted Grandma Moses Land, where her best-loved paintings have expanded in life-like three dimensions. There's Home for Thanksgiving, with the table all set. And the Quilting Bee and First Skating. Go over the bridge to the snowy woods. Out for Christmas Trees. Ah, what fun that was in those long-ago days! Wander through the old covered bridge where you'll have a glimpse of The Lone Traveler. And ahead are the cathedral-like hills of White Christmas and the cheery living room of Home for Christmas—just as Grandma Moses painted it.

It's all on our Tenth Floor Downtown. And naturally, Santa is there, too, waiting to give a fine coloring book to his little friends and to pose with them for Santa-Photos.

Over in the Lounge the George Latshaw Puppets will be doing shows every hour on the half hour . . . and you'll meet Mervin the Mischievous Mouse and his friend Blue Jay. Between times there's a truly inspiring 30-minute film about Grandma Moses, narrated by Archibald MacLeish.

The Twigbee Shop is open for young business. And there's Aunt Em's Kitchen. And Wallie Spatz the Silhouette Lady. And Bruce the Talking Spruce. In short, everybody's here for Christmas! You come, too!

Higbee's

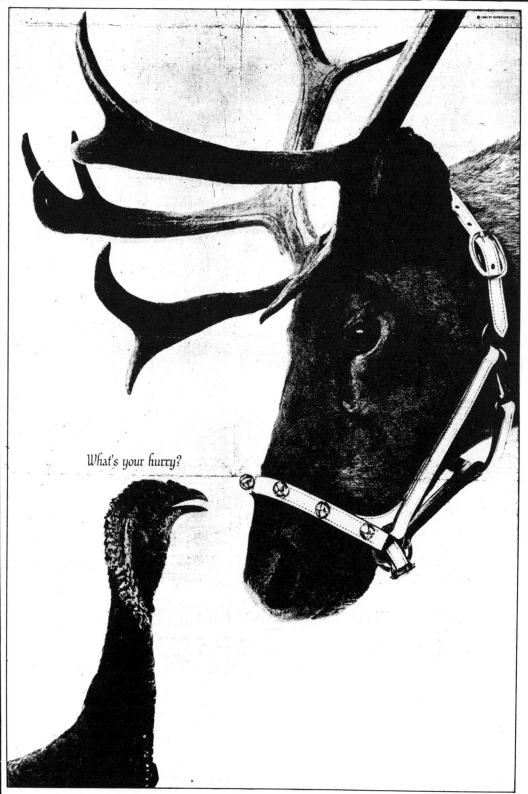

What's your hurry?

Below:

In this Christmas world of make believe it seems entirely fitting and proper to find Little Orphan Annie, and her famous dog, Sandy, talking about Santa and his arrival at the wharf behind Horne's. It's a joyous ad. Warf! Warf!

Left:
Christmas comes horning in before
the turkey has a chance.
Ohrbach's uses the early gift buying theme
to put across a thoughtful
store message.

The Christmas shirt that rings true. . .and gets remembered. Of course, a $40,000 Mercedes tops his Christmas list but he is willing to settle for one of the "affordable luxuries" Carson's says it specializes in. The $26 Halston shirt comes with a complimentary half-ounce of Halston fragrance for men, and we're sure that lots of Chicago men are now driving around in their Halston shirts. A memorable ad.

There are Antiques that sparkle in silver and gold

And rare Books to be treasured by both the young and old.

There's the Cozy Cloud Cottage where Santa keeps house,

And occasionally is visited by a friendly Fieldmouse.

There's Marshall Field's Delivery service right to your door,

And Electronic games that automatically keep score.

And what are the treats that everyone savors?

What else but Field's Famous Frango's® in fanciful flavors.

And when it comes to the gourmet we've filled every nook

In the Galley on nine with things for the cook.

And there's the H. Simmons Shop for every man's pipe dream,

And the Crystal Palace on Three serving up old fashioned Ice cream.

There's J.R.'s on Four, a place where juniors can shop,

And our own candy Kitchens where the sweets are non-stop.

And what does Marshall Field's have for the art-lover's pleasure?

Why Lithographs, Limoge porcelains, and Lladros to treasure.

And certainly Freddie Fieldmouse and Uncle Mistletoe

Are as much a part of our Christmas as the people of Chicago.

And Marshall Field's knows how to keep folks in stitches,

With Needlepoint, patchwork, and other handmade riches.

And certainly a sight that is most divine,

Is the annual display of Ornaments in the Christmas Court on Nine.

And if you're looking for gifts with a personal touch,

Choose beautifully engraved silver, and Pewter and such.

So when it comes to shopping, Marshall Field's ends your Quest,

With gifts from a selection that's better than the Rest.

Find Surprises for aunts & uncles & little girls & boys,

Wrap up the finest gifts in clothes, home accessories and Toys.

And when the shopping's all done, dine Underneath the great tree

Then take the little ones to Visit Santa, it's a Wondrous sight to see

And when your busy day is over, it's certain you'll agree,

Marshall Field's is an Xtra special place, where You'll find everything from A to Z!

Marshall Field's & Christmas

SOMETIMES I WISH I COULD BE
A SINGLE TREE BY THE SEA
BEDECKED IN CHRISTMAS FINERY...
THE SKY WOULD SMILE DOWN AT ME,
SOFT BREEZES WOULD KEEP ME COMPANY.
AND A MAGICAL STAR
WOULD BE THERE TO SAY
COME SHARE IN THE JOY
OF A LONG AGO DAY...
AND I WOULD BECOME A MAGIC TREE
FOR ALL THE WORLD TO SEE...
WHAT A WONDER THAT WOULD BE.

Left:

J. Bryons' "single tree by the sea" institutional ran Christmas Day, giving all of Miami a moment of magic. There was the beautiful illustration of the tree topped by a star fish and standing on a sandy beach right by the water. And the copy, a poem really. A Christmas message to remember.

Below:

From New York to Toronto requires a mere 55 minutes flying time; as this page by Eaton's indicates. This ingenious invitation to do your Christmas shopping in Toronto startled New Yorkers out of their complacency when they saw it smack in the middle of their favorite morning Times.

Next weekend, fly up north to Santa's store. Where your dollar is worth more than Santa's. Ho ho ho (sigh)

On Thanksgiving Day morning, CBS will broadcast the greatest Santa Claus Parade in the whole world. (Channel 2.)

The Eaton's Santa Claus Parade (which actually took place a few days ago) happens each year in Toronto. And has for the last 73 years.

Just 55 minutes from LaGuardia.

And each year, that parade comes to its end at the front door of Eaton's, in downtown Toronto. Santa's store.

One of the greatest department stores in the world.

You could watch the parade on CBS TV Thursday morning.

And by Thursday afternoon, after hopping an American Airlines flight to Toronto, you could spend the rest of the day actually shopping the great store that annually stages the original, ultimate Santa Claus Parade!

Here's what's in it for you.

Your U.S. dollars are worth $1.09* when you spend them in Canada.

Toronto is already basking in its reputation as perhaps the brightest, cleanest, safest, happiest big city on this continent.

But if you need another excuse to come spend a weekend of shopping, dining, exploring and theatre-going with us, it's right there in your wallet.

You see, right now our Canadian dollar isn't looking quite as rosy as our reputation.

So you can exchange your American buck for a buck-nine (or thereabouts) in Canadian funds.

In other words, $100 American buys you about $109 worth of food and drink, fun and accommodation in Toronto.

And that's before you even start Christmas shopping at Eaton's.

The things that Americans love to buy in Toronto now cost less than ever.

The new Toronto Eaton Centre, which houses Eaton's million square foot downtown store and 150 other fine merchants all under one glass-domed roof, is architecturally utterly dazzling.

The merchandise inside, the extraordinary variety and selection of leather and bone china and woollens and cashmeres and furs which traditionally delight Americans, is

now yours at about 10% less than just a few months ago.

And most of the original works by Canada's finest artists and craftsmen you'll find in and around our store are duty-free for home-bound Americans.

Sound good so far?

Once you decide to come it's easy sledding from there.

To make it easy for you to accept our invitation to Toronto, we've lined up some mutual friends to smooth your way.

American Airlines New York ticket office [(212) 661-4242] will look after your air arrangements. (It's not a long weekend in Canada, so there should be lots of seats available.)

The same airline, or your own travel agent, will arrange a fine Toronto hotel for you.

Our Canadian Government Office of Tourism in New York (in the Exxon Building, 1251 Avenue of the Americas, [(212) 757-4918] will give you all the facts and booklets about what's to see and do in Toronto at large. For free.

Once here, our Eaton's Ticket Office (right in our store) will arrange for theatre, concert or sports tickets.

You can get your free Eaton's store directory and U.S. customs regulations information at the Information Desk on Eaton's main floor.

And Eaton Trust, (right beside our main store entrance) will change those greenbacks into Canadian currency any time between 9:30 am and 9:00 pm on Thursday, Friday *and* Saturday.

Which, coincidentally, are the same hours that Eaton's is open and eager to help you fill your Christmas shopping Santa Sack Thanksgiving Weekend, and every weekend between now and Christmas.

Eaton's is Santa's Store.

EATON'S
TORONTO EATON CENTRE
Dundas and Yonge Streets, Toronto, Ontario.

*Currency exchange rate as of Nov. 10, 1977

Angela and Harold are talking out the timeless problems of shopping for Christmas. "Tempus fugit, Harold", is a reminder for all Joseph Horne customers that shopping time is short. This ingenious bed quilt carries that message, too, and who can fail to stop here? And see? And read? And remember?

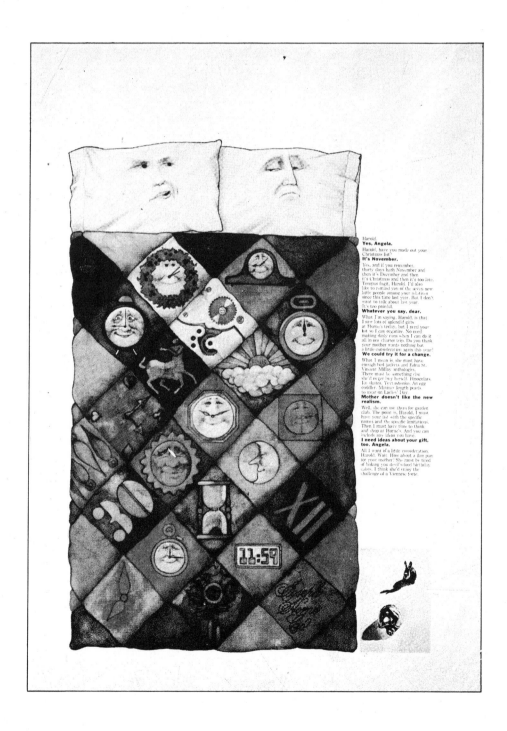

Harold.
Yes, Angela.
Harold, have you made out your Christmas list?
It's November.

Yes, and if you remember, thirty days hath November and then it's December and then it's Christmas and then it's too late. Tempus fugit, Harold. I'd also like to remind you of the seven new little people among your relatives since this time last year. But I don't want to talk about last year. It's too painful.
Whatever you say, dear.

What I'm saying, Harold, is that I saw lots of splendid gifts at Horne's today, but I need your list so I can organize. No need making daily runs when I can do it all in one charter trip. Do you think your mother wants nothing but a little consideration again this year?
We could try it for a change.

What I mean is, she must have enough bed jackets and Edna St. Vincent Millay anthologies. There must be something else she'd never buy herself. Binoculars, ice skates, Yevtushenko. An egg coddler. Matmec length pearls to wear on Ladies' Day.
Mother doesn't like the new realism.

Well, she can use them for garden club. The point is, Harold, I must have your list with the specific names and the specific limitations. Then I must have time to think and shop at Horne's. And you can include any ideas you have.
I need ideas about your gift, too, Angela.

All I want is a little consideration, Harold. Wait. How about a flip pen for your mother? She must be tired of baking you devil's-food birthday cakes. I think she'd enjoy the challenge of a Vienna torte.

To Joseph Magnin, their new dreamy gift boxes belong in show biz, and
they do. No wonder they are seen all over the west, a considerable
contribution to the glamour and color of California.

LOOK WHO'S GAINING ON YOU

Traveling like lightning. And before you know it . . . panicsville! Lest the panic be upon you, shop your favorite stores. Now. And get those gifts going to their final destination. Before the crowds gather. Some things have a way of sneaking up on you. If you let them.

The Columbus Dispatch

A bow to the Columbus Dispatch. This newspaper, starting the second week of November, gave the readers several reminders that Christmas was coming. "Traveling like lightning, and before you know it—panicsville."

Newspapers everywhere might take note of this performance by the Columbus Dispatch. This may be service beyond the call of duty but it is for the benefit, not only of the retail advertisers, but the people of the community as well.

"For the best Christmas under the sun" you can count on the May
Company in Los Angeles. "We're ready," the store says,
with all that's right and good. Of course there is Santa, California
style, complete with sun glasses and palm trees.
A sure-fire eye-stopper.

windows

_ a Christmas homecoming

Won't you join us today in our

New York love affair.

Come home to Christmas

at Lord & Taylor

—the happiest

journey of the year

Fifth Avenue at 39th Street

Lord & Taylor's Christmas window unveiling is more than a tradition. The people who line up on Fifth Avenue (families!) are living testimonials that Christmas is alive and well. It is only fitting and proper that this special gift which Lord & Taylor gives to New York should be celebrated and editorialized. Which it was!

Right:

Good old Santa. He's the star performer this week. Pizitz fills the page with his familiar face.

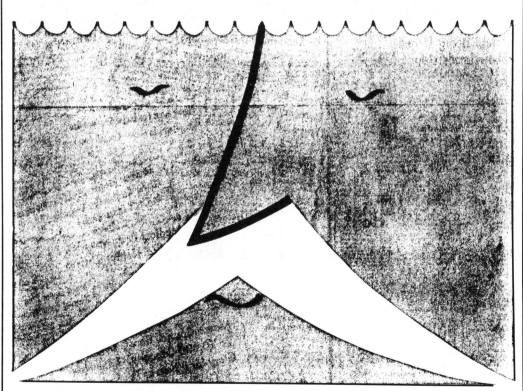

he was last seen entering his favorite store! the famous brand leader! serving Alabama in four locations! tomorrow, he will be on the sixth floor downtown with a gift for the kiddies! after your visit—browse around! see why we have been Santa's best friend for 65 Christmases! and be sure to see Santa's Enchanted Forest—it's a treat the kiddies shouldn't miss!

FALL STARTS AT JOSEPH MAGNIN WITH THE BEAUTIFULLY SEASONED SHANNON RODGERS FOR JERRY SILVERMAN COLLECTION. WON'T YOU JOIN US FOR AN INFORMAL PRESENTATION IN THE JM DESIGNERS' ROOM 11:00 TO 4:00, MONDAY AND TUESDAY, STOCKTON & O'FARRELL, SAN FRANCISCO AND WEDNESDAY, STANFORD SHOPPING CENTER. MR. JERRY UCHIN OF JERRY SILVERMAN WILL WELCOME YOU.

How else would you say it? Joseph Magnin uses one big, beautiful photo of bare trees to broadcast the fashion message: ''Fall starts at Joseph Magnin...'' This is the new communication and Magnin's tells it like it is.

Who is the early bird with fashion in Philadelphia? John Wanamaker indisputably occupies that position with advertising like this. An eloquent use of white space!

There is never just one look for a new fashion season. If anything, the presentations get more complex, with a mixed bag of tailoreds and frillies, pants and skirts, shorts and longs. How can a store explain it all and still keep the reader's interest? Take a look at the job M.M. Cohn did in a Sunday, February 1, ad in the Memphis Commercial Appeal. The retailer went for the single idea of spring, the appeal of a robin in the snow and a song of a headline: "How can we have spring fever, when it isn't even spring." Below the red-breasted robin, seven sketches from spring's mixed bag. Each look is described in the copy. The reader will study the new pants, the dropped-torso dress, the tunics. But what she will remember most of all will be that robin in the snow, a sign that M.M. Cohn was there first with the news of spring.

When spring comes Joseph Horne does something about it. Anybody walking into the store gets a lift of spirit and that spirit is everywhere. Especially in merchandise and how it is put on display. To top it off the advertising department does a beautiful job reflecting the spirit in the newspaper. Who can resist?

ll winter long, the woodland ferns stay fast asleep under a cover of frost and snow. Then the alarm goes off. And, one by one, the curly, sleepy fiddleheads begin to stir. They rise and take a look outside. They stretch. They slip out of their flannel nightgowns. And fling open their fresh green fronds to welcome spring. Whee.

Come. See. Something's stirring at Joseph Horne Co.

CHAPTER IX

SALES

This fall, a snappy Detroit Free Press writer got high-visibility editiorial pick-up in Knight-Ridder newspapers across the country with her article on the day she was "absolutely frozen in shock" at the retail price of a pair of unlined gray flannel slacks by Ralph Lauren. They were $378, not at just one store, but several in the metropolitan area. The popularity of her story shows the way the country is thinking about fashion these days.

"It's a change in lifestyle", analyzes Dan Cooper, principal in charge of retail consulting at Peat Marwick Mitchell, New York. "It used to be that customers would get points with their peers for buying designer. Now, people are getting points for buying off-price. With an almost 11 percent unemployment rate, if people can afford to buy a $400 pair of slacks they are almost embarrassed to do so".

"For department stores, selling at full price may well be the exception", says Cooper. "Retailers will have to justify selling merchandise at regular prices. It will have to be earned by broad assortments, in making themselves the headquarters store in specific categories", he reports.

Cooper and other retail observers warn that offering value for the money is different than simply offering low price. The word "sale" has lost some of its old magic. Now, when customers observe reputable stores offering sales of up to 75 percent off at the end of the season, they wonder if they haven't been bluffed when they part with their money at a 15 percent pre-season sale.

Today's sale ad must be much more than an eye-catching announcement. It must explain the quality of the merchandise. And it must offer good reasons why the customer should shop with the retailer. In these difficult times, it must restore some of the trust that has been lost.

After-Hours sales have been in the standard repertoire of many stores but none have given it the distinction and polish we see here by Dayton's. This page, printed in blue and black, is enormously attractive. The moon, half hidden in clouds, the well-lit windows and sign, the informative copy—it adds up to a superior advertisement.

396

Left:
The idea of paying back your bus fare is doubly significant in New Orleans because the bus system had not been in operation for months. This sentimental greeting to an "old friend" had to be the most talked-about advertisement the city had seen in a decade.

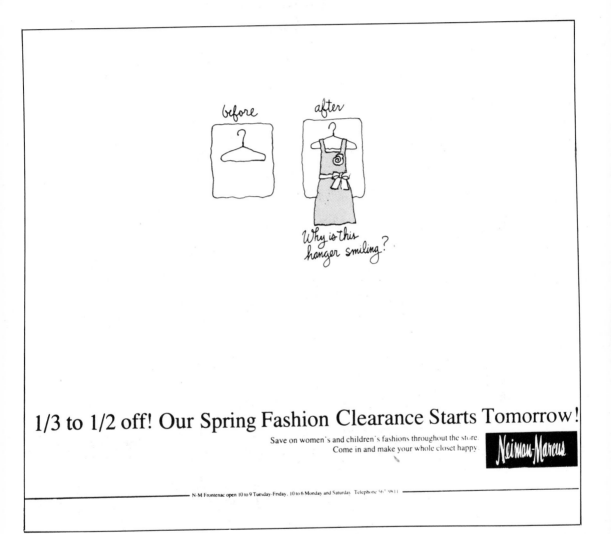

before   after

Why is this hanger smiling?

1/3 to 1/2 off! Our Spring Fashion Clearance Starts Tomorrow!

Save on women's and children's fashions throughout the store.
Come in and make your whole closet happy.

Neiman-Marcus

N-M Frontenac open 10 to 9 Tuesday-Friday, 10 to 6 Monday and Saturday. Telephone 567-9811

How do you announce a fashion clearance? You can't list items if they are few of a kind, and everybody in town blasts away with big type. Neiman-Marcus knows the benefits of doing it differently. This generous half page says it all—savings throughout the store and the urgency of Tomorrow. One caution before you rush off and do likewise—a store must have the terrific acceptance of N-M before doing things like this.

if

you've finally faced the fact that your wardrobe has had it, and you have to keep dimming the lights to make that old rug look better and there seems to be too much of "him" and too little shirt and you won't let your 12-year old leave the house because he has more patches than he has jeans and you always have to invite 4.8 people to dinner because those are all the place settings you have or you're dying to catch Cher in living color instead of old black and white and you've been counting on someone to come up with a great new calculator to help you figure your way through it all. And all the while looking for some money saving answers to your budget problems…and looking to the one store that has more of what you want, when you want it, at prices you want to pay…then my friend…

macy's fall sale is for you

And, it all starts tomorrow morning at all 16 stores.

The word "you" is direct, the shortest distance between two people. It's a powerful word and Macy's, New York, knows it. This sales announcement editorial is written with the reader in mind, the "you."

Right:
How do you say "everything's on sale"? Prange's says it ten times. It is a known fact that a positive statement repeated, piled up, one on top of the other, gains power enormously. Prange's makes a dynamic poster of the idea.

LAST 10 DAYS

EVERY 🪑 . . . IS ON SALE

EVERY 🛋 . . . IS ON SALE

EVERY 🪑 . . . IS ON SALE

EVERY 🔵 . . . IS ON SALE

EVERY 🪟 . . . IS ON SALE

EVERY 🖼 . . . IS ON SALE

EVERY 🔺 . . . IS ON SALE

EVERY 🛏 . . . IS ON SALE

EVERY 🛋 . . . IS ON SALE

EVERY 🎵 . . . IS ON SALE

EVERYTHING'S-ON-SALE
H🏠ME SALE

HOME SAVINGS: Upholstered and occasional furniture, rockers, recliners, mattresses, wall systems, dinettes, bedrooms, floor coverings, bed, window and wall coverings, and more. Famous makers include Drexel, Bernhardt, Hooker, Hammary, Selig, Kincaid, Futorian, Stearns & Foster, Hickory Fry, Karastan, Mohawk, Cabin Craft, Croscill, Cortlex, and others.
DELAYED BILLING: Through Sunday, February 28th, you can have billing delayed for 90 days after delivery when you charge your Home Sale purchases on your Prange's charge card.

PRANGE'S

"Sale-Homing Devices—the tools of law and order for each and every housebird who takes a special pride in the roof over her head." John Wanamaker makes the usual home sale unusual, and gives the customer a handsome tabloid-size insert that she will cherish, refer to, and act upon. After a nasty winter this is a particularly welcome, light-hearted introduction to spring house-keeping.

SALE-HOMING DEVICES

ADVERTISING SUPPLEMENT TO THE PHILADELPHIA INQUIRER, SUNDAY, FEBRUARY 27, 1972.

Right:

This portrait of a Macy's Kansas City buyer is distinguished for its accuracy and visual impact. It's about time a harried and worried personality is shown for what he is and does, from the pencil behind his ear to the means of locomotion under his feet. Every buyer has his day and we're glad.

HE SEES ALL; HEARS ALL; BUYS THE BEST!

HE IS ... FIGURING ALL THE ANGLES ... ER BUYS!

HE RELIES ON FACTS AND FIGURES TO MAKE SURE YOU ALWAYS DO BETTER!

HE IS NEVER WITHOUT HIS BADGE OF INTEGRITY . . A WHITE CARNATION!

COMPARISON SHOPPER REPORT

PASSPORT

MACY'S OWN BRAND

HE TRAVELS THE WORLD, AND BRINGS ITS BEST BACK FOR YOU!

CHANCES ARE HE WAS BORN AND EDUCATED IN KANSAS OR MISSOURI, KNOWS YOU AND YOUR PREFERENCES.

YOU'LL FIND A LOT OF MID-AMERICA IN HIS SELECTIONS!

HE IS AN ACTIVE MEMBER OF HIS COMMUNITY!

WOMEN'S COATS

BUYERS' DAYS SALE!

BOYS' WEAR

Portrait of a MACY★S buyer

FOR THE PAST SIX MONTHS, HE HAS BEEN TRACKING DOWN BIG VALUES FOR BUYERS' DAYS!

TO BUY OR NOT TO BUY, MACY'S BUREAU OF STANDARDS IS HIS CONSCIENCE!

HE HAS GONE TO EVERY EXTREME TO MAKE FRIDAY AND SATURDAY DAYS YOU WILL REMEMBER

MACY★S BUYERS' DAYS SALE STARTS TODAY!

In the mid-70's, Saks Fifth Avenue started a trend in first person conversation copy. (We see other stores finally picking up the idea.) This one, with two voices making two statements, is as audible as a flat newspaper page can get. It's a beautiful piece of writing.

The way I look at it,
with 40% to 55% off
the original prices, if
I bought two pairs
of shoes, one would be
practically free.

You know, I think you're right.
And then, when you figure out
what I'd save with ⅓ to ½ off the
original prices on clothes for me
and Jack and the children and
the dog and things for the house
and a present for Jack's aunt
and then...there's Christmas....
Remember that silk shirt?

...Well, the final clearance sale of summer fashions is on...
And it's at *Saks Fifth Avenue...*

Right:
It's thrilling to see a new approach to a sale announcement. Carson's horoscope is alive with interesting copy and art, mostly pertinent to the big event. Who could miss this message?

YOUR HOROSCOPE FORECASTS
· savings tomorrow!! ·

big day sale

GENERAL APPROACH FOR TODAY: this is a good day to be alert to the household and clothing needs of you and your family. Tomorrow is Carsons one-day BIG DAY SALE. General vibrations indicate great bargains for everyone.

OUTLOOK FOR THE FUTURE: cost of living may ease up or down a few points, the stock market is unpredictable but when you shop and **choose it and charge it at Carsons,** you're assured of superiority of selection and extra savings.

STATE STREET STORE ONLY

The Daisy Sale is a Higbee tradition and the problem of selling the sale recurs every year. To tie in with a musical theme and make broadcast an important factor has given this event a new dimension. The newspaper ad announcing the last day is made up of the music itself, winding up with, "So don't delay, it ends today; we're so sad but alas it's true."

In view of curtailed motoring the idea of a "telephone sale"
makes a lot of sense. The Bay (Montreal) offers 27 items from
Notions and Stationery in a neat, informal high-visibility
layout with strong human appeal.

"Tomorrow Ohrbach's is selling my famous brand dresses for less than I'd charge my own relatives."

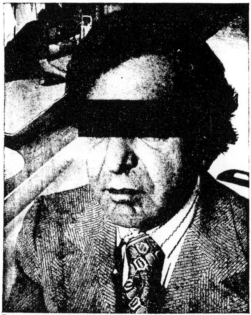

Famous manufacturer who prefers to remain anonymous.

We made this bargain with five famous manufacturers: We could cut their prices, if we would cut out their labels.

So tomorrow in our Miss Ohrbach's department, you'll see a lot of big name dresses without their big names. And without their big prices. In sizes 8-16 and 5-15.

You'll see short dresses, long dresses and one of a kind dresses. Layered looks and unlayered looks, pleats and A lines, slinky knits and innocent voiles, polyester blends and woven cottons. You'll see all kinds of fresh spring dresses in fresh spring colors for only **$22.** And **$25.**

Then there's a special group of impeccably tailored jacket dresses, straight out of the top fashion books. You'll see stripes and solids. Geometrics and prints. Cotton jacquard and linen-textured polyester. And you'll see a price tag that says **$42.** Which is pretty astounding even if you've got relatives in the business.

Ohrbach's.

It's what you get for the low price that counts.

This was Ohrbach's in 1972. One innovation after another to capture the customer's imagination. This one is tops. At least we get a glimpse of the glum "famous manufacturer" who has clothes to sell but wants his labels out. Great headline, great copy. This is advertising that gets seen, gets read and gets action.

406

NO PARKING

...**lot sale can last forever!** And ours is no exception. We'll be moving indoors tomorrow, Monday, at 9 p.m. . . . if there's anything left. Today and tomorrow you can still save on famous name TV, stereo, appliances, bedding, occasional pieces and much more as you shop in the great out-of-doors. Come out today, 12 noon till 6 p.m., or Monday, 10 a.m. till 9 p.m., and join in the fun . . . the savings. You couldn't pick a better time to use your Barker Bros. FLEXACCOUNT or to open a new one so that you can pick the type of payment schedule that best suits your family's budget. Shop the last 2 days of Barker Bros. Parking Lot Sale.

BARKER BROS.
clearance center
317 North Euclid Avenue, Ontario, or Call 983-9766

Sometimes it takes a staggering jolt to make people read copy. That's exactly what Barker Bros. does here, using type, words, and a second color in a layout nobody can miss. A great design job.

How can you advertise an auditorium dress clearance and show no dresses, and show no auditorium, and show no store, and show nothing but the skyline of the city silhouetted against the dawn? Does it pull? Come stand in line at Carson's. It extends all the way to the elevators.

Macy's has its own bouncing way to talk to customers and explain a sale.
Read it all and sense the excitement the customer feels.
No wonder Macy's never misses.

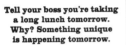

Tell your boss you're taking a long lunch tomorrow. Why? Something unique is happening tomorrow.

Ask your whole diet club to come along tomorrow. Why? Something satisfying is happening tomorrow.

Turn off your TV set tonight right after the news. Why? Something thrifty is happening tomorrow.

Call your mother-in-law to come baby-sit tomorrow. Why? Something exciting is happening tomorrow.

Cook a casserole for tomorrow's dinner tonight. Why? Something exceptional is happening tomorrow.

Change your dentist appointment for next week. Why? Something tremendous is happening tomorrow.

!?★✳&$
It's happening tomorrow

Macy's all-store, all-floor Spring Sale begins tomorrow. Exciting, exceptional, tremendous, thrifty, satisfying and unique. Miles of aisles of big, bountiful, savings-full sales. At your Macy's tomorrow. Come to **Macy's.**

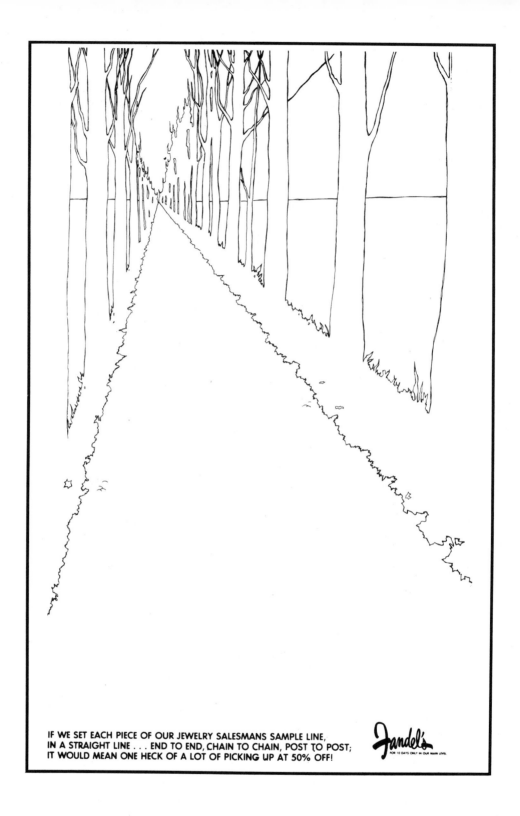

IF WE SET EACH PIECE OF OUR JEWELRY SALESMANS SAMPLE LINE, IN A STRAIGHT LINE . . . END TO END, CHAIN TO CHAIN, POST TO POST; IT WOULD MEAN ONE HECK OF A LOT OF PICKING UP AT 50% OFF!

This long lane into infinity staggers the imagination. Can't you see the citizens of St. Cloud gasping when they opened the paper? When you have a problem of a clearance or a sample line, and can't show specific items, something else must deliver the message. Fandel's has made it happen.

Since the news media made a point of bears, and how fat they are this particular year, it seemed proper to focus on one of those critters wrapped in a blanket. Stewart's offers four Fieldcrest items and talks about "energy saving blankets— reduce the chill factor—turn that thermostat way down and save." Needless to say this was the best seen ad that week in Baltimore.

411

INDEX OF AD CATEGORIES

INDEX OF ILLUSTRATIONS

ACKNOWLEDGMENTS

Many staff members and associates of RETAIL
REPORTING CORPORATION were instrumental
in adapting the original ads from our weekly
RETAIL AD WEEK and producing the new
material that appears in THE BEST IN RETAIL
ADS, Volume I. We appreciate their efforts
equally and thank those who were most involved.

J. Paganetti, Author
M. Seklemian, Author
Susan Lefkowitz, Art Director